Miguel,

To my teacher,
With eternal gratitude
and fondness. Thank you
for all your support & guidence.

Your student,

Joe

Financial Crisis in American Households

Financial Crisis in American Households

The Basic Expenses That Bankrupt the Middle Class

Joseph Nathan Cohen

PRAEGER™

An Imprint of ABC-CLIO, LLC

Santa Barbara, California • Denver, Colorado

Library of Congress Cataloging-in-Publication Data

Names: Cohen, Joseph Nathan, 1976– author.
Title: Financial crisis in American households : the basic expenses that
   bankrupt the middle class / Joseph Nathan Cohen.
Description: Santa Barbara : Praeger, [2017] | Includes bibliographical
   references and index.
Identifiers: LCCN 2016055250 (print) | LCCN 2017011057 (ebook) | ISBN
   9781440832215 (hard copy : alk. paper) | ISBN 9781440832222 (ebook)
Subjects: LCSH: Households—Economic aspects—United States. | Cost and
   standard of living—United States. | Middle class—United States. | Global Financial
   Crisis, 2008-2009. | Households—United States.
Classification: LCC HC106.84 .C634 2017 (print) | LCC HC106.84 (ebook) | DDC
   339.4/20973—dc23
LC record available at https://lccn.loc.gov/2016055250

ISBN: 978-1-4408-3221-5
EISBN: 978-1-4408-3222-2

21 20 19 18 17   1 2 3 4 5

This book is also available as an eBook.

Praeger
An Imprint of ABC-CLIO, LLC

ABC-CLIO, LLC
130 Cremona Drive, P.O. Box 1911
Santa Barbara, California 93116-1911
www.abc-clio.com

This book is printed on acid-free paper ∞

Manufactured in the United States of America

For Danielle, Naomi, Maya, and Galit

Contents

Acknowledgments

I want to extend my gratitude to colleagues and friends for their help. I am deeply indebted to my mentor, Miguel Centeno, for his never-ending support. I am grateful to work with so many exceptional colleagues at Queens College, and feel a particularly deep debt to Dana Weinberg, Andrew Beveridge, and Charles Turner for their guidance, mentorship, and support. I would also like to thank Sharon Zukin, Helaine Olen and Beth Ptalis, whose early attention encouraged me to develop this project. I thank my editor, Jessica Gribble, for her valuable feedback and support. I am grateful for valuable feedback from Nathan Stein, and from the participants of panels at the Queens College Sociology Workshop, the Eastern Sociological Society, and the American Sociological Association. Finally, thank you to my family. This book is dedicated to the memory of my grandmothers, Minerva Tanner and Hazel Bright.

Household Financial Crisis in the United States

For years, economic analysts have spoken of a long-term decline in the economic fortunes of the U.S. middle class. Stable, well-compensated jobs are disappearing. Wages have barely paced living costs. People save less, borrow more, and go bankrupt more often than a generation ago. The ranks of the middle class in the United States are said to be emptying out[1] on their way to becoming a modern-day proletariat.[2]

For years, many experts treated this sense of middle-class decline with some degree of credulity. They maintained that regular Americans' living standards had never been higher. Upward mobility partly explained the middle class's disappearance.[3] People have never been so well fed, enjoyed so many amenities, received so much education and healthcare, and lived so long. Our streets have never been safer. Obesity—not starvation—is the principal nutritional problem facing the poor. Critics often rejected talk of a declining middle class as an exaggeration.

The 2016 U.S. presidential elections made it clear that the voting public did not agree. There appeared to be a strong, widespread sense that the U.S. economy was not serving regular Americans well. Both political parties seemed to be running against American capitalism. Economic policies that once would have been celebrated as responsive to business and in accordance with modern economic theory were now painted as part of a corrupt conspiracy against families. There seemed to be a strong, bipartisan demand that politicians find ways to protect people from an economy that seems to offer little promise for a better future.

A closer look at the data suggests that there is merit to the view that Americans' living standards have never been higher. However, economic fortunes seem to be deteriorating in one clear respect: people are becoming less economically secure. Economic life is more of a tightrope walk. Work is becoming more precarious.[4] People's incomes have become more volatile.[5] The employer-provided insurances and pensions that sustained previous generations are disappearing.[6] Most families have little to nothing saved for retirement. Many of them don't have enough saved to cover a missed paycheck and don't know anyone who could lend them a few thousand dollars if they found themselves in a bind. Being short on money is a particularly serious problem in the United States, where running out of cash can endanger a person's access to healthcare, education, and work opportunities. The public institutions that might have helped compensate for these changes are widely seen as deteriorating under long-term neglect.

When discussions arise regarding the money problems faced by U.S. households, attention immediately turns to earnings problems. Explanations focus on the problems people face in getting money: income volatility, job precariousness, the decline of unions, income stagnation, and so on. Less attention is paid to the role of spending. In part, spending is not a focus because living costs are presumed to have been falling. In an era of $1 restaurant hamburgers, $50 Walmart touchscreen tablets, $12 Costco jeans, or free online newspapers and telephone calls, it makes sense to pay less attention to the role that living costs play in sowing money problems.

We should not ignore overspending, however. It is partly responsible for many Americans' financial problems. Even though incomes have stagnated for years, the presumption is that families could have kept saving by tightening their belts. Although it has never been easier to cut spending, people just haven't been doing it. Spending has continued to grow as it did during the golden age of the U.S. middle class in the mid-20th century—even if income has not.

This observation can lead many to conclude that Americans' money problems are the product of personal failures. They see growing household spending as the result of the United States' culture of consumerism, impulse control problems, gluttony, financial imprudence, or some other character flaw. In turn, this portrayal can foster an attitude that is more opposed to using public resources or regulation to help those with money problems. After all, if people's excessive lifestyle expectations or inability to exercise self-control is the cause of their money problems, wouldn't subsidizing their excess consumption be wasteful and unfair to those who manage their money well? Wouldn't people be more likely to correct their bad behavior if they were exposed to its natural consequences? Moreover, wouldn't these kinds of government intrusions in the free market ultimately undermine capitalism's capability to raise living standards by creating more, better, and cheaper products?

Although there are kernels of truth to this view, it also has a very critical weakness. Roughly ten years ago, research by then-Harvard law professor (and now U.S. senator) Elizabeth Warren and colleagues[7] found that families facing bankruptcy had fallen into trouble in part because they had difficulty keeping up with more basic expenditures, such as housing or medical care. This book presents a range of analyses suggesting that, a decade later, these spending pressures still drive the bulk of rising household spending, and they may have gotten worse. It is not that Americans are frittering away their savings on frivolous consumerism, but rather that the rising costs of key basic necessities (e.g., education, child care, or housing in nondistressed communities with access to jobs) have been spiraling upward. Moreover, these costs have risen during a period in which these necessities are become more essential to securing income. With the passage of time, sustaining a household without these types of basics is becoming more difficult.

In part, the cost of these necessities has been rising because the institutions that once would have absorbed them—such as employer-sponsored benefits, public services, and public assistance programs—have been disappearing, while the public institutions that would have picked up the slack have not kept up with rising needs. Political scientist Jacob Hacker[8] speaks of a Great Risk Shift, in which those who oppose these vestiges of mid-20th century welfarism sold a "Personal Responsibility Crusade" to policy-makers and voters. This Crusade maintained that people needed to stop relying on others to secure life's essentials and to seize responsibility for their own well-being. They argued that society would be stronger and living standards would ultimately be higher if they were to reject such communal welfarism.

What happened? Why did this Crusade not work? As discussed a bit later, part of the problem was an implicit assumption that unfettered capitalism would unleash innovations and efficiency enhancements that would ultimately deliver top-notch education, healthcare, housing, and other products at rock-bottom prices. This scheme ultimately worked across much of the economy, which is why we enjoy such low prices on apparel, autos, electronics, furnishings, food, reading materials, telecommunications, entertainment, personal care items, and many other products. While free markets have generally worked, they appear to have failed in key markets for basic essentials. The past thirty years' shift toward laissez-faire has not created a bounty of high-quality, inexpensive medical care, higher education, child care, or housing in the United States.

Along with examining these rising cost pressures and their effects on household finances, this book provides a data-intensive exposition of the proposition that the rising cost of basic necessities plays a role in deteriorating household finances. It probes the finer details of households' balance sheets and income statements while exploring the historical context in which these financial problems developed. This book engages some of the complicated social-scientific and philosophical problems with which one must grapple when formulating diagnoses of and prescriptions for these financial problems. Furthermore, it looks to other countries to explore whether there are viable alternatives to the approach taken by the United States.

While there are probably limits to what governments can do to stop the decline in household incomes, U.S. policy-makers might at least mitigate the problem by emulating other highly developed countries' practice of ensuring universal access to high-quality essential services. Doing so would help households restrain their spending and cut many financial obligations, which would ultimately buffer people from the negative well-being consequences of running out of money. Doing so will require that Americans confront some deeply held cultural beliefs about how the economy works.

A Thirty-Year Deterioration in Household Finances

We often assume that the middle class's financial problems were caused by the 2008 financial crisis and Great Recession. The presumption makes sense. The 2008 downturn was severe. It destroyed 8.1 million jobs and caused the unemployment rate to double.[9] An estimated 170,000 to 200,000 small businesses were lost.[10] The stock market lost roughly half its value, and home prices dropped by about one-quarter.[11] Even though the ensuing Great Recession was said to have ended in the summer of 2009,[12] much of the public continues to believe that these are bad economic times.[13] The gross domestic product (GDP) may be rising and the stock market booming, but much of the country feels as if it has not benefited considerably.

In seeing the middle class's money struggles as a product of a recession, we understand the problem as a by-product of economic cycles. Americans' money problems are understood to be a result of the economy's natural rhythms of ups and downs. Such a perspective makes it seem sensible to wait for things to turn around. There is no reason to doubt that the economy will rebound, and it makes sense to presume that everything will eventually return to the pre-Recession "normal."

The main problem with such a view is that households' money problems are long-term developments that have persisted across economic cycles.

Household finances have been deteriorating since at least the early 1980s, if not the end of the 1960s. It is not as if regular Americans' finances were generally in order before the 2008 crash, and then they got bad. By historical standards, household finances had deteriorated substantially during the economic boom that preceded the crash, and then people's money problems became much more noticeable (or less ignorable) after the crash. Rising financial insecurity looks more like a secular development than a cyclical one. These are not short-term problems caused by a temporary economic downturn. Instead, they more likely reflect a structural problem.

A Look at the Data

Figure 1.1 describes some of the ways in which household finances deteriorated over recent decades. It depicts four broad trends: (1) income stagnation (as represented in the top left using median real household incomes), (2) falling savings (bottom left, as a secular fall in the personal savings rate), (3) rising indebtedness (top right, in the exponential growth of household debt to GDP), and (4) an increased incidence of financial failure (bottom right, measured by the personal bankruptcy rate).[14]

Income Stagnation

One of the most widely noted manifestations of the middle class's economic struggles is *real income stagnation*, a situation in which household incomes are not rising relative to general living costs. This trend is depicted in the top-left quadrant of Figure 1.1. It shows how household incomes rose quickly during the mid-20th century but slowed in the decades that followed.

During the 1950s and 1960s, incomes grew at an average annual rate of about 3 percent per year. At that growth rate, a household earning $50,000 today would have an inflation-adjusted income of $67,196 ten years from now. Beginning in the 1970s, this rapid and steady pace of income growth slowed down. Median real wages stopped rising during economic downturns, and the overall pace of household income growth fell to just under 0.8 percent per year between 1970 and 2000. As a comparison, at that era's growth rate, a person who earns $50,000 today would have an income of $54,687 in ten years—roughly $13,000 less than would have been obtained mid-century. Between 2000 and 2012, median incomes fell from roughly $68,642 to $62,241. Since 2000, incomes have been stagnating across the income scale—not just at the median.[15] In essence, the vast majority of those who sustain a living through employment are not earning more money.

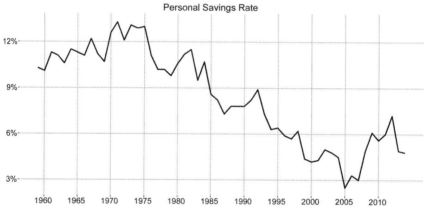

Figure 1.1   Signs of a Long-Term Deterioration in Household Finances.

Much of this stagnation is attributable to more difficulty securing jobs and pay raises. Hourly wages have barely moved for decades.[16] Getting more money often means working longer hours or sending more household members to the workforce, rather than finding better-paying jobs. People's access to work has become more precarious,[17] which means that even those who are earning good money today are more likely to lose those jobs or see their pay fall behind prices than in previous generations.

Slow wage growth is not the only factor at play. Incomes from private pensions have been declining as well.[18] Households' income from financial investments have also fallen, primarily because cash accounts yield little to no interest.[19] Personal incomes from businesses have stagnated with wages, perhaps as a result of an environment in which it is hard to compete with

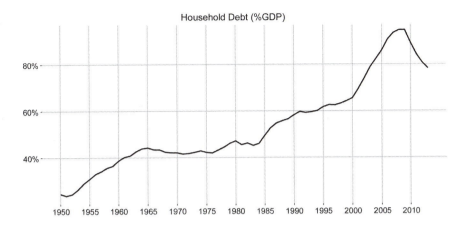

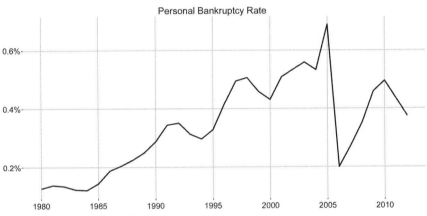

Figure 1.1 (Continued)
Sources: American Bankruptcy Institute (2014); Federal Reserve Bank (2014); Census Bureau (2014).

large firms and foreign enterprises.[20] Government assistance has tightened up for the working-age population, although Social Security recipients did well over the past several decades.[21]

Falling Savings

In the midst of these earning problems, household savings collapsed. The lower-left graph in Figure 1.1 depicts changes in the *personal savings rate*, the percentage of after-tax dollars that the average family saves in lieu of spending. Between 1960 and 1975, the personal savings rate fluctuated in the 10 percent to 14 percent range. After 1976, the personal savings rate declined steadily, eventually reaching near-zero right before the 2008 crisis. Since the Great Recession, many observers have celebrated a purported resurgence in savings, but the magnitude and expected durability of this rebound can easily be overstated. When savings rebounded to about 5 percent in 2013, it was reverting to levels that prevailed in the mid-1990s, not the mid-1960s.

This decline is enough to produce a substantial diminishment in long-term wealth accumulation. At mid-century rates, a household earning a $60,000 yearly salary would put aside between $6,000 and $8,400 a year. Over 30 years of compounding 5 percent real annual returns,[22] such savings would result in a nest egg of between $400,000 and $558,000. If that same $60,000-a-year family were to save at more recent rates (between 2 percent and 5 percent of their income, as opposed to between 10 percent and 14 percent), they would be left with a nest egg of $78,000 to $199,000. As we will see in Chapter Three, this is a very optimistic estimate of what people actually save and accrue over a lifetime.

Falling savings are often explained as the product of three factors: earning problems, easy debt, and excessive spending. Cheap debt is discussed in the following section, and spending choices are examined in depth in Chapter Five. Whatever its cause, the falling saving rate portends a situation in which people do not have adequate savings to cope with a rainy day or foreseeable financial shocks such as college or retirement. Differences in the savings rates of today versus the 1960s can amount to hundreds of thousands of lost dollars accumulated over a lifetime.

Rising Indebtedness

When people lack savings, they often rely on debt in its stead. Household debt ballooned in proportion to the overall economy over the past several decades. The overall value of household debt rose from about 24 percent of GDP[23] in 1950 to nearly 95 percent of GDP by 2009. In other words, household debts have quadrupled relative to overall economic output. More people borrow, and people borrow more.

Since 1950, household debt has grown in three bursts. The first burst occurred from 1950 to 1964, when household debts rose from 24 percent to around 42 percent of GDP. We might surmise that this is a result of the post-World War II reconstruction of consumer debt markets. Thereafter, household debts remained relatively stable until about 1984, after which they grew at an accelerated rate. This second boom in household lending followed substantial deregulation in credit markets, for example, by repealing legal restrictions on interest rates and interstate lending. Consumer debt also grew with the development of the U.S. financial sector, which was rapidly creating new markets for extending, trading, and liquidating loans. Opportunities to borrow began to proliferate.

Household debts then ballooned from 2000 to 2007, a period in which debt became cheap and bountiful. Several factors helped loosen debt markets, including financial deregulation, "innovative finance" schemes that allowed lenders to quickly extend and then sell off their loans, and an insatiable foreign hunger for U.S. dollars and debt. All of this resulted in a glut of consumer debt and that era's extraordinarily low cost of credit. We experienced these changes when it became much easier to get credit cards with larger credit limits, although they often had high and unpredictable charges attached to them. New mortgages (e.g., adjustable-rate or low down payment mortgages) made it easier for people to borrow more. Check cashing outlets proliferated. Stores more readily offered customers credit through co-branded credit cards. Debt became much cheaper and easier to incur.

Even if credit is cheap and abundant, this debt boom requires willing borrowers, and American households readily obliged. You need a spender to be a borrower. As discussed in Chapter Five, households' penchant to borrow is often portrayed as the product of some combination of materialism, impulse-control problems, short-termism, inflated lifestyle expectations, and social status jockeying. The implication of these views is that people's assumption of debt is mostly wasteful, avoidable, and tied to the sins of envy, vanity, gluttony, sloth, and so on. However, a closer look at household spending data suggests that the types of household products typically featured in these arguments—clothes, cars, leisure products, beauty and personal care products, and so on—are not driving rising spending and debt. Instead, much of the momentum driving household spending comes from a set of essential products that have not been getting more affordable over time.

Rising Incidence of Financial Failure

As households accumulate debt, they walk toward the precipice of financial breakdown. Their finances become a high-wire balancing act, and this balance can be thrown off by a job loss, medical event, or even a major car or home repair. With more people sitting closer to the financial precipice, more fall over the edge. The bankruptcy rate has risen steadily (bottom right of Figure 1.1), from 126 per 100,000 people in 1980 to 373 in 2012. This represents a 296 percent increase. In 2006, the federal government confronted this rising tide by making it harder to qualify for debt discharge under bankruptcy proceedings. These changes create the impression that financial failure fell in that year; but this decrease was more a product of the lack of availability of bankruptcy than a matter of people not being in a deeply troubled financial situation. In any case, the returns pressed bankruptcy rates down to levels that prevailed in the late 1990s, not the early 1980s.

A Structural Problem

There is clear evidence that household finances have experienced some long-term deterioration. Sometime between the late 1960s and mid-1980s, people stopped getting raises, cut their savings, started borrowing more, and went bankrupt more often. This long-term deterioration in household finances suggests that we are not dealing with the temporary effects of an extraordinarily bad economic downturn. Because this deterioration is an enduring problem, it seems unlikely that household financial problems will simply self-correct after the economy recovers. If economic recoveries have generally failed to produce substantially higher wages, better quality jobs, more savings, less debt, and so on, why would this recovery be so different?

In characterizing these problems as the result of "structural problems," we are implying that U.S. capitalism, as it is practiced today, has design flaws. It is not reacting to broader changes in the economy, politics, technology, or society in ways that strengthen regular Americans' financial situations. It may be that the United States requires substantial reforms before the middle class finds itself on firmer ground. The possibility of structural reforms makes this a high-stakes political and societal issue. Reform can create big winners and losers, and thus political conflict. We turn to these conflicting political views next.

The Politics and Science of Financial Problems

Polls suggest that these trends are not lost on the American public. An overwhelming majority of Americans register consistent disapproval of the U.S. economy's path. Economic issues are regularly cited as top electoral concerns. There is a widespread perception that the political system has been captured by and serves elites—not the interest of regular Americans. The pressure felt by the middle class is argued to help propel the antiestablishment politics experienced in the 2016 election.[24]

Attitudes vary widely with regard to what—if anything—to do about households' purported financial problems. Some believe that there is no serious problem with household finances and that many complaints about money come from those who want handouts. Some believe that U.S.

households' money problems exist but are temporary and that they will be resolved by the economy's impending recovery. Others believe that the problem is real but is a matter of people causing their own difficulties by mismanaging their money. Still others argue that these problems are the product of an economic system that fails to serve the interests of regular people.

Is It a Serious Problem?

Many observers believe that talk of Americans' money problems is over-blown. These skeptics' views should not be dismissed out of hand. Policies designed to reverse these trends have the potential to divert resources away from other goals. They also carry the risk of negative unintended consequences. Before endeavoring to solve a problem, it is worth pondering whether we are in fact dealing with a serious issue. Our answers will hinge on the problem's prevalence (how much of society is affected by it) and its severity (the harm done by it).

Financial Insecurity Is Prevalent

On one hand, insecurity is part of regular life. It should not be surprising that most Americans face some kind of financial insecurity. On the other hand, the data suggest that a very high proportion of society is, by basic financial planning standards, in very poor financial shape.

Chapter Three uses U.S. household finance surveys to gauge the state of U.S. families' financial security. It finds that (depending on the criteria used) between one-quarter and one-third of U.S. households are *economically dependent* in the present; that is, they are unable to sustain a very basic livelihood without outside help from family, friends, charity, or the government. Another third or so are *precariously independent*; that is, they are able to make ends meet but do so as a delicate balancing act. They effectively live check to check, and they are generally unprepared to weather the demands of unanticipated financial shocks, such as joblessness, illness, injury, divorce, or even a major home or auto repair.

This leaves us with about two-fifths of households that seem capable of covering their bills and withstanding minor bumps in the financial road. However, most of them seem destined for eventual dependency on public assistance. Most households have nothing saved in private retirement accounts (e.g., a 401(k) or IRA), private pensions are slowly disappearing,[25] and many of those with any retirement savings only have enough to cover a few years at the poverty line. Ultimately, their living standards will depend on public assistance programs such as Social Security and Medicare. Only a minority of households—around one-tenth—seem well positioned to maintain economic independence into old age.

Is the Problem Serious?

But is this a serious problem, or are people panicking over nothing? Isn't adversity and insecurity part of life? Isn't there a social safety net that keeps money problems from becoming life and death situations? Aren't a lot of money complaints a matter of inflated lifestyle expectations, efforts to jockey for social status (i.e., "keeping up with the Joneses"), or an inability to control their impulses in money matters? Moreover, if insecurity creates an incentive to work and manage our finances prudently, wouldn't we do harm by completely squashing it?

The criticisms underlying these kinds of questions have some substance. On one hand, there are reasons to see talk of a declining or impoverished middle class as overblown. In both a comparative and historical sense, the vast majority of Americans enjoy high and rising living standards, including many officially "poor" Americans. No previous generation of Americans has been more amply fed, better housed, more insulated from violence, more thoroughly entertained, and more surrounded by wondrous material possessions. There is no doubt that, in many respects, the average person today lives better than royalty lived in past eras. Some of the discontent surrounding the economic affairs of the middle class involves relative, rather than absolute, deprivation.

On the other hand, financial insecurity and money shortages have nontrivial implications for both those afflicted by the problem and society at large. Money buys access to life's necessities, and the personal onus of securing access to basic necessities is high in the United States. A recent analysis of the 2014 *American Values Survey* suggests that roughly 36 percent of Americans cut food consumption for financial reasons, and 29 percent put off seeing a doctor for financial reasons.[26] Financial concerns can prevent college-qualified students from pursuing higher education.[27] Those without money can face considerable difficulty securing child care.[28] Other highly developed societies subsidize or socialize medical care, higher education, or child care, much like K–12 education and policing services are socialized in the United States. There, money problems do not restrict access to nonemergency medical care, college, or the ability to work while parenting small children.

Beyond concerns about absolute material deprivation, there is much research suggesting that the experience of financial insecurity or poverty can adversely affect people's health and development. Some research suggests that, under economically adverse circumstances, populations are more likely to abuse alcohol and drugs, to experience depression and other mental health disorders, and to commit suicide.[29] Children and young adults who come of age in economically bad environments tend to self-report lower health levels later in life.[30]

Often, people approach the topic of household finances by asking why a person should care if their personal affairs are in order. Mass financial insecurity is not just a concern for those who are afflicted with financial problems. When financial problems become prevalent, their ill effects can spill over to the wider community, affecting those whose finances are otherwise in order. For example, people's home values are often hurt by neighbors' mortgage defaults.[31] Many working-age adults' finances are strained by the aid they extend to relatives, and people often go bankrupt as a result of having to care for family members.[32] A rising tide of distressed people can strain social assistance programs, erode local tax bases, and exacerbate public budget deficits. Mass financial insecurity can also increase the economy's exposure to systemic financial and economic risks. It is worth considering whether things would have turned out differently in 2008 had people saved enough collateral to get high-quality mortgages, put aside enough emergency savings to cover the costs of temporary joblessness, or hadn't been so under-saved for an imminent (and possibly involuntary early) retirement that they were speculating with money that they couldn't afford to lose.

Setting aside any concerns related to 2008, the fact remains that the weak state of household finances may tie our policy-makers' ability to make decisions they deem fit. For example, it is hard to tighten consumer lending when so many under-saved households and businesses rely on cheap consumer credit, even if policy-makers feel that the economy would be better off with less consumer debt. When so many people's personal retirement plans or pension funds depend on a booming stock market or housing market to make up for years of under-saving, a central banker faces some disincentive to let the air out of financial bubbles. When much of the country's wealth is tied up in homes whose values depend on ultra-cheap mortgages and tax inducements to buy homes, it is practically difficult to stop funneling societal resources into buoying real estate markets. Of course, these problems do not, in and of themselves, prevent the government from making economic policies that prevent over-indebtedness or market bubbles, but they do create additional disincentives to do so.

Widespread financial insecurity is not a good thing for society. If we do concede that society ought to try to do something about the problem, what are its best options?

Generic Responses

The political conflicts involved in debates about how to respond to household financial insecurity involve three poles of thought. The first is to do nothing. The second is to use government power and resources to engage and, hopefully resolve, the problem. The third is to maintain—or even strengthen—our commitment to laissez-faire, free market capitalism.

Do Nothing

It is probably fair to say that doing nothing is society's default response to social problems in general. There are many reasons to favor doing nothing as a rule of thumb. Government attempts to micromanage the world around it have a historically demonstrable risk of negative unintended consequences.[33] Societal problems are often transitory, and an ill-conceived response can be unnecessarily expensive, disruptive, and self-defeating. Governments cannot solve all of society's problems, and there may be more pressing problems that merit attention and resources. There are reasons for that disposition to do nothing in the face of households' financial problems.

Doing nothing seems like an unlikely solution in this particular case. Deteriorating household finances is a chronic problem that seems to have been developing over decades. As we will see in the chapters that follow, many of the forces that have been damaging household finances remain intact and may even by strengthening. This does not seem like a problem that will self-resolve, and its consequences may be harder to ignore over time.

Government Initiative

Another possibility to address households' financial problems is to use the government's power and resources to ease whatever pressures are causing household finances to deteriorate. This may involve developing laws, regulations, and government programs that socialize the cost of essential goods and services, redistribute money to those under financial pressure, or alter the rules (and bargaining power) underlying private economic transactions. In short, these solutions involve socialism, redistribution, and regulation, which are concepts that Americans have widely viewed negatively during the past several decades, although such views have been softening in recent years.[34]

Often, discussions involving the concept of socialism and redistribution can quickly descend into Cold War-style polemics that contribute little to sensible policy discussions. Some level of socialism and redistribution are deeply engrained features of just about any modern economy. Moreover, there is ardent bipartisan support for some forms of socialism, redistribution, or regulation, even if they denounce them in principle. Political differences over redistribution mainly involve disagreements about the relatively small proportion of social spending directed toward the working-age poor. While such programs include those explicitly targeted to the poorer households (e.g., food stamps, Medicaid, the Children's Health Insurance Plan, Pell Grants, or minimum wages), they also include programs that benefit wide swaths of the U.S. economic hierarchy's lower and middling ranks (e.g., public schools, libraries, the interstate highway system, Stafford Loans, first-time home buyer help, public recreational facilities, and the two giant social programs—Social Security and Medicare).

Over the past several years, policy proposals of this sort included things such as free community college, raising the minimum wage, expanding public housing or transportation, or raising tax cuts and credits for lower income people. The largest program of this sort, which this study's findings ultimately suggest will be of great consequence if successful, is the Affordable Care Act (ACA). It is hard to pass final judgement on the ACA's effectiveness, but it represents the United States' clearest and most substantial step in this direction.

Redoubling Our Commitment to Neoliberalism

Others see these problems as the result of ill-conceived government intrusions on private markets and believe that a redoubled commitment to neoliberalism is key to restoring household finances. *Neoliberalism* is an economic paradigm or ideology that stresses the societal benefit of deregulated, private markets and an economic system that channels resources through private businesses and investors. It is reviewed at length in Chapter Four.

This view sees household financial struggles as the product of the types of social policies mentioned previously. Adherents of this view often maintain that the high taxes and economic regulations that come with social programs often discourage growth and jobs creation, which makes it harder for people to earn income. Moreover, it sees policies that insulate people from financial pressures as preventing the kind of market discipline that inculcates financially prudent decisions. It sees the pains of poverty as motivating people to work harder to earn money, while encouraging them to make the types of financially prudent decisions that prevent financial failure.

Concretely, those who believe that household finances would ultimately be fortified by neoliberalism favor policies such as labor market deregulation, low minimum wages, social program cutbacks, and tax cuts (especially on businesses and investors). They often describe such reforms as catalysts for virtuous cycles of private investment, job creation, innovation, and ultimately the material enrichment of society. Conversely, they see socialism, redistribution, regulation, and other government intrusions on private people's or businesses' prerogatives as damaging.

Conclusion

Opinions about how to respond to the deterioration of U.S. household finances often gravitate among these three poles of thought. The first is inclined to do nothing. The second is to strengthen social programs. The third is to redouble our commitment to free market capitalism. Ultimately, the discussions that follow engage these three poles and use data to explore the viability, possible benefits, and potential costs of each.

Value Neutrality

Discussions about household finances are politically contentious and fraught with philosophical differences and value judgments that make them difficult to resolve conclusively using the tools of science. Many such questions involve concerns about how people *ought to* live, the lifestyles or level of economic security that people *ought to* expect, or the degree to which the government *ought to* accept responsibility for people's financial situations. To paraphrase the early-20th-century psychologist Viktor Frankl, these "ought to" questions are largely moral matters that are more in the wheelhouse of philosophers or clergy than social scientists. Science cannot answer "ought to" questions. It is better at making inferences about what has already happened, which is different from telling people what they ought to do in the future. But that doesn't mean that the tools of science are useless.

The defining hallmarks of science are that it uses observable information to test ideas about how things operated during an experiment or quasi-experiment. Scientists strive to explain how certain facets of an observed phenomenon cause other facets to occur. A scientist might look for causal relationships in physical objects, chemical interactions, or living organisms, as many natural scientists do. Or they may look for such relationships in observed human societies, as many economists, sociologists, or political scientists do. In this particular case, we are searching through observable demographic, macroeconomic, public finance, and household finance data in an attempt to discern the historical incidence, causes, and consequences of heightened household financial insecurity.

One major problem with these types of endeavors is that in order to observe phenomena such as household insecurity, its various possible causes, and many possible consequences, we have to define them. If we are going to present data on concepts like financial insecurity, public insurance, economic adversity, or human well-being, we have to establish their concrete meaning or referent explicitly. We are forced to develop provisional answers to the "ought to" arguments described earlier.

The requirement to develop provisional definitions unavoidably sullies the scientific purity of any attempt to engage politically or philosophically contentious issues. Some people use this insight as a launching point to question the neutrality of any scientific venture to study such issues. In other words, they argue that every scientist has an implicit agenda and, perhaps by extension, that there is no reason to treat scientific commentary on these issues as having anything special to say.

These arguments have some element of truth, but this does not mean that scientific information is useless. Just because we cannot fully and unequivocally reach some ideal (e.g., honesty, kindness, ethicality, or value-neutrality) does not mean that we shouldn't strive for it. Likewise, it does not imply that such efforts are necessarily fruitless. If social scientists can develop provisional answers to morally or philosophically complicated questions, be open and explicit about these assumptions, and do their utmost to adopt reasonable assumptions that would be widely accepted, then they can contribute to public debate on these types of contentious issues by testing ideas or gleaning impressions from historical records.

The tools of science and modern statistics provide us with an occasion to test some of the common wisdom that prevails in public discussions. Scientists and nonscientists develop arguments about economic or other social affairs by making assumptions or speculations about how the world works. Disagreements often hinge on the fact that two parties are approaching a common problem with different assumptions or beliefs about the objective facts surrounding household finances. The tools of science provide some means of testing the strength of these assumptions. Where it is assumed, for example, that welfare spending improves human well-being or that higher taxes cause unemployment, a scientific engagement of socioeconomic data helps us discern whether these theories seem to have been true in the past. Assumptions that have some root in past experience are perhaps more worthy of credibility. To the degree that we can use the tools of science to sift less credible arguments out of public debate, we can improve the quality of our collective problem-solving.

The View That Emerges

Several key points emerge from the study that follows. The first key insight, established previously, is that the deterioration of household finances is a long-term phenomenon. This deterioration has developed slowly over the past 30 to 40 years and seems more likely to be an enduring, structural problem rather than a temporary consequence of the Great Recession. This implies that household financial problems are structural in nature and are rooted in some combination of long-term environmental changes and/or long-term problems with the organization of the economy.

The deterioration of household finances cannot be boiled down to one simple cause. Multiple factors are at work. Part of the problem is with earning incomes. Many U.S. workers have fought a losing battle for work against foreigners and machines, and they are not being absorbed elsewhere. The population is aging, and older people face many challenges finding gainful employment. Pensions, benefits, cost-of-living adjustments, and even steady work are becoming rarer, and more of the country ekes out a living through short-term contract work and the "gig economy." More people live alone, and single people tend to be poorer.

Earnings problems clearly cause some of the financial hardship facing the middle class, and many of the societal forces that cause these earnings problems are practically difficult—if even possible—to reverse. However, part of the problem seems more squarely within people's ability to control: their spending. Runaway spending is part of what is causing household finances to deteriorate. Arguably, in an era of cheap imports and low-markup retail (e.g., Walmart, Costco, and Amazon), it has never been easier to cut spending. Given the tough jobs environment, it would make sense for people to save money. Americans have both reasons and opportunity to tighten their belts—but it isn't happening.

The long-term rise of household spending in the midst of earning problems leads many observers to conclude that those with money problems are chiefly responsible for their situations. Most households do not budget[35] or even understand basic concepts of personal finance.[36] Many analysts cite the emergence of a spendthrift culture of consumerism, whereby people's materialistic impulses push them to spend money on frivolities that they cannot afford. These types of diagnoses can color our attitudes about how to respond to the middle class's financial problems. If wastefulness and irresponsibility are to blame for people's money problems, then using public resources to help them seems tantamount to pouring money down a black hole. There is no limit to what people can spend on impulse, hedonism, or keeping up with the Joneses. One might even argue that the pains of money problems are necessary to push people to manage their money responsibly.

In several respects, there is substance to this "culture of consumerism" argument, but a closer look at household finances suggests that this line of reasoning misses an important dimension of household overspending, and this oversight may ultimately hinder the development of productive responses to the problem of financial insecurity. Over the past several decades, it appears that families have been spending less, relative to incomes, on the products typically featured in "culture of consumerism" arguments: clothing, cars, home furnishings, appliances, grooming products, electronics, food, and so on. It is not so much that people are buying less of these things, but rather that the modern U.S. economy has become very good at delivering these products at rock-bottom prices. During this period, household cash flows have been strained by a more specific set of expenditures, particularly housing, healthcare, child care, and education. For several reasons, our economic strategy of relying on technology, foreign outsourcing, and market competition has not resulted in a similar bounty of affordable, high-quality products as in many of the aforementioned consumer markets. Prices for these essentials have gone up, and there are several indications that higher prices are not the result of comparatively better products.

In some measure, people's money problems partly represent a failure of the U.S. economy; they are not strictly a product of people's personal failings. Medical care and education are extraordinarily expensive in the United States, and it is not clear that Americans get higher-quality products for the higher cost they pay. Moreover, other societies organize these markets differently, such that securing these basics does not have such a strong impact on personal finances. If basic medical care bankrupts someone, is it really a personal failure? Canadians and Brits don't have to foot big medical bills, even if they are struck by some serious illness. The Finns don't have to pay for child care. The Dutch and Germans don't pay university tuition. In most highly developed countries, moving into cheap housing need not imply moving into communities with broken schools, severe crime, poor public services, and generally low living standards for one of the world's most developed economies.

This puts people in a difficult dilemma. Even if they were able to tighten their belts and solidify their financial situation by forgoing health insurance, a college education, or a home in a neighborhood with reasonable access to jobs, K–12 schools, or emergency services, it is not altogether clear that doing so is a good choice. The problem is that cutting these expenditures could ultimately endanger people's absolute well-being and even leave them in more financially vulnerable positions. Forgoing health insurance to balance your books works until you get sick. Saving money on child care and education may ultimately make it even harder to earn a livelihood. It is hard to say whether or not one's children are better served by saving less money by living in a bad school district or by cutting one's financial margin of error while raising the kids in neighborhoods and school districts that seem to produce healthier, safer, and more economically independent children. At the same time, failing to save enough money poses a risk that people will be cut off from these essentials if they run into problems down the line. This dilemma can seem like a "damned if you do, damned if you don't" situation. Families often find themselves enmeshed in a lose-lose dilemma in which they can have sound finances or quality essentials, but not both.

The rising burden of essential products is partly a by-product of government policies. Over the past several decades, U.S. policy-makers have increasingly relied on economic policies that are often described as "neo-liberal."[37] This ideology, which is examined in greater depth in Chapter Four, is premised on the principles of laissez-faire and trickle-down economics. The former principle maintains that society benefits when the government maintains a "hands-off" approach to economic governance and leaves control of the economy to largely deregulated private enterprises. The latter principle maintains that if the government is to reallocate resources to any group, it should be investors and businesses, who are expected to use these resources to create more jobs, products, and prosperity, which leads to higher living standards.

Neoliberalism has a strong logic that should not be dismissed out of hand. Arguably, it has helped sow economic prosperity and helped enrich Americans in terms of consumer goods; for example, clothing, food, home furnishings, personal electronics, transportation, telecommunications, and a range of other products have become very inexpensive. It can also claim credit for having helped bolster job prospects at the lower tiers of the job market and for improving Americans' tremendous access to credit.

Whatever their success in other consumer product markets, neoliberal policies have not led to a bounty of high-quality, highly affordable healthcare, education, and housing. Many of the techniques we use to make food, clothes, or electronics cheap—such as importation from low-wage countries, highly automated production, or self-service—do not work as well in these markets. In fact, the rather laissez-faire system in the United States has resulted in *higher* costs and, in some respects, lackluster results, in healthcare, education, and housing. Other highly developed countries do not put their people in such difficult dilemmas. Of course, having money confers advantages in any society. However, other countries offer a range of examples that show how social programs can contain the personal burden of accessing reasonably good-quality healthcare, child care, education, and housing. While these other societies are certainly not untroubled utopias, their ability to deliver better results in terms of household finances and well-being is worth noting.

Emulating mid-20th century/European-style government-directed policies to ensure universal accessibility is not an uncomplicated solution. It entails costs and sacrifices whose weight will fall harder on some people than others. Moreover, Europe has problems of its own, including household financial ones (see Chapter Seven). On the whole, however, universal accessibility to quality healthcare, education, and housing is likely positive on balance, and such policies could help defray the pressures that are causing household finances to deteriorate and may also reduce the well-being consequences of having money problems.

Ultimately, Americans must collectively face a choice about how society should respond to their money struggles, as they have for decades. Although these choices are difficult and all bear risk of failure, the U.S. public should not presume that they are collectively consigned to struggle with money. Governments do have the capacity to at least ease the burden of these problems, and other countries offer ideas about how this can be done.

Book Preview

Chapter Two provides a snapshot of U.S. household finances and develops a more concrete view of the United States' poor, middle class, and upper class. We typically understand household finances through the prism of our personal situation and generally assume that our personal circumstances are typical or middling. The chapter provides a concrete view of richer and poorer Americans, particularly who they are, how much they earn, and what they own and owe. The analysis makes sense of the perch from which we personally look at household finances.

Chapter Three defines financial insecurity and assesses its prevalence and depth in contemporary U.S. society. The analysis suggests that about one-third of society is economically dependent on others and unable to sustain a basic livelihood on their own. Another third balance their books as a day-to-day juggling act but are ill-equipped to confront life's many unanticipated—but not rare—financial shocks. Much of the remaining third may be able to deal with the shock of a temporary job loss, illness, or home repair, but they have not saved enough to finance an independent livelihood in old age. The vast majority of society seems destined for the public rolls. It is hard to see how society will maintain generally high living standards, or even avoid mass poverty, without extensive social programs.

Chapter Four examines the long-term deterioration of U.S. household finances, and several important concurrent—and possibly contributory—political, economic, and social developments. Although we often think that households' financial problems are the product of a once-in-a-lifetime economic downturn, this deterioration has been developing over decades. While many of the forces that have challenged household finances are being felt across the highly developed world, there is reason to believe that the United States' comparatively strong commitment to neoliberal economic policies makes matters worse.

Chapter Five examines why Americans have not tightened their belts in response to the financial pressures they face. This chapter establishes the degree to which household spending—and in turn financial insecurity—is driven by the rising personal burden of healthcare, child care, education, and housing. Households are overspending in part because the U.S. economy has proven unable to deliver highly accessible, high-quality education, healthcare, housing, and other products that are essential to well-being.

Chapter Six provides a deeper exploration into the rising personal burden of these essentials. It probes questions about what people need, whether or not their spending on essentials is worthwhile, and how the choices of economic policy-makers have contributed to this rising burden. There are clear reasons to believe that education, healthcare, and housing expenditures influence people's overall well-being. Although some of this expenditure is wasted in terms of well-being benefits, the burden for even basic essentials is clearly high and rising. Cutting out these expenditures in the pursuit of financial well-being is a risky gamble.

Chapter Seven looks abroad to describe how other highly developed societies organize these essential markets and asks how their policies affect household finances, public finances, and human well-being. It finds that, despite the United States' comparatively great wealth, both its household finances and overall well-being are rather middling compared to other highly developed societies. The United States may be remarkable in its antipathy toward the socialism and "big government," but it is hard to see how regular Americans have benefited from the policies that stem from this antipathy.

Chapter Eight describes how Americans' deep faith in neoliberalism keeps U.S. society from adapting sensible solutions that have succeeded in other developed countries. Although its proponents warn that the consequences of violating the tenets of their free market faith portend doom, Americans have good reason to shed this orthodoxy. Free markets work sometimes, but not all the time. There are good reasons to violate these orthodoxies in healthcare, education, and housing.

CHAPTER TWO

A Snapshot of U.S. Household Finances

Talking about other people's money is generally considered impolite. Many people don't share financial information with friends and family. For this reason, we tend to have a vague sense of other people's financial situations. Maybe we know that a $50,000 income is considered mid-range nationwide and that a six-figure income is relatively good. We might know how much someone has to earn to move up in tax brackets or qualify for social assistance programs. Often, the only financial details that people grasp are their own, and much of society doesn't even understand much about their own personal circumstances.

Most people see their financial situation as normal, typical, or average. A 2012 Pew Research Center survey asked Americans to identify the economic class to which they belonged. About 91 percent of respondents self-identified with some part of the middle class (about 8 percent saw themselves as poor, and 1 percent as rich).[1] On this basis, we might infer that the U.S. middle class earns between the 8th and 99th percentiles of income or wealth. Data from the Federal Reserve Bank's *Survey of Consumer Finances*[2] suggests that, in 2013, these class dividing lines imply that the middle class has incomes between $12,000 and nearly $700,000 per year. Their net worth is implied to range between nearly $8 million and less than zero. In other words, a large number of people in very different financial circumstances think that their economic situations are typical.

This penchant to see our financial situation as typical is partly a result of our social environment's insularity. We tend to work and live among others whose financial situations are roughly comparable to our own. We mix with people who live in the same community, share a workplace, or have children who go to the same school. In an economically segregated society, people are surrounded by others under similar circumstances. Although we may know people who are somewhat richer or poorer, the bulk of our social relations have economic circumstances comparable to our own, and we tend not to mix with people whose circumstances are dramatically different. When everyone around us is similar to us, it is natural to assume that we are typical.

All of this can skew our understanding of household finances in general. The issues that might press a wealthier household into financial problems (e.g., overpriced higher education, overspending on lattes and designer clothes, or not having enough retirement savings to retire comfortably) are very different from those faced by people closer to the bottom of the economic hierarchy (e.g., the cost of not having access to an affordable bank account or the strains of finding basic child care or transportation to work). Most of the country more closely resembles the bottom class than the upper-middle class (though the market for scholastic policy analysis skews wealthy).

To provide a more concrete anchor to this book's discussions, this chapter examines how much money Americans earn, own, and owe. It describes the basics of household finances, parses out how household finances differ across major U.S. demographics, and attempts to flesh out a more detailed picture of the U.S. economic hierarchy.

Understanding Households' Financial Circumstances

What does it take to be rich in the United States? A 2011 Gallup poll asked this question to a random sample of Americans, and more than half settled on an annual income of $150,000 a year *or less*. These estimates often draw laughs of incredulity. The audiences for academic presentations about household finances skew more educated and wealthy, so many of them live in, or come from, households that would fit this definition of "rich." Most of them flatly reject the idea that they are rich. However, a look at the broader distribution of wealth makes it clear that a family with two $75,000-a-year jobs is very well off in comparison to the rest of the country. They may not be among the top 1 percent, but they have more money coming in than 9 out of 10 U.S. families. It is hard to see a household that out-earns 90 percent of those living in one of the world's richest societies as being in hard-luck circumstances.

Most people focus on income because the numbers are easy to comprehend. Our annual incomes are printed on our pay stubs, we have some ability to map income estimates to people's job titles, and we see income differences laid out on tax forms and job posting sites. However, income is only part of a household's financial picture. What constitutes a "high" or even "sufficient" income depends on people's living costs, which can vary widely depending on geography, household composition, household members' health, and a range of other circumstances. Moreover, people with similar incomes can be in very different overall circumstances that are determined by wealth and debt. There are lower-income Americans with considerable wealth, and there are high-income Americans getting crushed by debt.

These considerations illustrate some of the complex issues involved in judging the state of household finances and the utility of starting our discussion about U.S. household finances with an exposition of the basic balance sheet and income statement concepts that determine a family's financial situation. We start our discussion with a brief exposition of basic personal finance concepts.

Incomes

Incomes are money flows into a household's accounts. Households can receive income from a variety of sources. In 2013, about 72 percent of households received money from wages (payment from an employer for doing a job). About 42 percent received government checks. Just under one-quarter (22 percent) received financial (e.g., investment portfolio) income. About 8 percent received income from a personal business. Less than 5 percent received alimony or child support.

Gross income refers to pretax income. The distribution of U.S. households' gross income is depicted in Figure 2.1.[3]

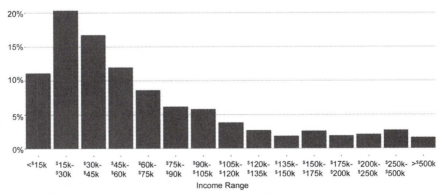

Figure 2.1　The Distribution of U.S. Household Income, 2013.
Source: Federal Reserve Bank (2014), *Survey of Consumer Finances.*

The data suggest that the median household received roughly $47,000 of income in 2013. This is household income, which in many cases represents the combined earnings of multiple earners. The middle 50 percent—those between the 25th and 75th percentiles—received between $24,000 and $90,000. The data estimate that 13.5 percent earn less than a poverty-line income, and about one-tenth earn six-figure incomes or more. The top 1 percent took in an income of $696,000 in 2013.

The bulk of household income comes from two sources: wages and government payments. Among all households that earned wage income, the median took in $48,000 from this source. The median take from government payments was $15,000, with the middle 50 percent (the 25th and 75th percentiles) taking in between $8,400 and $24,700. Among the 22 percent of households receiving financial income, the median proceeds from these investments was $958, and one-quarter of this group took in less than $10 a month from this source. Personal businesses also often yielded small incomes; of the 8 percent of households receiving business income, only about 1.8 percent received the equivalent of a median household income from that source.[4]

About 18 percent of households received no wages, financial income, or business income. The median household in this group earned about $19,000 in income in 2013, and the middle 50 percent took in between $12,000 and $33,000. Much of this money came from government payments (with a median take of $12,000, primarily through Social Security), supplemented with private pensions, familial transfers (e.g., alimony and child care), or other atypical sources. Social Security is by far the biggest type of government payment received, with several times more beneficiaries receiving several times larger checks than from other government payment programs (e.g., unemployment insurance or workers' compensation programs, or Supplemental Nutritional Assistance Program [SNAP], Temporary Assistance for Needy Families [TANF], or Supplemental Security Income [SSI] welfare programs for the poor).[5]

Taxes on Income

Taxes on income shape the amount of income that is ultimately available for households to spend. There are two major types of taxes on income. What we typically call *income taxes* are federal, state, and sometimes local governments' tax levies on household incomes. These are the federal and state income tax lines on people's pay stubs, which are mainly involved when people file their 1040s and their state/local equivalents in April. These income taxes are generally progressive (some states have flat taxes), which means that wealthier people pay more than poorer people. For example, in 2013, a household earning less than $8,925 owed 10 percent in federal income taxes, whereas one earning $100,000 owed 28 percent, and one earning more than $400,000 owed almost 40 percent. Higher income families are often able to pay less in taxes than the rates listed in federal tax return bracket tables because households have a range of deductions and credits that ultimately reduce their obligations. Although tax rates seem highly progressive, the larger tax structure is designed to enable people to move down in tax bracket by structuring their financial reports in ways that make their incomes nontaxable or taxable at lower rates.

A second type of income tax is *payroll taxes*, which are levied on employment (including much self-employment) income. Payroll taxes have increasingly replaced personal (and corporate) income taxes as an income source for the federal government.[6] These are the Social Security and Medicare tax lines on your pay stubs. Payroll taxes are often construed as a form of nontaxes, both in political debate and in major household finance data sources. The tax status of payroll taxes is complicated by the fact that they are nominally tied to some (vague) future promise of receiving health insurance and cash payments in old age. As such, it resembles a pension investment. However, it also resembles a regular tax and associated welfare program, in the sense that Social Security is a pay-as-you-go system where today's workers pay for the benefits of today's elderly. Presumably, today's young workers will receive similar benefits when they are old. To the extent that they do not, then payroll taxes are simple taxes that pay for the working-age population's elderly contemporaries, much like tax-financed welfare programs pay for their poor contemporaries.

Federal payroll taxes are flat taxes levied against employment income that, in 2013 (the survey year), amounted to a rate of 7.65 percent on the first $113,700. This income cap helps drive down the rate paid by higher income households. The data suggest that the median households earning less than $50,000 paid 7.61 percent of their income in payroll taxes, and the middle 50 percent paid between 5 percent and 7.65 percent. In contrast, households that were earning at least $250,000 paid 5.3 percent of their income in payroll taxes, with the middle 50 percent of that group paying between 4.4 percent and 5.7 percent. Higher income households pay proportionally less in payroll taxes due to these caps. The net result is that this is partly a regressive tax, as poorer people pay proportionally more of their income. The program is also regressive in the sense that people who earned more money in their working years receive bigger cash payments. Richer people actually receive the biggest Social Security payouts.

Financial Obligations, Discretionary Spending, and Savings

In addition to taxes, often families are tied into several contractual *financial obligations*, which are legally binding payment obligations. For example, households have to repay debts, such as a vehicle lease or rent. Some households are required to pay child support or alimony. Federal Reserve estimates maintain that the average U.S. household owes about 15 percent of its posttax income in mortgages or rents, property tax payments, home insurance, and service payments on consumer debts.[7] Note that this is an average. As discussed later, much of the country carries little debt, and many households have already paid off their mortgages. These averages are pulled up by a narrower set of households that carries larger obligations.

The amount of income left after a household pays its taxes and meets its financial obligations is available for *discretionary spending*. These are spending choices that the household has the ability to make or forgo. Money that is left unspent is *saved*, which can be used to build a households' wealth.

Wealth

We tend to understand people's economic situation with reference to their incomes. People are classified as poor when their incomes fall below the poverty line. Many of us assume that people are "rich" if their incomes are high. Wealth is an equally critical—some might argue more critical—determinant of households' financial security. *Wealth* (or "net worth") is the value of a household's assets, less the value of its outstanding debt. Figure 2.2 describes the distribution of household wealth.

Data from the *Survey of Consumer Finances*[8] suggest that the median household had a net worth of about $81,000. The distribution of wealth varies more widely than income. The middle 50 percent—those between the 25th and 75th percentiles—registered between $9,000 and $315,000 in net worth. About 13 percent of households have a negative net worth (i.e., they owe more money than the value of their possessions). In contrast, about 18 percent are worth at least $500,000, 9 percent at least $1 million, and 0.6 percent at least $10 million.

Households hold their wealth across a range of *assets*, that is, property that can be converted into money. The most common forms of assets held by households are cash accounts (held by 93 percent of households), vehicles (86 percent), homes (65 percent), retirement accounts (49 percent), nonretirement financial investments (42 percent), or owned businesses (10 percent). Generally, these holdings are modest. For example, the median

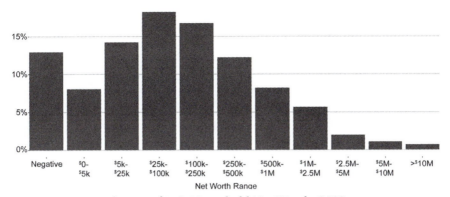

Figure 2.2   Distribution of U.S. Household Net Worth, 2013.
Source: Federal Reserve Bank (2014), *Survey of Consumer Finances.*

cash account held about $4,520, and 25 percent of households' cash accounts hold less than $900. The median owned home was worth $170,000. Few households have retirement savings that could cover more than a few years at the poverty line.

The value of assets is offset by *debts*, that is, borrowed money that a household is contractually obligated to repay. Debt is an important part of asset acquisition. The acquisition of major assets, such as a home, vehicle, or, in the United States, a postsecondary education, can require more money than families typically have saved. They must borrow money to ultimately accumulate money.

About 74 percent of households carry debt. The most common forms of debt are home-related, such as mortgages, home equity loans, or lines of credit. About 42 percent of households (66 percent of homeowners) carry these types of loans, and these debtors owe a median of $60,000 (or 15 percent of household assets) on these kinds of debt. Home-related debt is by far the biggest debt on household balance sheets. Education debt is a second important form of debt. Roughly one-quarter of households carried education debt, with a median debt of $16,720 (18 percent of household assets). Credit card debt is often discussed, but it is a minor item on household balance sheets. About 42 percent of U.S. households carried credit card balances, and the median balance carried by this minority was about $2,300 (or 1.5 percent of household assets—credit cards are generally extended to people with incomes and assets).

These are the basic parts of households' financial picture. A household must manage inflows and outflows of money, save money, and accumulate money while managing debt. Some households successfully juggle these moving parts, while others find this balancing act more difficult. Who tends to succeed, and who is more prone to difficulty? We turn to this question next.

Demographic Differences in Financial Fortunes

Demographic comparisons are useful in helping us understand what is going on with household finances. Knowing who is faring better or worse in terms of earning income may help shed light on what is happening with U.S. household finances. In this section, we concentrate on seven types of demographic categories that demarcate meaningful differences in financial situations: sex, race, age, education, marital status, labor force status, and parental status.

Table 2.1 spells out some of these differences in terms of what people earn and own. In reading these statistics, remember that these categories overlap and cut across each other. Households are more likely to be headed by someone who is married, in the working-age population, white, employed, male, and with less than a college degree's worth of educational attainment. These characteristics describe general tendencies rather than provide a profile of the majority. Only about 11 percent of U.S. households are headed by a working-age, married, employed white man with a high school degree or less.

Income

Household incomes tended to be higher in households headed by men, non-Hispanic whites, the college-educated, the employed, and those who were paired (married or cohabiting). Households headed by a female, nonwhite, Hispanic, young, undereducated, unemployed, or unpaired person were more likely to be poor.

Some of these differences make sense. For example, younger people are often studying or just starting out in their careers, and they have been hit hard by unemployment in recent years. Older people are less likely to be working or are working less than they did during their peak earning years. Paired adults earn more because there are more potential earners, or a division of labor enables one member to commit more fully to earning than he or she would as a single person. The college-educated are presumably better trained for better jobs. Traditionally, women and nonwhites have been subject to discrimination in job markets, and nonwhites' difficulty in accumulating wealth has been compounded by housing discrimination.

Table 2.1 Demographic Profile of U.S. Household Heads and Their Finances, 2013

	# HHs (Millions)	% HHs	Income			Net Worth			
			Median	% Poor	>$100k	Median	<$20k	>$200k	>$1M
Total	123	100%	$46,668	14%	21%	$81,456	33%	34%	9%
Sex									
Male	88	72%	$59,857	10%	27%	$113,440	28%	39%	12%
Female	35	28%	$27,265	23%	5%	$29,660	46%	21%	3%
Race									
White, Non-Hispanic	82	67%	$55,799	9%	26%	$142,122	24%	43%	13%
Nonwhite or Hispanic	40	33%	$33,480	23%	11%	$18,184	51%	16%	3%
Age									
<35	25	21%	$35,103	24%	10%	$10,433	62%	8%	1%
35–44	21	17%	$60,872	13%	28%	$46,978	37%	26%	6%
45–54	24	20%	$60,872	11%	28%	$104,970	29%	37%	10%
55–64	23	19%	$55,191	10%	26%	$165,068	24%	46%	15%
65–74	16	13%	$45,897	9%	21%	$232,282	14%	54%	19%
75+	13	11%	$28,204	13%	7%	$195,574	16%	49%	9%
Education									
<HS	13	11%	$22,522	34%	2%	$17,278	52%	15%	1%
HS	38	31%	$36,726	16%	8%	$52,287	38%	24%	3%
Some College	23	19%	$40,987	14%	14%	$47,080	39%	27%	6%
College	48	39%	$79,539	6%	39%	$218,904	21%	52%	19%

(continued)

Table 2.1 (*continued*)

	# HHs (Millions)	% HHs	Income			Net Worth			
			Median	% Poor	>$100k	Median	<$20k	>$200k	>$1M
Total	123	100%	$46,668	14%	21%	$81,456	33%	34%	9%
Marital Status									
Paired	70	57%	$70,408	7%	32%	$148,328	24%	43%	14%
Unpaired	53	43%	$28,001	22%	5%	$31,880	45%	22%	4%
Labor Force									
Working	87	71%	$56,002	11%	25%	$118,060	28%	39%	9%
Not Working	35	29%	$29,421	19%	9%	$69,112	35%	32%	10%
Life Cycle									
Under 55, Unpaired, and Childless	17	14%	$31,694	23%	6%	$14,195	55%	13%	2%
Under 55, Paired, and Childless	11	9%	$63,611	4%	26%	$59,370	36%	28%	4%
Under 55, Paired, and with Children	31	25%	$75,278	10%	35%	$75,996	32%	33%	9%
Under 55, Unpaired, and with Children	11	9%	$28,204	32%	4%	$8,396	65%	7%	1%
Over 55 and Working	22	18%	$69,191	4%	33%	$260,490	15%	56%	22%
Over 55 and Not Working	30	24%	$31,450	15%	10%	$157,148	22%	44%	10%

Source: U.S. Federal Reserve (2014).
Note: Households counts may not add up to 123M due to rounding.

These individual demographic factors are related. For example, female households are more likely to be single (as paired households tend to identify the male as the "head"). Single adult households are disproportionately younger or older. Younger or older people are more likely to be unemployed, as are those without a college education. Whites have higher rates of college attainment relative to nonwhites/Hispanics as a whole. We could go on and on with these chains of relationships. The main point is that the individual effects of these demographic factors need to be parsed by using an analytical method called regression analysis,[9] which separates out the independent explanatory factors on a particular outcome. The procedure helps us discern the degree to which sex, race, education, age, marital status, or parenting status coincide with higher earnings, net of each other. The results are presented in Table 2.2.

The results suggest the typical female-headed household can be expected to earn about 7 percent less than a household headed by a man of the same race, age, education, and marital, labor force, and parental status. A household headed by a nonwhite or Hispanic person earns almost one-quarter less than an otherwise similar household headed by a white person. Households headed by older people tend to earn double that of a younger household with similar labor force status, educational attainment, and so on. The typical college graduate is estimated to earn 2.5 times the income of an otherwise similar household headed by a college dropout. Parents earn slightly more than nonparents. Income-earning advantages are accruing to men, whites, older people, the more highly educated, people who are paired, people who are working, and people with children.

Wealth

The differences in wealth are far starker than differences in income. Table 2.3 describes the results of a similar regression analysis predicting household wealth.

Some of these results are more straightforward to explain. For example, older people have much more wealth than younger people, in part as a result of the young not having had enough time to accumulate wealth of their own. Moreover, older people are more likely to have inherited any family wealth that might exist. More educated households have more wealth, in part because their higher incomes have allowed them to save more money and accumulate more wealth. Lower incomes and potentially higher living costs might also explain why single people are estimated to have one-quarter the accumulated wealth of their paired counterparts. Wealth differentials for those who are working might also exist for the same reason.

Table 2.2   **Demographic Predictors of Household Income, 2013**

	Estimate	Coeff.	SE
Baseline Income	$17,891	9.792	0.043
Sex (Baseline: Male)			
Female	–7%	–0.072	0.035
Race (Baseline: White Non-Hispanic)			
Nonwhite/Hispanic	–23%	–0.268	0.022
Age (Baseline:<35 years)			
35–44	+50%	0.403	0.032
45–54	+51%	0.412	0.036
55–64	+70%	0.533	0.033
65–74	+98%	0.685	0.036
75+	+85%	0.614	0.038
Education (Baseline:<HS)			
HS	+41%	0.342	0.030
Some College	+66%	0.505	0.038
College	+162%	0.962	0.029
Marital Status (Baseline: Paired)			
Unpaired	–54%	–0.774	0.036
Labor Force (Baseline: Not Working)			
Working	+64%	0.497	0.026
Parental Status (Baseline: No Children)			
Has Children	+13%	0.123	0.027

Model predicts logged household income.
Coeff. = Coefficient (predicted effect of category on logged income).
SE = Standard error of estimated effect.

Source: U.S. Federal Reserve (2014).

The Economic Classes

As noted at the outset of this chapter, most Americans have a vague grasp of other people's financial situations, and they often understand society-level financial issues through the prism of their personal situation and the situations of those around them. Our understanding of how household finances differ often involves a vague three-category typology. The widespread sense is that we have a prosperous and privileged upper

Table 2.3 Demographic Predictors of Household Net Worth, 2013

	Estimate	Coeff.	SE
Baseline Net Worth	−$30,954	12.30	0.03
Sex (Baseline: Male)			
Female	−11%	−0.11	0.02
Race (Baseline: White Non-Hispanic)			
Nonwhite/Hispanic	−19%	−0.21	0.01
Age (Baseline:<35 years)			
35–44	+25%	0.22	0.02
45–54	+54%	0.44	0.02
55–64	+92%	0.65	0.02
65–74	+142%	0.89	0.03
75+	+143%	0.89	0.03
Education (Baseline:<HS)			
HS	+8%	0.21	0.02
Some College	+24%	0.59	0.02
College	+79%	0.59	0.02
Marital Status (Baseline: Paired)			
Unpaired	−29%	−0.25	0.02
Labor Force (Baseline: Not Working)			
Working	+22%	0.20	0.02
Parental Status (Baseline: No Children)			
Has Children	+1%	0.01	0.02

Model predicts logged household net worth (Shifted + 250000).
Coeff.=Coefficient (predicted effect of category on net worth).
SE=Standard error of estimated effect.

Source: U.S. Federal Reserve (2014).

class, as well as an underclass that struggles. In between these two groups, we understand there to be a middle group of regular people, whose economic fortunes are the topic of debate. In the abstract, the scheme is easy to grasp.

When we move beyond these broad generalities, it becomes quite clear that people's grasp of household finances differs. Very poor people think that they are middle class, as do many multimillionaires. As discussed at the outset of this chapter, this is probably related to the fact that most people are surrounded by others who are in roughly the same financial position. We tend not to mix with people who are markedly richer or poorer than us, which leaves us with a very weak sense of the financial situation faced by people who aren't like us. Table 2.4 presents a better-specified view of how household finances differ across the U.S. economic hierarchy.

At the top of the economic pyramid, there are the wealthy and near-wealthy. These two groups are distinguished by their considerable accumulated wealth, which seems roughly sufficient to guarantee that a person never has to work again (as long as they keep their lifestyle expectations in check). At the bottom of the economic pyramid, there are those conventionally considered society's poor. They tend to earn and own little. Between these two extremes, there are three groups termed the "middle class." They may earn a living wage and only sometimes accumulate much in the way of wealth, most of which is invested in a house. The middle class comprises about 86 percent of society.

The Wealthy

When most people think about the wealthy's possessions, they imagine the accoutrements of the rich—fancy homes, fine art, expensive cars, designer clothing, vacation homes, and so on. However, these are not the possessions that define wealth. Income-generating assets make wealthy people wealthy. The bulk of the wealthy's accumulated wealth is held in income-generating property, such as businesses, financial investments, and nonresidential real estate. Over the past several decades, these types of assets have been spectacularly profitable, both in comparison to how profitable they were in the mid-20th century and in comparison to labor today.[10]

Questions about the wealthy must always deal with the nagging question of where to draw the line between the rich and nonrich. Just how much money does it take to be considered "wealthy"? Different people harbor different definitions. As noted earlier, more than half of the country believes that it takes a yearly income of $150,000 to be "rich." At the other end of the spectrum, there are people like Louisiana Congressperson John Fleming, who argued that his household could not bear paying more taxes despite his $6 million annual income because after "you pay 500 employees, you pay rent, you pay equipment, and food," you are left with "a mere fraction of that"—"by the time I feed my family, I have maybe $400,000 left over."[11] People harbor different ideas about who should be considered rich.

Table 2.4 A Typology of U.S. Economic Classes

	Overall	Poor Income Below PL	Lower- Middle Income Below 200% PL	Middle-Class Income 2x–4x PL	Upper-Middle Income Above 400% PL	Near Wealthy Net Worth Above $1.4M	Wealthy Net Worth Above $5.3M
% U.S. Households	100%	13%	23%	28%	29%	5%	2%
Median Income	**$47k**	**$11k**	**$25k**	**$46k**	**$101k**	**$192k**	**$520k**
[25th, 75th Percentile Values]	[$24k, $90k]	[$9k, $16k]	[$18k, $32k]	[$37k, $61k]	[$75k, $142k]	[$110k, $311k]	[$259k, $1M]
% Receive [Median Received]:							
Wages	72% [$46k]	52% [$10k]	59% [$25k]	76% [$44k]	87% [$91k]	68% [$157k]	70% [$222k]
Government Payments	44% [$12k]	66% [$8k]	58% [$16k]	42% [$17k]	27% [$17k]	41% [$27k]	39% [$27k]
Business Profits	16% [$15k]	6% [$4k]	9% [$12k]	14% [$12k]	19% [$17k]	48% [$41k]	72% [$123k]
Financial Income	23% [$958]	4% [$602]	8% [$244]	18% [$300]	35% [$588]	72% [$16k]	87% [$78k]
Median Net Worth	**$81k**	**$5k**	**$16k**	**$77k**	**$225k**	**$2.3M**	**$8.5M**
[25th, 75th Percentile Values]	[$9k, $316k]	[$0, $34k]	[$1k, $86k]	[$14k, $218k]	[$89k, $585k]	[$1.8M, $3.2M]	[$7M, $14M]

(continued)

Table 2.4 *(continued)*

	Overall	Poor Income Below PL	Lower-Middle Income Below 200% PL	Middle-Class Income 2x–4x PL	Upper-Middle Income Above 400% PL	Near Wealthy Net Worth Above $1.4M	Wealthy Net Worth Above $5.3M
% Possess [Median Value]:							
Home	60% [$180k]	23% [$92k]	42% [$120k]	61% [$150k]	81% [$225k]	95% [$539k]	92% [$1M]
Vehicles	86% [$19k]	62% [$7k]	80% [$10k]	92% [$15k]	95% [$24k]	93% [$33k]	96% [$47k]
Cash Accounts	92% [$7k]	72% [$556]	86% [$1k]	97% [$4k]	99% [$13k]	99% [$71k]	100% [$193k]
Retirement Accounts	47% [$53k]	5% [$4k]	21% [$9k]	49% [$24k]	77% [$80k]	88% [$443k]	89% [$780k]
Financial Investments	24% [$25k]	7% [$5k]	11% [$7k]	24% [$10k]	41% [$20k]	73% [$551k]	85% [$2.4M]
Business Equity	10% [$100k]	3% [$22k]	4% [$23k]	8% [$29k]	12% [$60k]	36% [$784k]	72% [$3.2M]
Demographics (% Headed by):							
White	70%	48%	58%	74%	81%	91%	94%
Under 35 Years	21%	37%	24%	21%	15%	1%	2%
Over 65 Years	24%	18%	28%	26%	17%	38%	38%
Married/Cohabiting	57%	30%	44%	59%	72%	84%	88%
College Degree or More	39%	16%	20%	34%	60%	82%	84%
Employed	71%	60%	61%	72%	83%	72%	77%

PL = poverty line, k = thousands, M = millions.
Source: U.S. Federal Reserve (2014).

Drawing a practical dividing line between the wealthy and nonwealthy is difficult, unless you set it at some patently uncontroversial level, such as a net worth in the hundreds of millions or billions of dollars. Many single-digit millionaires reject the idea that they are wealthy. Many nonmillionaires have difficulty envisioning how someone with that much net worth could be worried about money.

Where to draw the line? At some point, an analysis needs to set provisional definitions in order to move past measurement debates and start interpreting data. The analysis for this book is based on two thresholds. The higher threshold, which is designated the "wealthy," includes households with a net worth of $5.1 million or more. The lower threshold, designated the "near-wealthy," has a net worth of $1.4 million or more. The former group comprises about 2 percent of society, and the latter comprises about 5 percent. Moving forward, references to wealthy Americans, refers to both groups.

Explaining the Thresholds

Why these thresholds? Here, "wealthy" is defined as having enough wealth to finance a typical or comparatively privileged income into perpetuity. A wealthy person has enough wealth to be reasonably assured of maintaining a regular person's lifestyle without ever having to work again. They are in a position of supreme security, and the money worries faced by this group are probably more fairly characterized as concerns with maintaining a privileged lifestyle and transmitting that advantage to future generations than with genuine fears of absolute deprivation. We use these two criteria to demarcate two groups: the *wealthy*, who are in a position of supreme security, and the *near-wealthy*, who are in a reasonably secure position.

These are the standards used to distinguish the wealthy and near-wealthy from the rest of society. We want a level of wealth that can generate sufficient living income indefinitely, where people can survive "on the interest" without spending away their principal (original) investment.[12] We presume that the near-wealthy can survive on a median income and that the Wealthy can survive on a 75th percentile income (accounting for cost-of-living increases).[13] Regarding the amount of risk assumed for our lower, near-wealthy standard, we will assume an asset portfolio that is wholly invested in financial assets (no proprietary businesses or real estate) with 25 percent of its funds invested in T-bills, 50 percent in Treasury bonds, and 25 percent in an S&P 500 index fund.[14] This type of allocation is roughly similar to what the investment analysis firm Morningstar would describe as a conservative investment portfolio.[15] For our higher standard, we consider a 25 percent T-bill/75 percent T-bond allocation, which mirrors

Morningstar's recommended allocations for an "Ultra Short-Range" income-oriented portfolio for retirees. Most financial planners would agree that these allocations are very conservative.

Between 1928 and 2010, blue chip stocks (as measured by the S&P 500) appreciated by an average annual rate of 11.3 percent, or 8.2 percentage points above inflation.[16] Blue chip long-term debt (as measured by the 10-year Treasury bond) averaged a real (inflation-adjusted) appreciation rate of 2.1 percent annually. Short-term debt (measured by the 3-month T-bill) averaged 0.5 points over inflation. This renders an expected real annual rate of return of 3.2 percent for our lower standard and 1.7 percent for our higher standard of risk aversion.[17]

If we want to receive $90,000 (inflation-adjusted) into perpetuity, at a real return rate of 1.7 percent, the formula suggests that we would need about $5.3 million. A person with $5.3 million in accumulated wealth is extremely secure in the expectation that they can live among society's top 25 percent forever, or at least the rest of their lives, without having to work or assume much in the way of financial risk. To receive $45,000 at a real return rate of 3.2 percent per year, we would need about $1.4 million. A person could secure a median income with a quite conservative investment portfolio. We use these thresholds to divide the wealthy and near-wealthy from the rest of society.

Highly Diversified, and More Invested in Businesses and Finance

In addition to having more money, these wealthy are also distinguished by the diversification of their income and assets. Whereas most households tend to earn the bulk of their money from one or two sources and have most of their assets stored in one or two assets, wealthy households are diversified.

First, wages play less of a role in sustaining wealthier households. The median middle-class households and upper-middle-class households receive 88 percent and 95 percent of their income from wages, respectively. Wages contribute 45 percent of the median near-wealthy household's income, and just under one-quarter of the median wealthy households. Wealthier households earn money from a wider variety of sources. Just under one-third of wealthy households received income from at least four sources (among wages, proprietary businesses, financial proceeds, retirement pensions, government payments, rents, or royalties), while only 2 percent received income from only one source. Income streams tended to be less diversified among the near-wealthy, but their income still tended to be much more diversified than those in the middle class.

In comparison with the rest of the population, wealthier households receive much more money from proprietary businesses and financial investments, and they have much higher financial and business holdings. Strong business earnings suggest that much of the wealthier classes are composed of successful businesspeople. This does not imply that starting a business is a likely way to get rich. First, some selection effects are at work here. Proprietary business incomes have stagnated alongside wages over most of the income scale during the past 30 years,[18] but unsuccessful businesspeople quickly cease being business owners and get reabsorbed by the labor force. Second, some of these businesses are minority shares in a business in which they take a passive role; that is, they had money and then invested in the business, rather than starting a business and getting rich.

The wealthy have substantial financial holdings from which they receive considerable income. These holdings are certainly part of the reason that the wealthy have become wealthier. Financial markets have boomed over the past several decades, both relative to other asset classes and in comparison to financial investments in earlier eras. The wealthy have the resources to take part in these profits.

About 33 percent of households in this group receive government payments. This unexpectedly high incidence is due to the fact that wealthy people tend to be older, and this group collects Social Security payments. The median take from this source was $25,200, which is high compared to the amount received by poorer households. Social Security gives higher payments to those who earned more in their working years.

A Demographic Portrait of the Wealthy in the United States

The wealthy are disproportionately older, whiter, more educated, and more often married compared to other groups. Although most wealthy and near-wealthy households are headed by someone in their sixties or older, only minorities of people in their sixties or seventies are part of this group (the data suggest at most 3 percent for the former, and less than 7 percent for the latter). The wealthier classes may skew older for at least two reasons: they have had time to earn and accrue wealth, or they have reached an age in which family wealth is likely to have been passed on to them.

Many millionaires are likely late-career professionals or executive-level workers who earned enough to accrue into the low single-digit millions in net worth with their high incomes and accompanying latitude to save and invest money. Their ranks probably include many retired doctors, lawyers, dentists, engineers, small businesspeople, mid-level executives, and others who got educated, got and stayed married, saved regularly, and managed their money reasonably well over a lifetime. The dominance of earned wealth among the ranks of the wealthy is probably truer of those with net worth in the single to tens of millions. As one moves higher up the ranks of the wealthy, inherited wealth becomes more prevalent.[19]

Thomas Piketty[20] suggests that the wealthy were more likely to maintain their position through inheritance before the 1950s. By 1950, the degree to which societal wealth was transferred across generations was falling in proportion to the total amount of household wealth accumulation, and it remained quite low during the 1960s and 1970s. In more recent decades, the concentration of wealth and the high returns to accrued assets relative to wages have likely bolstered intergenerational wealth transfers among the wealthy and pushed us back toward where we were before the 1950s.

Money is not the only resource transferred across generations. Noncash intergenerational transfers helped place today's and future wealthy people into a position to maintain their status. For example, this group enjoys high education levels, which may have been a function of their parent's ability to cover the costs of higher education or attain a foothold in better school districts. The wealthy are more likely to be homeowners and business owners, and much of this "earned" wealth may have been financed initially with parental aid. These forms of early-life help put young people in a position to begin accruing wealth early, which is important if someone of more modest means hopes to become a millionaire.

The Poor

Conceptually, the poor are distinguished by economic deprivation. They do not have enough money to secure the things they need. Deprivation is often described as being one of two types. In *relative deprivation*, people believe that, given their personal status or station in society, they ought to have access to particular goods and services. For example, it is relative deprivation if a person does not own a car but feels he ought to have a car by virtue of his age, background, or occupation. Relative deprivation exists where someone is not afforded access to a good, service, or right that is expected to be afforded to people of a particular status, ability, or ethic to which the deprived person self-identifies. In contrast, *absolute deprivation* occurs when someone lacks access to a good, service, or right that is necessary to meet some uncontroversial basic standard of living that transcends people's status or personal characteristics. This involves things presumed to be necessary to ensure survival, basic social integration, or minimal levels of well-being. Starvation is a form of absolute deprivation—all people undoubtedly need food, and, on the whole, society accepts the notion that no person should be hungry. Not having a car might be considered a form of absolute deprivation for the 45 percent of Americans who have no access to public transit,[21] if we presume that all people should have some reliable conveyance to work, school, shopping, or healthcare. The key difference is that these types of needs associated with absolute deprivation are not seen as contingent on a person's status. These two different conceptions of deprivation play an important role in shaping public debates over how society should respond to people's money problems. Voters are more inclined to support fights against poverty in the form of absolute deprivation, but they are less inclined for poverty as relative deprivation.

Officially "Poor"

Conventionally, households are designated as "poor" if their gross income falls below the Census Bureau's or Department of Health and Human Services' poverty thresholds.[22] The official poverty line is society's most conventionalized method for differentiating society's poor from the nonpoor. These thresholds are used when discussing the poverty rate, a metric used to determine the prevalence of poverty in society. This measure is widely used by government programs to determine eligibility for public assistance. This line is also widely used by scholars in poverty research. The specific income level that one needs to earn to be considered "officially poor" changes from year to year, and it varies by the number of adults and children in a household.[23] In 2013, it ranged as follows: $11,534 for an elderly single-person household; $24,008 for a two-adult, two-child family; and $52,430 for the rare nine-adult household.

Despite its widespread use, the traditional poverty line is a crude measure. This line is calculated as three times the inflation-adjusted cost of what the U.S. Department of Agriculture estimated to be the cost of a minimum food diet in 1963.[24] The original poverty line in the United States was drawn roughly 50 years ago. At its drawing, it was presumed that one could sustain a minimally acceptable lifestyle on a pretax income that was three times the estimated market cost of what USDA officials deemed to be a modest food diet. After that threshold was set, the Bureau adjusted the figure annually according to the Consumer Price Index (CPI).

Are the "Poor" Really Poor?

The crudeness of the official poverty line has led some analysts to ask whether the "officially poor" are absolutely poor. Whether poverty is relative or absolute is important to debates about the state of household finances. If poverty is overwhelmingly relative and not absolute, then discussions about poverty primarily involve matters of distributional equality.

Distributional inequality does not imply that people are desperate. If a billionaire joins a community of 100 middle-class families, the community becomes very unequal even though no one has become poorer in an absolute sense. Some observers, such as the Heritage Foundation's Richard Rector, advance this type of assertion in noting that many of those who are officially poor enjoy a range of material comforts that were considered luxuries in previous generations, such as air conditioners, dishwashers, flat screen TVs, or video game consoles.[25] Obesity, not starvation, is the principle nutritional problem facing the poor. Many "poor" own their own home, and the average poor person has a home with more living space than the typical resident of Amsterdam or Paris.[26] Although situations of absolute deprivation do occur (e.g., homelessness or hunger), these situations tend to be temporary or transitional situations, rather than a permanent state of affairs.[27] Moreover, these estimates may ignore the effect that expansive social programs in the United States have on the incidence of genuine poverty.[28]

These observations evoke questions about whether people's money problems are indeed serious, as opposed to a matter of people simply wanting to enjoy a better lifestyle than their incomes permit. Opponents of progressive redistribution often ground their policy views on the belief that absolute poverty is a rarity in the United States, that U.S. living standards are in fact rising rapidly and across the board, and that most people's complaints about money involve poor personal financial management, "class envy," and a desire to raise their own living standards at the expense of society's "makers" (as opposed to "takers"). In many corners of public debate, concerns expressed about the economic problems faced by the poor and middle class are construed as being more a matter of frustrated lifestyle aspirations and less about the threat of real, serious economic deprivation.

In the next chapter, we probe household finance and cost-of-living data to explore questions about absolute deprivation's genuine extent, particularly given the existence of the U.S. social safety net. In the following section, we take this conventional poverty line as given, in part because this threshold is a useful dividing line that is used to discern who merits public assistance from those who do not. Next, we explore the details of this group's finances.

Poor People's Money

The median poor household earned $11,000 in 2013, and its "middle 50 percent" (those between 25th and 75th percentile incomes) earned between $8,000 and $15,000. This amounts to a monthly income of $666 to $1,250 per month. Despite any disagreements about whether the poverty line represents a precise dividing line between the economically desperate and not desperate, it seems likely that most readers would find it challenging to sustain what they would personally consider a basic livelihood on this income.

About two-thirds of these households received income from government payments. Just under half of this group received money from welfare programs (e.g., TANF or SNAP), about 30 percent from Social Security, and 15 percent from both welfare and Social Security. A smaller proportion received income from other programs, such as workers' compensation or unemployment insurance. Among those who received any payments, median receipts from government assistance were $8,360–$3,600 for welfare recipients and $8,520 for Social Security recipients. This suggests that about one-third of poor households receive no assistance.

The second most common source of income comes from employment wages. About 50 percent of poor households earned income from this source. Among all poor households that earned any wages, median earnings from this source was $9,600. This is equal to 1,280 hours of work at the federal minimum wage, or 32 weeks of full-time, 40 hour-per-week employment. These are the "working poor." Many of them are low-wage workers who experienced some employment or income disruption during the survey year. Others are elderly workers who work to bridge shortfalls in their public or private pensions. The data suggest that the poor are sometimes partly sustained by retirement pensions, financial income, or business income.

The poor generally have few assets, and the assets they do possess tend to be stored in one of three asset types: automobiles, cash accounts, and owned homes. About 70 percent of households in this group owned a cash account, 61 percent owned a vehicle, and 22 percent owned a home. Cars depreciate in value fairly quickly, and most retail cash accounts lose real purchasing power over time. Prevailing deposit rates have been lower than inflation for several years. The median vehicle owner's cars were valued at $7,200, and the median bank account holder had about $510 stored in cash or near-cash instruments. Both assets depreciate in value over time—vehicles lose value under any circumstances, and cash accounts do so when interest rates are lower than inflation. Combined with the fact that low-value homes are least likely to appreciate, this means that the poor's asset base stagnates (if it does not erode) over time, rather than appreciates.

Theoretically, the poor could help themselves by investing in higher-performing assets, such as stocks. This idea has motivated some policymakers to propose schemes that encourage financial investment among the poor. For example, in 2015, the federal government launched the myRA program, a tax-sheltered, low-fee, small-denomination retirement program that was designed to encourage the poor to make more financial investments. In general, it is hard for the poor to "play the market" with banking and financial fees heavy on low-asset households. Many market schemes designed to help the poor invest are larded up with high fees, and, of course, this group does not have much money to invest in the first place. This last piece was a more critical flaw in this program, and similar ideas that investment promotion will help the poor. If a poor family were to put aside an extra $50 a month (a considerable part of their disposable income) for 30 years, the program's own estimates suggest that he or she would be left with a nest egg of just under $27,000—two years of poverty line income replacement. These schemes do not do much if social programs are not generous.

Note that the poor are less likely to be indebted, relative to the middle class. This low indebtedness is probably a matter of this group's poor access to credit. Lenders typically won't extend credit to this group, so this group tends not to borrow. Often, the credit that is available to the poor is extended on onerous terms. For example, credit markets make loans available to anyone who receives a regular paycheck through payday loans, whose interest costs can run into the hundreds or even thousands of percentage points on an annual basis. A 2012 analysis by the Pew Research Center suggests that about 8 percent of Americans earning below $15,000 per year use such loans, a rate that seems commensurate with the lower-middle class and middle-middle class (see the next section).[29] For the most part, the poor are comparatively less disposed to incur debts and are not particularly inclined to use the debt arrangements most available to them.

Profiling the Poor

Overall, the poor are more likely to be younger or older (not middle aged), single, less educated, nonwhite, and nonemployed. These are general demographic tendencies. The poor are more demographically diverse than these broad characterizations suggest.

About 20 percent of poor households are headed by someone who is disabled, and another 17 percent are headed by retirees. This group may face considerable obstacles to earning money through markets, generally receives few to no wages, and most of this group (well over 90 percent) receives government assistance. In addition to the fact that both groups almost universally receive government payments, public assistance through the Social Security program is comparatively generous for these two groups. On average, members of these two groups receive around $9,300 in government assistance, which is about two to four times more than other poor groups. Of the various poor demographics profiled here, only retirees have a substantial proportion of group members with some accumulated wealth. The data suggest that 25 percent of poor retirees have $128,500 or more in net worth, often invested in homes. Overall, though, this group's access to accumulated wealth is limited.

Another 21 percent of this group is headed by single parents or guardians. This category includes households with nonmarried/cohabiting heads of household and at least one resident child. A large majority of this group (~86 percent) has low education levels (high school or less). Most of this group is young (median age is 37), but about 10 percent are headed by someone aged 57 or older. Over half of this group earned wages in 2013. Employment rates were higher in black and Hispanic single-parent households (61 percent and 65 percent, respectively) than in white households (53 percent). Despite higher employment rates, the median single-parent black household earned just over half the wages received by whites or Hispanics ($5,000 versus $9,000 and $9,700, respectively).

Another 12 percent of poor households are headed by the young, aged 25 or less. Employment is very high in this group (87 percent), but incomes tend to be low because their ability is adversely affected by weak job market conditions in the survey year, their lack of experience, and the more time demands of schooling. Forty-one percent of this group self-describes as students. About 23 percent of these youth-headed households have resident children.

These four groups—those headed by the disabled, retirees, single parents, and the young—represent about 70 percent of the country's poor households. The distinguishing characteristics of this group include low educational attainment (82 percent less than college), disproportionate joblessness (30 percent self-reported as unemployed), and disproportionate Hispanic representation (28 percent Hispanic vs. 48 percent white). About half of these households have resident children.

The Middle Class

When we remove the poor, the near-wealthy, and the wealthy, we are left with 82 percent of U.S. households representing the middle class. The defining feature of the middle class is that they are too wealthy to receive extensive help from the government, but they are not wealthy enough to be guaranteed a middle-class livelihood without the ability and opportunity to maintain gainful work. This group can be understood as comprising three groups.

The Lower-Middle Class

Lower-middle-class households have incomes that lie between 100 percent and 200 percent of the poverty line. The median household in this group earns $23,000, and the middle 50 percent earns between $18,000 and $30,000. These incomes are generally sustained by a blend of wages, government assistance, and, to a lesser extent, pensions. Roughly 24 percent of U.S. households fall into this category.

As a group, they are not altogether different from the poor. Some analysts treat this group as the "near poor," and the fact that their incomes qualify them for a range of government payments and programs suggest that they are institutionally recognized as being in a financially precarious situation. Many of them could fall into official poverty were it not for their continuous employment, the continuity of their cohabitation arrangements, and, for retirees, their private pensions or Social Security payments (Social Security is not a means-tested program, which means rich and poor people get checks). Like the poor, many of those in the lower-middle class are heavily invested in their automobiles, although a larger proportion of this group owns their home than the poor.

About 28 percent of the lower-middle class is headed by someone older than 65. Although these households often do earn wage income, they more often are sustained by the Social Security program, which provides a median income of $13,200 to all senior-headed households in this class. For many elderly households, this public assistance program is sufficient to keep their household out of official poverty. Without the Social Security program, an estimated 59 percent of elderly lower-middle-class households would fall below the poverty line (see Chapter Three). Sometimes, this group supplements its income with modest private pension payments.

About 71 percent of the working-age lower-middle class (roughly half of the entire lower-middle class) earns enough money through wages to stay above the poverty line. This group includes many single-income families either because the household has only one adult head or one of its heads experienced unemployment. They tend to be less educated and thus earn less money when employed. This group also includes many single-income and highly educated households whose income was completely disrupted for some period during the year. This group can be considered the "working near-poor" and they effectively become the "working poor" in years where their income is interrupted by things such as a job loss or illness.

In general, this group has little accumulated wealth. Median net worth in this group is less than one year's poverty line income. The average household has more than one-third of its wealth stored in vehicles, which are nonperforming assets. Only about 23 percent own a home, and the median value of owned homes in this group was $120,000. Other assets are less widely held: 16 percent of them have any sheltered retirement savings, and 10 percent have any nonsheltered financial investments. The median household in this group has $600 in its bank accounts.

The Middle Class Proper

The middle-middle class includes the 30 percent of U.S. households earning between two and four times the poverty line. Median income is $45,000, and the middle 50 percent earns between $36,000 and $60,000. Median accumulated wealth is about $60,000, which is generally invested in a home. Aside from their cars and homes, this group tends not to accumulate much in the way of assets. About 43 percent have retirement accounts, and the median middle class retirement account has about $20,000 in holdings.

This group's demographic differs from that of the lower-middle class in several respects, particularly race, marriage/cohabitation, and full employment. As a whole, this group is not strikingly more educated than the lower-middle class (e.g., college attainment rates are roughly similar). This group's members are whiter, more likely to live as couples, and are more likely to have enjoyed uninterrupted employment. A household headed by the average, fully employed head is likely to fall here.

The Upper-Middle Class

In this book, households who earn more than 400 percent of poverty line income are designated as upper-middle income earners, but they lack sufficient wealth to be counted as wealthy or near wealthy. Younger members of this group seem well positioned to be wealthy with effective financial planning and the prevention of some major economic calamity. However, many members of this group are older and are struggling to establish a base of retirement assets that can work in conjunction with government payments programs such as Medicare and Social Security to render a reasonably comfortable retirement. Roughly 30 percent of U.S. households fall into this upper-middle class.

The members of the upper-middle class earn several times more than poor households and often accumulate some wealth over their lifetimes. This group is disproportionately white, middle aged, educated, married, and employed. It might include couples who are college-educated and reasonably well employed or later-career workers whose pay has risen over time. The median household in this group earns $100,000, and the middle 50 percent earn between $74,000 and $142,000. This income generally comes from wages.

Like the rest of the middle class, the upper-middle class is largely invested in their homes. Home ownership is high in this group (82 percent), and the median value of an owned home is $230,000. Members of this group are more likely to have other kinds of assets, and the value of these assets tend to be larger than that of other members of the middle class, but the degree to which these households are well diversified and wealthy should not be exaggerated. The median household in this group has no nonsheltered financial investments and about $28,000 in retirement accounts. Only about 68 percent of households in this category have any retirement savings, and the median account has about $75,000 in it, which is roughly six years of poverty-line income. The median household has about $12,000 in liquid holdings.

This group pays more taxes than other members of the middle class and tends to receive less direct government aid over their working years. However, this group does enjoy high public retirement benefits, and they benefit from several government programs that are designed to help them accumulate net worth.

Conclusion

This chapter presents an overview of U.S. household finances. We tend to interpret personal finance issues by using our personal situation as a baseline comparison. The problem is that we have limited exposure to people in substantially different economic circumstances from our own. By sharpening our understanding of the variety of economic situations in which other Americans operate, we have a better cognizance of our own economic situation and how household finances differ on the rungs above and below us.

The data suggest that somewhere somewhat less than one-tenth of society has considerable accrued wealth, such that they would be able to live a livelihood similar to that enjoyed (or endured) by a plurality of Americans without ever having to work again. In many respects, their financial problems seem more likely to be a product of lifestyle expectations or, as we will see later, attempts to secure a position for their children in the upper ranks of society during a period in which economic mobility is low and inequality is rising. This top 10 percent is more likely to be headed by older, college-educated, married whites, although other demographics are represented in this group.

At the other end of the economic hierarchy, there are society's poor, a group primarily composed of the very young, very poor, uneducated, non-whites, Hispanics, and single parents. The economic situation of these groups is far inferior to the upper class and even middle class, although there is some debate about whether the deprivation experienced by this group is relative or absolute (a theme we will pursue later). This group roughly comprises one-seventh of society, and their situation is not altogether different from another 23 percent or so of society that is part of the lower-middle class. In many respects, having the good fortune of not losing work, experiencing a health condition, or running into some other economic misfortune separates the poor and lower-middle class. In any case, together these two groups comprise about 40 percent of U.S. society.

The remaining 50 percent of society is the middle class. They can be divided into two groups. The upper-middle class tends to be whiter, middle-aged, better educated, and married/cohabiting, all of which translates into better employment opportunities, higher income, and ultimately more opportunity to accumulate wealth. The middle-middle class is highly employed, like the upper-middle class, but they tend to have less education, more nonwhites or Hispanics, and more single people.

These are the various perches through which we can view the issue of household finances. Knowing where we sit on the economic pyramid provides a sense of whether the mental baseline presented by our own financial circumstances is more typical or outlying relative to the rest of the country.

The audience for an academic book on household finances likely skews educated and, as a group, is probably wealthier and earns more money than the general population. Readers can easily cross-reference their personal circumstances with the population at large. While most of us consider our situation to by typical or middling, it is probably "typical" for our social milieu in a society that is highly segregated economically. Much of the country feels like it is struggling financially, and it can be instructive to see how others do so with fewer resources at their disposal.

As noted in the preceding discussion about the poor, there are many observers who question whether or not those who sit at lower stations in the economic hierarchy are really struggling with serious economic adversity. Are the middle and lower classes struggling with serious money problems? We turn to this issue next.

CHAPTER THREE

Financial Insecurity

> Private school: $32,000 a year per student. Mortgage: $96,000 a year. Co-op maintenance fee: $96,000 a year. Nanny: $45,000 a year. We're already at $269,000, and we haven't even gotten into taxes yet.
>
> Allen Salkin, *New York Times*[1]

The concept of financial insecurity is intuitively straightforward but harder to pin down in concrete terms. Most of us have vague ideas about what it means to be financially secure. It might involve being able to cover the bills and maybe save some extra money for the future. It might involve not staying awake at night worrying about money. Some people see it as having no limits on their spending. Apparently, there are Manhattanites with half-million dollar incomes who feel insecure, even though about half of U.S. households survive on less than that nanny's salary of $45,000 a year (and many probably do so believing that their finances are in order).

These definitional differences can cause people to talk past each other in discussions about financial insecurity, so it is worth being explicit about what is meant by the term. This chapter explores the concept of "financial insecurity," develops a scheme for assessing it, and tries to estimate its prevalence and severity in contemporary U.S. society. The data suggest that most households are insecure. At least one-quarter of the country's households are unable to sustain a very basic livelihood without outside assistance, and thus they seem incapable of functioning as independent financial concerns. Perhaps another quarter of the country lives month-to-month, a tenuous situation that could easily start unraveling if confronted with unanticipated—but reasonably commonplace—shocks, such as illness, injury, divorce, or even a major home or auto repair. Even if a household is able to maintain some degree of financial independence during its working years, the vast majority of Americans are under-saved for old age and seem ultimately destined for eventual dependency on the public rolls.

These findings suggest that Americans' economic security ultimately depends on the government's readiness to help them. Given these findings, one might question the proposition that Americans' economic security and wellbeing could be improved by limiting or diminishing the government's role in economic life. It is hard to envision how households could become more economically secure by weakening an institution upon which the vast majority of them depend. It is reasonable to ask whether a society can even maintain modern living standards without "government handouts."

Financial Insecurity as an Emotional State

Many people understand "financial insecurity" as an affective (or emotional) state. By this standard, people are considered to be financially secure if they *feel* secure. Surveys suggest that somewhere between one-third and one-half of Americans view their financial situation negatively,[2] so we might infer that this is the percentage of society facing financial struggles.

There are several reasons to pause before relying on people's self-perceived situations as a basis for assessing the prevalence and severity of financial insecurity. First, such sentiments can be divorced from people's objective financial situation. A 2012 U.S. Trust survey of multimillionaires found that more than one-tenth of respondents felt financially secure in the present, and roughly 30 percent do not expect to be financially secure into the future.[3] Likewise, many people are probably oblivious to the precarious state of their finances or have come to accept their own precariousness as normal, reasonable, fair, or a fact of life. Most people do not even track their finances,[4] and much of society lacks the tools to make sense of any financial information they might possess.[5] All of this is to suggest that most people's capacity to assuredly diagnose their financial situation as "secure" is questionable.

Moreover, feelings of financial insecurity may not reflect an objectively dire financial situation. Many fears surround the potential loss of comfort, privilege, or luxury, rather than of some more absolute form of deprivation. People often define their present lifestyles as being minimally acceptable.[6] So, for example, a wealthy household's distress may be rooted in fears of not being able to enjoy a lifestyle that most people could never maintain, or not being able to insulate their families from the financial pressures that most people deal with on a regular basis. While these types of worries produce emotional distress, it is hard to see them as sufficiently serious as to warrant a societal reaction.

Self-perceived financial insecurity is also a problematic measure of financial insecurity because there are people who are anxious in general, and this generalized anxiety extends to money matters. Emotional dispositions may be ingrained personal traits. For example, research suggests lottery winners eventually return to baseline negative affective states after the initial thrill of winning subsides, just as those who have experienced a serious personal loss (e.g., of a limb) can eventually come to terms with their new situation and return to their baseline positive attitude about their lives.[7] To some degree, people are emotionally disposed to anxiety or calm, and those generalized dispositions influence their personal financial assessments.

All of this suggests that subjectively perceived financial insecurity is probably an unreliable and potentially invalid measure of people's objective financial situation. For this reason, we might try to develop objective standards of financial security, which are divorced from people's personal goals, feelings, lifestyle expectations, risk tolerance, and so on. To do this, we can delve into the particulars of people's income statements and balance sheets.

People's Money Needs

While it may be true that life's most important things are free—family, friendship, sunrises, and such—it is also true that free things cannot sustain a modern livelihood on their own. Money buys food, shelter, basic utilities, clothing, hygiene products, education, medical care, transportation, and a range of other products that shape a person's prospects for survival, health, safety, and a meaningful place in society. Moreover, people need money to make legally obligatory payments—a person can go to jail for not paying taxes or child support—so money, to some extent, purchases one's freedom. At its root, financial insecurity involves the risk that money shortages will force people to forgo things that they genuinely need.

If financial insecurity involves not having enough money to cover basic essentials, we need some conception of what is included in these essentials. We need some idea of what goods and services people need to maintain a basic living standard. Much poverty research presumes that these money needs are roughly captured by the official poverty line. As discussed in Chapter Two, the official poverty rate is a very crude measure. Implicitly, it assumes that people's basic living costs (BLCs) are reasonably approximated by taking the inflation-adjusted cost of what the U.S. Department of Agriculture deemed to be a "minimum" diet in 1963, multiplied by three. Crude measures are a fact of life in the analysis of household finances, but this particular measure is so rough that it can reasonably considered to be meaningless. Yet, these estimates are the basis for determining people's eligibility for social assistance, redistributive tax credits, or health insurance subsidies.

More recently, researchers have sought to develop a better-specified view of people's money needs by explicitly specifying and pricing out the out-of-pocket costs incurred in the acquisition of necessary goods and services.[8] Doing so involves making determinations about the goods and services people need, as opposed to those that they want. *Needs* are things (e.g., goods, services, rights) whose acquisition is essential in the sense that their denial causes some kind of harm.[9] People need food, shelter from the elements, or emergency medical care because they help prevent death. It is unhealthy for someone not to use personal hygiene products (e.g., toothpaste or soap). It is hard to play a meaningful role in society without clothes or some means of conveyance to work. It might be hard to find a meaningful role in the economy if you lack basic education or training. Not paying taxes can land you in jail.

The expansiveness of our definition of "needs" will influence the proportion of society that we see as financially insecure. For example, health insurance is expensive. If we deem it necessary, then the many families who forgo health insurance due to affordability problems can be deemed to have forgone a necessity for lack of money and are thus construed to be in a state of financial failure. However, if we deem it optional—more like a video game console than indoor heating or plumbing—then this family is not forgoing a necessity, and thus not in a state of financial failure.

In contrast, *wants* are things that people desire, but their denial seems likely to have little to no impact on people's basic levels of well-being. So, for example, people need a diet with protein, but might want that protein to be delivered through high-quality cuts of beef, as opposed to eggs and beans. People might want to wear designer clothing, but their basic needs for warmth or the social need to be clothed in public are just as easily satisfied with generic label clothes.

Arguments about what constitutes a "need" versus "want" can go on interminably. Some basic products are clearly necessary (e.g., basic shelter, food, clothing, or emergency medical care), and others are clearly nonessential (e.g., designer clothing, video games, or premium cuts of beef in lieu of eggs). In between these two extremes, there are products whose necessity or essentiality is the subject of disagreement. For example, people may harbor different views about whether people need preventative healthcare, postsecondary education, child care, cell phones, Internet access, fresh vegetables, or organic milk. Some see these things as genuine necessities that everyone in society should be able to access, and others see them more as the perquisites of economic success, which can reasonably be denied to someone who does not have the money to pay its costs.

At some point, an analysis must settle on some provisional definition about what constitutes a need. By the principle of conservatism, we should set this provisional definition in a way that makes it harder for us to arrive at the findings we anticipate seeing. Concretely, this means that, if we think that financial insecurity is prevalent, our case would be helped by adopting a minimalist definition of people's needs. A minimalist definition means that our analyses are disposed to *underestimate* the prevalence of insecurity. If we find high rates of insecurity, then we can be assured that these are low-ball estimates and that financial insecurity is probably even more wide-spread (by more commonplace notions of what constitutes needs).

Table 3.1 describes the products used to calculate households' Basic Living Cost (BLC), which try to estimate the costs of a basic, market-secured live-lihood. The products included are adapted from the Census Bureau's *Supplemental Poverty Measure* and Economic Policy Institute's *Family Budget Calculator* projects.[10] They are not intended to be an accurate estimate of people's basic needs but rather a strongly conservative estimate that is dis-posed to under-estimate the true prevalence of financial insecurity. So, if the reader believes that things such as health insurance, child care, home furnishings and appliances, higher education, cell phones, or home Internet access are part of a minimum living standard, then they should read finan-cial insecurity estimates based on these BLCs as underestimating the true prevalence of genuine insecurity.

Note that these BLC estimates do not consider questions about what constitutes minimally acceptable quality levels. It does not ask whether a person's diet is genuinely adequate if their budget is restricted to the USDA's *Thrifty* plan. It does not consider whether inexpensive housing is located in an adequate school district or whether crime levels are reasonable.

What Are the Costs?

Our estimates, which are based on cost estimates for the basket of prod-ucts described previously, suggest that the median U.S. household needs about $19,574 a year to cover the basic rental housing, utility, food, trans-portation, apparel, personal care, and minor healthcare expenditures. A family of two adults and two children are expected to need $24,966. This is a minimal living standard, which presumes that public or interpersonal assistance will provide free health insurance, child care, and any other essential goods and services that readers might seem necessary. These costs can escalate quickly in the absence of assistance. For example, if we were

Table 3.1 Assessing the Burden of Basic Necessities

Product Category	Based on Premise That Minimum Standard of Living Includes:	Standard Used for Defining "Minimum"	Data Source
Shelter	Personal living quarters	Median national rent ($850).	ACS
Food	Basic nutrition	Average national costs of USDA Low-Cost Food Plan.	CNPP
Utilities	Basic plumbing and power	Expenditures on natural gas, electricity, other fuels, and water for households summed with other CEX-derived estimates, and basic costs assumed to be empirical 25th percentile for total CEX-measured costs.	CEX
Transportation	Means of accessing workplace, markets, and other out-of-home amenities or enterprises	Expenditures on vehicles, vehicle financing, fuel, service and repairs, insurance, public transportation, and other charges summed with other CEX-derived estimates, and basic costs assumed to be empirical 25th percentile for total CEX-measured costs.	CEX
Medical Care and Drugs	Out-of-pocket costs of medicine and medical care	Expenditures on medical services, prescription drugs, and medical supplies summed with other CEX-derived estimates, and basic costs assumed to be half of empirical median for total CEX-measured costs.	CEX
Apparel	Clothing and footwear	Expenditures on clothing, footwear, and apparel-related services summed with other CEX-derived estimates, and basic costs assumed to be empirical 25th percentile for total CEX-measured costs.	CEX
Personal Care Items	Access to basic hygienic products	Expenditures on soaps, shaving products, deodorants, haircuts, and so on summed with other CEX-derived estimates, and basic costs assumed to be empirical 25th percentile for total CEX-measured costs.	CEX

Sources: Data from ACS = American Community Survey, CCA = Child Care Aware (2013), CEX = Survey of Consumer Finances (Federal Reserve Board, 2015), CNPP = Center for Nutrition Policy and Promotion (2013).

U.S. Department of Agriculture, Center for Nutrition Policy and Promotion. (2013). *USDA food plans: Cost of food report for September 2013.* Retrieved from https://www.cnpp.usda.gov/sites/default/files/usda_food_plans_cost_of_food/CostofFoodSep2013.pdf

U.S. Census Bureau. (2015). American community survey. Retrieved from https://www.census.gov/programs-surveys/acs

to include Affordable Care Act partially subsidized insurance and market-rate child care,[11] this two-adult, two-child family would require $34,127 per year. Note that, for 92 percent of our households, estimated BLCs are higher than their official poverty-line income. On average, an official poverty-line income was about $2,700 a year (or $225 a month) lower than their estimated BLCs. Of course, these living costs might overestimate the living costs facing nominally "poor" or "near-poor" households. What about government assistance programs, such as Medicaid, housing vouchers, food stamps, and the like? What about parental aid? Shouldn't these single parents be receiving child support? We turn to this issue next.

Economic Independence and External Aid

Exposure to financial insecurity is shaped by personal finances as well as the degree to which government programs and interpersonal (mostly familial) aid allow us to secure the basics off markets. In other words, you don't need money if family, charity, or the government can help you secure life's necessities. To the extent that other agents or institutions step in to safeguard our living standards when we're short on money, financial pressures present a less menacing threat to people's living standards. There are three major sources of such aid: public assistance, private charity, and interpersonal assistance.

Public assistance refers to government policies and programs that provide people with essential products, defray the out-of-pocket costs of accessing essentials, or directly give people money to buy essentials. The United States has a wide array of social programs that do all of these things. Governments deliver free K–12 education, libraries, parks, road infrastructure, and emergency services. They provide some people with subsidized postsecondary tuition (or at least educational loans), mortgages, and health insurance. They give money aid to the poor, the unemployed, the disabled, and the elderly. These programs either provide supplemental income or control households' out-of-pocket expenses, and help insulate people from the well-being consequences of running out of money.

Public assistance varies across states and countries. For example, healthcare is fully socialized in the United Kingdom, such that people's budgets are not strained by the cost of premiums, so the risk of losing health insurance due to financial problems is minimal. In contrast, health insurance costs weigh heavily on many U.S. household budgets, and many Americans forgo health insurance as a result of money strains. Tuition-free college or child care is more common in Northern Europe (much like K–12 education is in the United States), and the strain of postsecondary schooling on household budgets is lower in these countries, and being short on money seems less likely to result in people having to forgo these services. Likewise, public funding for public higher education is higher and tuition lower in Alaska and Wyoming, whereas it is more expensive in New Hampshire and New Jersey.[12] Publicly assisted child care is more generous in New Jersey, for example, than in Georgia.[13] Public assistance also differs in how readily it is granted to different demographic groups; for example, the U.S. federal government more readily offers money and health insurance coverage to the elderly but is less generous with the working-age population and, to a lesser extent, children.

Institutionalized private charity is a second mechanism by which people's basic well-being is insulated against economic failure. These are the local food banks, soup kitchens, clothing drives, and other assorted privately funded and administered delivery of essentials to cash-constrained households. In 2014, Americans are estimated to have donated $359 billion to charitable endeavors.[14] This is a considerable amount, though a lot of this money is not directed toward causes that help financially distressed households. Many large-scale donations ultimately benefit causes that serve privileged people (e.g., donations to elite schools, nonprofit cultural institutions, or public goods in wealthy communities). Others finance donors' personal consumption of goods and services but are structured as donations for tax purposes (e.g., religious institution memberships, private nonprofit club membership fees). Even if all philanthropy in the United States were directed toward programs that help shore up household finances, they would be far underfunded relative to major government social programs. The Old Age and Survivors Insurance benefits from the Social Security program cost more than $700 billion annually on their own—double the amount of the whole country's annual charitable donations. One government program (albeit a big one) dwarfs the entirety of all private charity.

Interpersonal assistance refers to situations in which a household receives products, money, or some form of economic insurance from a personal relation (a relative, co-parent, or cohabitant). Interpersonal transfers also play an important role in shaping household finances. For example, child support or alimony payments can strengthen the finances of a single-parent household. The independently poor children of wealthy parents enjoy higher living standards and more economic security than their personal finances warrant. Students who receive parental help in their postsecondary education are better positioned to graduate free of debt (or even graduate at all).[15] The bedroom in Mom and Dad's basement is a form of economic insurance, and parental gifts, loans, or inheritances can confer instant home ownership, retirement savings, or wealth in general.

Interpersonal assistance can be a major factor in determining someone's ultimate vulnerability to financial problems. For many households, friends or relatives can provide some form of economic assistance in times of need. Having a parent with a room into which someone can move is a major form of economic insurance. However, personal relationships can also incur financial liabilities. Studies find household often go bankrupt as a result of obligations to care for a relation.[16] Family obligations can make it hard for people to work and raises living costs. They can do harm as well as help.

Financial security is a matter of people being able to access the money they need. People's money needs are a matter of the out-of-pocket costs associated with securing access to the essential goods and services for well-being. These out-of-pocket costs can be defrayed by governments, private charity, or personal relations. After these out-of-pocket costs are established, assessing people's financial insecurity involves developing some sense of the likelihood that a household will not be able to cover its essential expenses. A household with a higher likelihood of running out of money is more insecure.

Prevalence and Severity of Financial Insecurity

Financial insecurity is not a black-and-white issue in the sense that someone either is or isn't secure. Instead, it is a matter of degrees—people are more or less secure. That being said, our understanding of these various shades of gray can be aided by some simplification. One way to think about household insecurity is through a typology of four states, which range from less secure to more secure.

Economically Dependent

The economically dependent lack the earnings or accumulated wealth to cover BLCs. Their access to life's necessities depends on public assistance or private charity. One might characterize a household situation as having "failed" in the sense that it is unable to sustain itself independently as an ongoing enterprise. This is the least secure kind of household, whose livelihood is sustained by external aid.

Short-Term Precarious

Short-term precarious households are earning or receiving enough money to cover BLCs, but they lack the resources to withstand the financial demands of an unanticipated, but reasonably commonplace, financial shock. These kinds of households might be characterized as "living paycheck to paycheck." Their economic independence is precarious, and many of these households cycle through states of dependency and precariousness.

Long-Term Unsustainable

Long-term unsustainable households are able to cover living costs and save some money. However, a household needs considerable savings if it wishes to cover its living costs in its later years. These are years in which people find it more difficult to earn income and when a household can confront considerable healthcare and long-term care bills, even with U.S. socialized health insurance for its elderly. Households that seem financially viable during its working years, yet unprepared to weather the costs of old age, are considered to be long-term unsustainable.

Long-Term Sustainable

Finally, there are households that seem well-positioned to maintain a comfortable lifestyle into old age. Although they may collect Social Security, they seem unlikely to depend on it to sustain a basic livelihood. This group includes older households who seem well-positioned to enjoy this level of security in old age, as well as younger households who seem on track to accumulate enough money to finance a secure, independent retirement.

Income Inadequacy

Our most basic standard of economic security is short-term basic financial independence. If a household is not able to come up with enough income to finance a most basic lifestyle, it is taken to be in a state of financial dependency. In effect, the household fails as an ongoing financial concern, and relies on external aid to maintain a most basic living standard. Here, we try to assess the prevalence of financial dependency by seeing how many of the country's households are earnings-adequate.

The concept of *earnings adequacy* asks whether people earn enough money to cover their BLCs. *Earnings* include money received through market transactions, such as wages, financial investments, personal businesses, private pensions, and other transactions resulting in proceeds from personal labor or personal property. An earnings-inadequate household does not earn enough money on markets to cover the market costs of basic housing, food, and other essentials. Such households requires outside assistance, debt, or accumulated wealth to cover the shortfall and ensure their access to basics.

To draw comparisons, we also consider the prevalence of income inadequacy. A household is *income inadequate* when its total income (e.g., from public aid, personal transfers, and market earnings) are not enough to cover

BLCs. Most of the difference between earnings and income inadequacy is a matter of government aid, such as welfare, food stamps, Medicare, Medicaid, or Social Security. This difference can be used to gauge the degree to which different groups are treated preferentially by society's social safety net. Where income and earnings-adequate rates are similar, governments don't really channel much in the way of payments to group members. Where the differences between these rates are larger, government programs are more aggressively edifying household finances through income payments.

How many households lack enough earnings or income to cover the costs of a very basic livelihood? One way to develop estimates is to see how much of the country has market earnings that are sufficient to cover a household's estimated BLCs. Remember that these are intended to be rock-bottom living cost estimates, so the resulting estimates of earnings or income inadequacy are minimum levels. A more extensive definition of basic living standards—including healthcare, child care, basic household appliances and furniture, Internet access, telephone access, and a range of other products—would result in higher estimates of economic dependency across society at large.

Table 3.2 depicts the prevalence of earnings and income inadequacy across U.S. households. It shows that more than one in four households don't earn enough money to sustain a basic livelihood without government or interpersonal aid. More than a quarter of U.S. households do not earn enough money on their own to cover the costs of a very basic livelihood. Earnings inadequacy is more prevalent among the unpaired, the unemployed, the less-educated, nonwhites, and the elderly. A substantial part of these groups needs external support to secure access to the most basic necessities.

Despite arguments that U.S. capitalism affords easy opportunities to save money and accumulate wealth, a surprisingly large plurality of households fail to do so. If an economic system has a 28 percent failure rate on something as basic as putting people in a position to earn enough to secure basic food, clothing, shelter, and personal care items—forget about healthcare or education—it is hard to see that system as one that easily delivers high living standards on its own. Raw capitalism on its own cannot produce the high living standards that we enjoy today. At least, no society has ever accomplished it on capitalism alone. All highly developed societies widely sustain access to life's necessities through government programs. They are all effectively somewhat socialist.

Nowhere is the failure of market-sustained livelihoods so clear, and the profound impact of U.S. social policies so obvious, as with the elderly. Earnings inadequacy is particularly high when the heads of households

Table 3.2   Incidence of Income Inadequacy across U.S. Households, 2013

Income Basis	Earnings Inadequacy (%)	Income Inadequacy (%)
Overall	28	16
Young (Head < 35 Years)	30	26
Older (Head > 65 Years)	49	17
Married	13	7
Nonmarried	38	27
Household with Children	23	18
Household without Children	30	16
Whites	24	12
Nonwhites	38	27
Head Fully Employed	12	10
Head Not Fully Employed	53	27
College-Educated	7	4
Not College-Educated	31	18

Source: U.S. Federal Reserve (2014).

are 65 or older, a group in which just under half lack sufficient earnings to cover basic costs. Other demographic groups that are vulnerable to earnings inadequacy include the unmarried, nonwhites, and those whose head of household was not fully employed (i.e., the head experienced unemployment, was disabled, or retired). In contrast to seniors, these groups receive less help from public programs, at least insofar as income payments are concerned. While government payments seem to halve the proportion of society that lacks enough income to cover the costs of a basic livelihood, the unmarried and nonwhites receive far less help from guaranteed income programs, as do parents, those without college degrees, and those from the working-age population. The elderly also receive socialized healthcare.

Of course, cash aid is not the only form of help extended by social programs. The government also subsidizes or directly provides many essentials to financially strained households, such that their money shortage does not directly translate into material deprivation. For example, the poor are eligible for housing vouchers, child care and education grants, and Medicaid. Eligibility for these programs often requires that a family be officially impoverished, which, as noted earlier, often involves incomes that are well below people's BLCs. In other words, someone can earn too little to cover basic costs but earn too much to be poor. This means that many earnings-inadequate families do not officially qualify as poor and are thus at risk of being denied help from programs for the poor.

How many households are ultimately denied access to necessities after the effects of these programs are considered? These questions have been pursued in detail by the Census Bureau's Supplemental Poverty Measure project, whose estimates found that about 15.5 percent of Americans might not be able to secure access to basic necessities even after government payments and subsidized provisions are considered.[17]

Liquid Assets

Some households are able to cover the costs of a basic livelihood, but their situation is a precarious one that could unravel if faced with unanticipated problems. For this reason, financial planners often recommend that households keep at least three months of replacement income or regular expenditures in cash accounts. The idea is that, if a household runs into some type of unanticipated financial shock (e.g., a job loss, medical event, or some other financially damaging incident), they have enough money to cover their costs without fast and dramatic cutbacks, onerous debts, or the liquidation assets at inopportune times (and thus at fire-sale prices).

How much of society meets that three-month liquidity standard? Table 3.3 describes households' *liquid asset coverage*, which is the amount of time that a household's accrued assets could sustain its basic costs without receiving any income. Gross income coverage is the sum of households' cash savings, money market accounts, and certificates of deposit, divided by its monthly pretax income. The resulting figure tells us how long a household could substitute completely lost income by using its liquid assets. *Basic cost* coverage uses our BLC estimates from earlier and suggests how long families could sustain a minimum living standard with liquid holdings.

In 2013, just under half of the country's families had less than $4,100 in liquid assets, and two-thirds had less than $15,000. Only about one-third of the country's households hold three months' worth of gross income in liquid assets. About half have less than one month in income, and a quarter have less than one week. About 22 percent have less than $500 in liquid assets, putting them at considerable risk of a cash shortage if they needed to cover the typical co-pay of an insured auto accident. This suggests that roughly half of the country subsists on a nearly month-to-month basis and that their cash reserves could be exhausted if confronted with an expenditure exceeding a few thousand dollars.

Table 3.3   Liquidity Metrics, U.S. Households, 2013

Type of Income Coverage	Gross Income	Basic Costs
Median Time Coverage:	4.3 w	11.0 w
Less than 3 months	67%	52%
Less than 1 month	50%	37%
Less than 1 week	26%	20%
Younger (head under 35)	3.0 w	5.0 w
Older (head over 65)	3.8 m	8.7 m
Married	6.3 w	5.0 m
Nonmarried	3.0 w	5.3 w
Minors in Household	2.4 w	5.5 w
No Minors in Household	6.5 w	3.8 m
White	6.8 w	4.6 m
Nonwhite	12 d	2.7 w
College-Educated	4.7 m	1.8 y
Not College-Educated	3.5 w	8.2 w

d = days, w = weeks, m = months, y=years.

Source: U.S. Federal Reserve (2014).

Liquid coverage varies across demographic groups. Age plays an important role, in part because older households have had a longer time to accumulate wealth, because they are supposed to keep a greater proportion of their wealth in low-risk liquid assets, and because older household's incomes tend to be lower than that of the working-age population (so there is less income to replace). The median household with a head older than 65 had about 3.8 months of gross income, whereas younger households only had enough to cover about 3 weeks of income. Married households had about twice the level of liquid asset coverage as unmarried households, a sensible result given that they generally have twice as many earners in the household unit. The differences between whites and nonwhites is striking (4.7 months versus 12 days, respectively), as was that between the college and noncollege-educated (5 months versus 3.5 weeks, respectively).

Gross income replacement is arguably a comparatively liberal standard with which to measure the adequacy of people's emergency savings. It assumes that we use the continuation of people's current living standards (as approximated by their gross income) as a basis for judging whether or not they have enough cash holdings. Arguably, people can tighten their belts when confronted with financial problems. What if we adopt a more restrictive standard, which considers people's ability to cover their BLCs instead? The median household comes closer to reaching financial planners' 3 months of coverage standard—it has enough cash to cover about 11 weeks of living costs. Groups who already tended to be better insulated by their cash holdings seem capable of covering their basic costs for extended lengths of time—the median elderly household is able to cover almost 9 months of basic costs, married people and whites are covered for about 5 months at the median, the childless have enough for almost four months, and the median college graduate enjoys a whopping 1.8 years.

However, demographics that seemed to have liquidity problems under the former standard also register as such using the BLC standard because their regular incomes are near-subsistence level from the outset. The median household headed by a nonwhite has an estimated 2.7 weeks of basic expenses in liquid assets. The median younger household has just over a month. The unmarried and parents have about a month and a half. And those without college degrees have nearly 2 months at the median. About one-third of all U.S. households have less than a month in BLCs, and one-fifth have less than a week.

Overall, a large proportion of U.S. households do not have much money with which to confront unanticipated financial problems. About two-thirds register as having less than the prescribed three months in income replacement. According to research by Lusardi and colleagues, those without cash savings would expect to resort to liquidating other assets (e.g., nonhome physical property, retirement accounts), borrowing money from family, using credit cards or other forms of debt, or working overtime to make ends meet.[18] These strategies work if someone has assets, access to debt, family or friends who are able and willing to lend money, or opportunities to work overtime. Not everyone has these recourses and are thus dependent on government aid unless they are to forgo essentials.

What About Insurance?

Households are expected to carry insurances to protect themselves against unforeseen calamities. While we do not directly examine insurance coverage here, other sources suggest that much of the country lacks major forms of coverage. In 2014, about 13 percent lacked health insurance coverage.[19] According to industry advocates' estimates, 13 percent of drivers are said to lack auto insurance.[20] About 30 percent of households have no life insurance.[21] A majority of Americans lack short- or long-term disability insurance.[22] It is estimated that only about a third of renters have rental insurance.[23] Large parts of society face the risk of commonplace calamities with only their (often limited) personal assets and government aid to protect them.

Wealth Accumulation

Our final criterion for assessing financial security is accumulated wealth. The topic of wealth was engaged in Chapter Two. It shows how about 8 percent or so of society has enough wealth to sustain a squarely middle-class lifestyle into perpetuity (as long as they are willing to settle for such a living standard). Most of society does not have so much accumulated wealth. Half of the country has less than $81,000 in net worth, and a quarter has less than $9,000. While a majority of households are able to self-finance a basic livelihood in the present, they are not accumulating wealth. Low wealth accumulation portends a situation of eventual economic dependency. It might not happen during a household's working years, but it seems hard to avoid in old age.

An analysis has to engage three questions to estimate the adequacy of people's accumulated wealth. First, it needs some sense of how much money the household needs in retirement. Second, it requires an understanding of how much a household needs to have accumulated to be reasonably assured of having enough money in retirement. Finally, it needs to examine how much wealth has already been accumulated and judge whether the households is "on track."

The Poor Financial Shape of Older Americans

The U.S. Federal Reserve's *Survey of Consumer Finances* (SCF) data suggests that the median net worth of a household headed by someone in their sixties is $162,180, including their homes. Without homes, median net worth is about $60,000, or about five years of poverty-line income at 2014 prices. To avoid absolute poverty, people need to cover the difference with jobs, public assistance, family help, or charity.

Public assistance plays a key role in preventing elderly poverty. About 9 percent of seniors are officially poor.[24] This low rate (relative to many other demographic groups) is primarily due to Social Security payments. The median senior household received just over $14,000 in Social Security payments in 2013. In 1959, about 35 percent of seniors were poor, compared to 27 percent of children. More than 50 years into the program, senior poverty has dropped by almost 75 percent, whereas child poverty has dropped by less than a quarter (to 22 percent).[25] Moreover, seniors benefit from a wide range of social programs that are quite generous, compared to those extended to other Americans. For example, they receive socialized basic health and prescription drug insurance. These benefits are in addition to those offered to other Americans, like food stamps and Medicaid. Without this extensive Social Safety net, the United States would likely have a far bigger and more severe elderly poverty problem.

Many seniors expect to cover living costs by working longer. The problem is that many seniors are involuntarily pushed out of their jobs, if not thrust out of the workforce entirely. Although older workers are often better protected from layoffs because they tend to have more seniority, those who do lose their jobs often face considerable difficulty finding work and are often forced to accept considerable pay cuts[26] (assuming they are able to work). A recent survey by the Associated Press and National Opinion Research Center found that about one-third of retirees report feeling that they were forced into retirement.[27] Roughly 61 percent of those who leave the workforce involuntarily do so as a result of health-related issues, and another 18 percent did so to care for a spouse or other family member who needed help.[28] In a labor market environment that has been unforgiving to the working-age population, it is hard to envision how a rising tide of elderly Americans will be able to sustain themselves by working well into retirement.

If personal savings, work, and public assistance aren't enough to cover the costs of one's livelihood in old age, family support is another possibility. Parental support has become more commonplace, just as it has become more common to provide financial aid to one's adult children. This phenomenon has produced what is widely known as the "Sandwich Generation"—a generation of middle-aged Americans who are pressed into supporting both their predecessors and successors financially. According to Pew Research Center estimates, about 15 percent of all middle-aged adults provided financial support to both a parent aged 65+ and a child in 2012.[29] Roughly 58 percent of this survey's respondents reported either already providing care for an aging family member or see it as "very likely" that they will do so in the future.

How Much Money Do You Need to Retire?

Our first task is to discern how much wealth is required to finance a retirement. We adopt three standards. The high—or moderately "wealthy"—standard follows our discussion in Chapter Two, which proposed that a net worth of about $1.4 million could deliver a median income into perpetuity with reasonably low financial risk. We will term this a moderately "wealthy" retirement. This is probably a lofty retirement savings target for most households, which delivers an income that is better than about half the country without public aid or loss of investment principle. Our second, "basic" retirement saving goal is for a portfolio whose principle and investment returns could yield an inflation-adjusted median lower-middle-class income ($25,000) over the household heads' life expectancy. Our third, "poverty-line" retirement goal seeks to secure a poverty-line income over the life expectancy of the household heads.[30] Here, we use the assumption of a $14,000 per year income as near-poverty.

To calculate the amount of savings required to finance a "basic" or "poverty-line" retirement, we need a sense of how long someone will live, how much prices will rise, and the returns one can yield from financial investments in retirement. We use the inflation (3.1 percent per year) and investment returns (6.4 percent)[31] assumptions established in Chapter Two. We calculate the net worth requirements to render these incomes by calculating each retirement plan as a *discounted cash flow*, a financial formula for determining the present value of a regular payments plan that incorporates consideration of principle investment appreciation. Using life expectancy estimates from the Social Security Administration,[32] along with the preceding assumptions about retirement income, investment returns, and inflation, we can estimate that a household would need $376,623 and $210,909 to finance a $25,000 and $14,000 per year retirement, respectively, over its life expectancy. Households whose heads have survived until age 80 are expected to need $217,558 to receive an inflation-adjusted income of $25,000 per year for its predicted remaining 8.8 years, or about $121,000 for a $14,000 a year retirement. These assumed cash needs over all elderly years will be drawn out momentarily.

Being "On Track"

Younger households are expected to accrue their retirement funds over a lifetime, and these savings are expected to be bolstered by compounded investment returns. We describe a younger household as being "on track" if their current net worth, along with some presumed future savings commitment, is sufficient to render the target retirement nest egg of $1.4 million, $377,000, or $210,000 (depending on whether one is aiming for a wealthy, basic, or poverty-line retirement as described previously).

Like our calculations of required retirement nest eggs, we need some estimate of investment returns and inflation, and we opt for a rough estimate that assumes a real return rate of about 7.4 percent per year[33] (a figure that can be altered by assuming more or less risk, or by histori-cal overperformance or underperformance on the markets). We presume that an on-track household will put 10 percent of its gross income into sheltered retirement investments (an obviously optimistic estimate for most of the country, given that so few households have *anything* saved) and that their incomes will roughly pace general prices.

With these basic inputs, we are in a position to estimate how much a household should have acquired to be on track for a particular retirement goal. We do so by calculating the present value of a households' expected future retirement contributions (10 percent of gross income) from the present value of its target retirement nest egg.[34] Figure 3.1 presents the results.

Lower-income households will have needed to accumulate more in wealth because they are presumed to be unable to contribute more to retire-ment in the future. A person earning $25,000 per year is estimated to need a net worth of more than $16,000 to be on track toward a $1.4 million nest egg. In contrast, a person earning $50,000 per year does not need to start saving until 22 years old. A $100,000 a year salary allows savings to be postponed to 31. A $250,000 yearly income can postpone savings until 43.

Although a higher income allows people to delay retirement savings, most households need to start saving relatively early in their working years to have adequate retirement savings. Even a household earning $250,000 a year needs to start saving in its late forties to reach our modest basic retirement goal, unless they plan on saving more than a tenth of their income annually. To finance a poverty-line income, these high-income households still need a decade of savings. A more typical home, earning a median wage, needs to start saving a tenth of their income in their early-to mid-forties.

Retirement Savings Adequacy

So how much of the country is adequately saved? Using our three retire-ment goals, our assumptions about long-term inflation and financial returns, and the presumption of a 10 percent rate of gross income saved, we can arrive at some crude estimates. Given that these estimates depend on many assumptions—reasoned ones but assumptions nevertheless—readers should focus on gross magnitudes rather than finer distinctions.

Our results suggest that about 23 percent of U.S. households have either accumulated $1.4 million in net worth or appear to be on track to do so. About 48.5 percent of households are either adequately saved for, or on track to save enough for, a basic retirement of $25,000 per year. Roughly

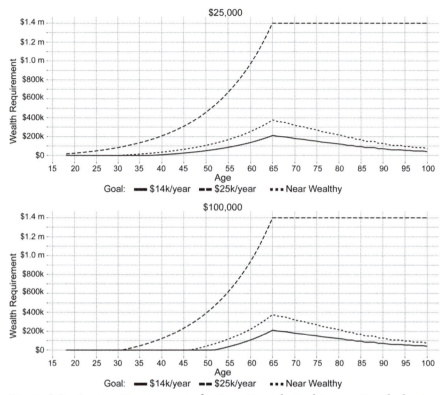

Figure 3.1   Savings Requirements for Four Hypothetical Income Levels, by Age and Retirement Goal.

64 percent are on track to finance a poverty-line retirement. Nearly two-fifths of U.S. households have either failed to save enough to finance, or be on track to finance, a poverty-line retirement.

Moreover, two caveats are in order. First, keep in mind that these savings goals are based on households' total net worth. They are assumed to liquidate all of their assets into a financial portfolio that will finance their retirement, including their residences. Many elderly people are reluctant to let go of their homes—it is cheaper to live in a home after it is paid off, an owned home may provide some economic security for younger family members, and a person may consider their home to be a major facet of their living quality. If we were to consider only nonhome investments, only about 54 percent seem prepared for retirement, and we approach half of the country being unready to finance a poverty-line retirement.

Who tends to be prepared for retirement? Aside from those with higher incomes, retirement savings are more likely to be adequate in households

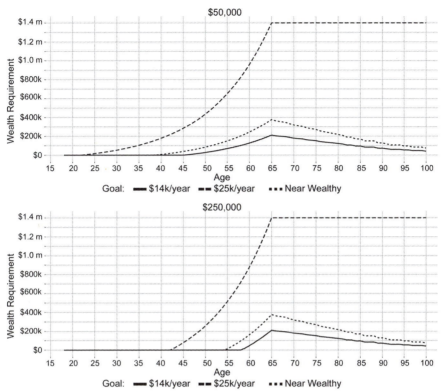

Figure 3.1 (Continued)
Source: Author's calculations.

headed by the college-educated, the employed, and the very young (although this is most likely a by-product of the fact that this last group requires no savings to be considered on track for more modest retirement goals).

What About Social Security?

At present, the average elderly Social Security recipient receives $1,335 per month from Social Security payments. In and of itself, these payments are sufficient to finance a poverty-line retirement, and they greatly reduce the need for savings to cover a basic, $25,000-per-year retirement. As we saw previously, Social Security plays a major role in providing the elderly in the United States with enough income to cover their basic bills. In effect, the United States avoids a massive elderly poverty problem through what is nearly tantamount to a guaranteed income program for older people.

How do we interpret the effects of Social Security on our estimates of people's preparedness for retirement? This analysis maintains the view that Social Security is a social program, like welfare or food stamps. As such, any program that relies on these payments is construed to be economically dependent. They do not function as independent financial concerns.

That being said, the existence of Social Security shields the elderly from the consequences of their having under-saved for their older years. Social Security enables older households who lack assets or employment income to subsist, and it lowers the consequences of money problems for today's elderly. What about younger households? As noted earlier, it depends on the continuance of the program. Social Security is under persistent pressure to be cut, and these cuts are often made salable by only applying them to younger people (e.g., those under 55). Doing so allows older voters to champion austerity and "fiscal responsibility" without biting the hand of the social program that feeds them personally. If these cuts materialize, then today's younger Americans will be more subject to the well-being consequences of having inadequately saved for retirement. If the program continues without cutbacks, today's youth will enjoy the same benefits as the older Americans who are the recipients of their payroll taxes.

Most of the Country Relies on Public Assistance

Although people often like to consider themselves to be financially independent, in reality, the vast majority of people seem to be in a financial position that is either highly dependent on a public safety net at present or ultimately destined for future dependency. Many of those who maintain some level of present-day financial independence are just one unanticipated— but not altogether rare—disruption (e.g., job loss, illness, etc.) away from financial dependence.

Given this level of dependency, it is hard to understand how cutting social supports could ultimately improve people's security and well-being. Public assistance is stigmatized in U.S. culture, despite the fact that so much of society relies on it. Americans seem obsessed with the possibility that some people cheat the welfare system, use it to avoid work, or spend public assistance money in unsavory ways. It draws their ire, leads to questions about why people should waste their tax money on dishonest or slothful people, and often marshals support for policy-makers who favor a broad abolishment of the welfare state to the greatest extent possible. In so doing, they may be lending support to a policy movement that will cut the financial legs out from under them.

Americans are broadly dependent on the government to provide an economic backstop. It is not only lazy young people, welfare cheats, and other assorted unsavory caricatures who rely on public assistance. Virtually everyone, except society's wealthiest third or so, lack the resources to establish secure financial independence. Dismantling the welfare state means dismantling the ultimate guarantor that members of a society that is widely insecure financially will be able to get what they need.

CHAPTER FOUR

The Big Picture

In the years following the 2008 financial crisis, many saw households' money struggles as a *cyclical phenomenon,* a by-product of the economy's natural rhythm of boom and bust years. The Great Recession may have been an extraordinarily bad economic downturn, and the recovery that followed may have seemed extraordinarily sluggish, but many harbored the view that household money problems would resolve themselves when the economy eventually recovers. Now, nearly a decade has passed since the 2008 financial crisis, and this hopeful view seems harder to sustain. It seems likely that U.S. households face *structural problems*; that is, more deeply rooted circumstances or flaws in U.S. capitalism cause these money problems.

The problem with viewing household money problems as a cyclical phenomenon is that rising financial insecurity has been developing steadily over decades. It is not as if U.S. households were in good shape in 2007, and then they got worse in the years that followed. Household finances deteriorated over decades through an iterative process of deep recessions followed by increasingly disappointing recoveries into progressively worse "new normals." The causes of household financial problems run far deeper than an unlucky economic downturn. We are dealing with a long-term phenomenon whose causes are probably rooted in similarly long-term developments.

This chapter considers some of these possible long-term causes. It contemplates the exhaustion of the post-World War II economy that is widely seen as the middle class's golden age. Globalization and technological advancement are discussed, which are two extremely important changes with complicated effects on households. Finally, the chapter also considers how key sociodemographic changes, such as an aging population or the decline of marriage.

Many of these big-picture forces are difficult, if not practically impossible, to reverse. One might question whether Americans would even want to reverse some of them were it possible. However, there is an additional factor—economic policy—that is easier to change. The choice to change policy seems much less complicated if it is damaging households' finances. Throughout this long deterioration in household finances, economic policymakers have reformed economic laws, regulations, and government programs in ways that embrace libertarian, free market, antigovernment, and antisocialist ideologies. At a minimum, these policies have failed to create an environment in which household finances could overcome these long-term pressures. At worse, they have exacerbated Americans' money problems.

The U.S. middle class faces many big-picture stressors that seem unlikely to reverse themselves anytime soon. This gives us reason to be pessimistic about the possibility that a simple rebound in the economy will restore household finances to their precrisis condition. However, the middle class can demand policies that help buffer their finances from the effects of these big-picture forces. A reversal of these antigovernment policies may be one way of engaging household money problems effectively.

The Exhaustion of Postwar Capitalism

Chapter One discussed how U.S. household finances have deteriorated steadily since the 1970s. At root, diagnoses of middle-class decline involve comparisons between today and the decades following World War II. Compared to the mid-20th century, today's households' earnings have stagnated, savings have fallen, debt has risen, and bankruptcies have become more common. That era was a golden age for the middle class, and Americans' current economic fortunes seem inferior by comparison.

In broad historical terms, the mid-20th century was a period of extraordinary prosperity. Figure 4.1 depicts the average economic growth rate across decades since 1820. During the 1950s through 1970s, the economy not only enjoyed a rate of growth that nearly doubled any other three-decade stretch since 1820, but this growth was also more stable. In the 19th and early 20th centuries, economic growth and prices fluctuated more wildly. Financial crises were much more common.[1] In the mid-20th century, the boom years were very prosperous, and the recessions were comparatively mild.

What happened? This prosperity grew out of a confluence of factors. The United States emerged from World War II as the only major economy

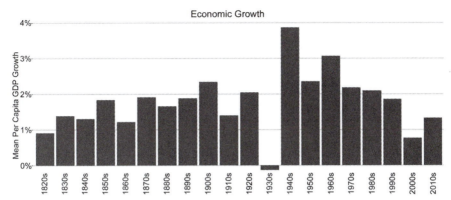

Figure 4.1   Historical U.S. Economic Growth by Decade, 1820–2015.
Source: Bolt, J. & van Zanden, J. L. (2014). The Maddison Project: Collaborative research on historical national accounts. *Economic History Review, 67*(3), 627–651. Available from http://www.ggdc.net/maddison/Historical_Statistics/horizontal -file_03-2007.xls

that was not left in shambles, so international competition was weak. Coming out of the war with considerable political, economic, and military power in international affairs, the United States wrote the rules that would govern international economic affairs over the next several decades.[2] The country seized opportunities to grow through industrialization and infrastructure development. Many of these developments capitalized on fundamentally transformative technological advancements, such as electricity, modern chemistry, and the automobile.[3] The country had made tremendous research and development investments during the war, which would serve as a basis for many civilian industries for years.

That era's prosperity was fueled by a booming manufacturing sector, fast-rising household consumption, a great deal of investment in physical structures, and, up until the 1970s, a dramatic growth in the public sector.[4] The scope of the government's growth during this period is striking, as depicted in Figure 4.2. The figure compiles data from two separate measures of government spending, relative to the overall size of the economy, since 1820.[5]

The figure shows how the U.S. government grew several times larger during and after the World War II. Even during the U.S. Civil War, government spending was a fraction of its present-day levels. This enduring growth emerged during the Great Depression, in the midst of a massive, politically destabilizing breakdown in the Western capitalist economies. The government began raising taxes on higher-income households and corporations, although it eventually transitioned the country's tax burden on

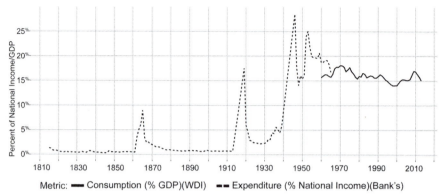

Figure 4.2 Government Outlays Relative to Overall Economy, 1820–2014. *Sources:* Banks (1976); World Bank (2015).

lower-income targeted personal income taxes (e.g., payroll taxes).[6] These funds paid for a range of new public programs and initiatives. In finance, the government established new, stringent regulations on financial institutions, established important financial regulatory agencies such as the Securities and Exchange Commission (SEC) and the Federal Deposit Insurance Corporation (FDIC). The government developed public works programs to absorb the Depression's unemployed, and it eventually came to be the economy's biggest investor and employer by a wide margin. The government established the Social Security program and, eventually, Medicare, Medicaid, and a range of other social programs. It financed a massive expansion of the education system. The government established the National Labor Relations Board (NLRB) and developed a system of more stringent regulations governing employment relationships. And, of course, the government maintained a massive military budget, which financed World War II, the Korean War, the Vietnam War, and the military activities of the Cold War.

Compared to today, the economy was much more equal,[7] so the fruits of this prosperity were more strongly channeled to the middle class. The tax system was far more progressive, with more revenue coming from corporations and high-income taxpayers (in 1950, a single person earning more than $200,000—about $2 million in 2015 dollars—faced rates of 91 percent). The dramatic growth in social programs led to dramatic falls in poverty[8] and a substantial rise in living standards.[9]

However, the system's ability to sustain this prosperity showed signs of wear. Business profitability started to sink almost as soon as the war ended and came to be buoyed by a persistent stream of tax cuts and a redistribution of society's tax burden onto households.[10] Much of this prosperity took place within a broader political and social compact that subjugated women and minorities. The country spent aggressively on the military and war. Reascendant Europe and Japan soon came to assert themselves in economic dealings with the United States, and other developing countries soon followed.[11,12]

At a pivotal moment in modern economic history—1972—Middle East oil exporters joined those who asserted themselves against the United States in mounting an oil embargo. The embargo created a shock in oil prices and set off a chain of events that would ultimately lead the postwar economy to unravel into the stagflation crisis of the 1970s, an unfortunate mix of chronic recession, high inflation, and high unemployment.[13]

Stagflation brought persistent labor conflict and economic frustration, which, along with a revolt against political reforms that sought to equalize the political, economic, and legal status of women and minorities, caused fissures in the Democratic coalition that had underwritten mid-20th-century economic policies. Whites, particularly those in the South, defected en masse to a new Republican coalition. These events culminated in the political ascendancy of Ronald Reagan and the rise of Reaganomics—a policy strategy that sought to restore the U.S. economy by undoing postwar reforms to government's role in the economy and moving U.S. capitalism closer to something more reminiscent of 19th-century capitalism.

In contemporary political and economic policy debates, people often look longingly at the mid-20th century. The U.S. middle class seemed to do very well during this period. Can household finances be helped by turning back the clock and reembracing the economic policies and strategies that prevailed during this golden age? In many respects, mid-20th-century capitalism operated in a different world. It was a world in which foreign competition was more limited, and the country could sustain growth by building factories that did not have to compete with those in low-wage countries. Part of what kept unionized white men in a position to earn good money was that women and minorities were systematically denied the opportunity to compete in these job markets. The government could boost the economy by developing a new program or making new investments, but the government cannot grow forever.

Although the clock cannot be fully turned back, there is reason to believe that some of our departure from postwar capitalism damaged regular households' financial fortunes. While there are clearly implausible ideas underwriting mid-20th–century U.S. capitalism—like the notion that the government could micro-engineer the economy to an eternal state of stable, perpetual prosperity—there is reason to believe that we overcompensated and took antithetical ideas about the benefit of laissez-faire too far. We will discuss this possibility later in this chapter.

Globalization

Postwar U.S. capitalism operated in a highly insulated economic environment. Some of this insularity took root during the Great Depression, an era of trade wars and desperate attempts to stabilize currencies.[14] Some of this insularity was maintained, and sometimes even strengthened, after World War II as part of an endeavor to stabilize the Western economies (and their political systems)[15] and in part because a destroyed European economy made export-oriented economic strategies less viable.[16] The mid-20th century was one in which the United States and other countries largely insulated themselves from international economic pressures and cooperated to maintain each other's insularity.

The postwar era decline in international trade is illustrated in Figure 4.3, which depicts the ratio of U.S. imports and exports to the gross national product (GNP) (a proxy for the overall size of the economy) since 1870.[17]

The figure shows that, through the late 19th century, the U.S. economy traded the equivalent of about 15–20 percent of its GNP with the rest of the world. This rate spiked temporarily during World War I, fell slightly during the interwar years, and then collapsed to less than 5 percent of gross domestic product (GDP) during the Great Depression. Through the 1950s and 1960s, trade stood at roughly half its pre-World War I levels, and the United States maintained a small trade surplus (i.e., the country exported more than it imported). These trade surpluses were primarily buoyed by a boom in international markets for chemicals, capital goods, and cars.[18] However, as the U.S. economy grew larger and wealthier, the hunger for—if not reliance on—foreign consumer goods, fuels, commodities, and other

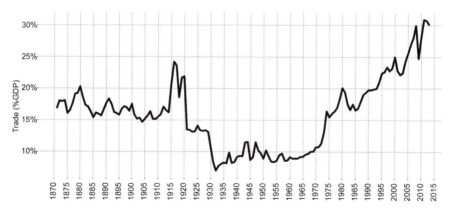

Figure 4.3   U.S. Trade (% GDP), 1870–2015.
Sources: National Bureau of Economic Research (2008); World Bank (2016).

basic production inputs grew. Eventually, Europe and Japan were able to stabilize and retrench their economies, and they developed the ability to compete with the United States in markets for consumer goods and advanced manufacturing (e.g., vehicles, capital equipment). Several East Asian countries were on the path to doing so as well.

By the 1970s, several factors pushed the United States along a path away from mid-century protectionism and toward its eventual embrace of globalization. The Bretton Woods system that governed mid-century exchange among the United States, Europe, and other highly developed countries broke down.[19] Other East Asian countries found ways to forge profitable niches in the global economy and eventually became internationally competitive. The pace of East Asia's development soon outperformed other middle-income countries that were trying to develop with protectionist policies (e.g., those of Latin America), helping push much of the world toward a trade-oriented economic strategy. Over the 1980s and 1990s, as Third World dictatorships fell, and the Soviet system collapsed, free trade became part of a larger project to integrate the world's countries in a politically and economically liberal world order.[20]

Within this globalized international economic order, the U.S. worker found it increasingly difficult to compete with foreigners. Falling trade barriers, along with technological advancements, decreasing transportation costs, and both economic development and better governance in developing countries meant that companies could produce products more cost-effectively with Eastern European or East Asian workers. Workers could be paid far less in those countries and often proved capable of producing as well as their low-skilled U.S. counterparts. The United States assumed a niche that specialized in high-skill activities (e.g., product design, engineering, research and development, marketing, business development, and the operation and maintenance of complex procurement and production systems) and less on lower-skill ones (e.g., manual assembly or processing). U.S. manufacturing remained productive, continuing to grow in terms of revenue, but the manufacturing jobs that remained here tended to be oriented toward high-skill and capital-intensive ones, while the simpler, more labor-intensive tasks moved abroad. This played a role in the slow but steady collapse of U.S. manufacturing jobs (see Figure 4.4).

The decline of manufacturing work (and a similar though smaller decline in natural resource extraction and production, such as mining and logging) resulted in the disappearance of jobs that once provided lower-skilled Americans with a middle-class livelihood. These jobs tended to be unionized, comparatively well-paid, and relatively secure. Over time, manufacturing jobs were replaced with those in the education, health, business

Figure 4.4 Manufacturing Workers (% Total Labor Force), 1939–2015.
Source: Bureau of Labor Statistics. (2016). Employment, hours, and earnings from
the Current Employment Statistics Survey (national), series CES0000000001 and
CES3000000001 [Online database]. Retrieved from http://data.bls.gov

services, and finance sectors. Some of them were well-paid and absorbed
younger generations of better-educated Americans. For the most part,
however, they did not, and the U.S. middle class was left with poorer-quality
jobs.

All of this paints globalization's effects on the middle class negatively,
but that is only part of the story. Globalization not only affected households'
incomes but also their living costs. As manufacturers moved their operations abroad, their cost savings generated intense price competition. In the
next chapter, we will see that this resulted in stable—and often *falling*—
prices across many product markets, including food, clothing, home furnishings and supplies, appliances, and consumer electronics. Globalization
is what delivers our $15 Costco jeans, $60 Walmart Blu-ray player, our
$100 IKEA dining room set, and much of today's bounty of unprecedentedly
cheap products. It not only delivers cheaper physical products but also services. For example, 24/7 customer service was virtually nonexistent decades
ago—it would have been a rare luxury to be able to call someone at 2:00
a.m. (or even during a weekend) for help with personal electronics, appliances, utilities, or just about anything else. Today, its prevalence is in no
small part due to the cost-effectiveness of foreign call centers.

This leave us with one of the big dilemmas involved in policies designed
to bolster middle-class finances. On one hand, the loss of manufacturing
jobs represents the loss of a major avenue of good pay and economic security
for regular Americans. These jobs have been leaving the United States and
leaving the middle class stuck with poorer job opportunities. However, this
exodus of jobs is part of what keeps our living costs low, and protectionist

policies would probably cut financially embattled families from the lifeline of cheap goods that sustain household consumption. Moreover, globalization has produced export markets that have been an engine for creating higher-skill, well-compensated jobs. This situation makes it difficult to address household financial problems by cutting the United States off from international trade. To protect those whose work has been sacrificed by globalization, we might need to forgo low consumer prices and a number of well-paid, high-productivity jobs. These are not trivial sacrifices.

Technological Advancement

It is often recounted that, at the dawn of the Industrial Revolution, the cloth spinners of Blackburn smashed James Hargreaves' spinning jenny, a machine that allowed a single person to do the work of multiple weavers. The story stands as an example of how technological advancement can destroy people's livelihoods, how people can rise up against the machines that displace them economically, and ultimately the futility of rebelling against technological advancement. It is hard to imagine how manual weavers could have permanently stopped automated cloth production, and, in retrospect, their failure seems like a good thing. Without the mechanized production of cloth, textiles would be rarer and more expensive. There would certainly be no $15 Costco jeans.

More generally, technological advancement plays a critical role in raising living standards over the long run. Still, these advances entail sacrifices to someone's livelihood. Just as the spinning jenny harmed the livelihood of Blackburn's 18th-century spinners, the automobile destroyed that of the horseshoe smith, and so on; technological advancement has displaced many workers and threatens to continue to do so in the future.

MIT scholars Erik Brynjolfsson and Andrew McAfee argue for this notion that technology is displacing workers in ways that may ultimately be harming the finances of the middle class.[21] They note how rising worker productivity and robust economic growth has not resulted in widespread rises in real incomes. The fruits of economic development increasingly accrue to those who own the machines (capital owners) and the high-skill workers who design and operate them. So, the millions of store owners and clerks employed in small local retail stores in the United States have been giving way to the designers and administrators of big-box stores, such as Walmart, Best Buy, IKEA, or Barnes & Noble, and online retailers such as Amazon and eBay. The same story can be told of typists who lost their jobs to Microsoft Office or the bank tellers and cashiers who gave way to ATMs and self-checkout kiosks. With the passage of time, technology has been claiming higher-skill jobs. Whereas thousands of accountants once prepared people's taxes, the task is now performed by TurboTax for far less cost, and proceeds in the tax-preparation area accrue to the Intuit Corporation, its managers, and those who develop and maintain its online platform. The list of occupational categories whose numbers have been whittled down by machines could go on and on, and this list seems poised to grow. For example, think of the millions of vehicle operators whose jobs are imminently being threatened by self-driving vehicles.

Presumably, the jobs destroyed by technology are offset by the new jobs they create. For example, the car may have destroyed the horse harness business, but it created a market for gas stations. Theoretically, these lost secretarial, cashier, or line assembly jobs free people up to perform higher value-added work, such as computer programming, marketing, or machine engineering jobs. The main problem is that many cutting-edge advancements require far fewer personnel than the major economic developments of previous generations. Many observers have noted that the powerhouse technology companies have actually produced very few jobs. A "new economy" retailer such as Amazon has a market capitalization of about $262 billion and 222,000 employees, while a similarly large "old economy" retailer such as Walmart has a market capitalization of $216 billion with 1.4 million employees. Today, the engines of economic progress get by on a smaller group of highly skilled workers. It seems implausible to absorb millions upon millions of workers who once would have worked in lower-skill, largely repetitive work by employing them as computer programmers, research scientists, and business managers. The flip side of these lost jobs is similar to that of globalization. Technology may damage particular people's livelihoods, but it also helps deliver more, better, and cheaper products. Even if it were practical to combat the march of technology, it is not entirely clear that we would want to do so.

This is one of two major concerns about technology and the economic circumstances of regular Americans. The second concern, which has most recently been advanced with much attention by economists Tyler Cowan[22] and Robert J. Gordon,[23] maintains that part of the problem is that the United States is going through a long-term technological showdown. For Cowen, much of the economic prosperity of previous decades were purchased by "low-hanging fruits" out of easier accomplishments whose time has passed—untapped land, expanding basic education, and transformative basic technologies (e.g., cars, telephones, or rail). We are now pressed to eke out growth through tougher endeavors, such as accessing resources while trying to limit environmental damage, expanding tertiary education, or refining these earlier basic innovations (e.g., low-fuel-consumption or self-driving cars, phone apps, or high-speed rail). The engines of yesterday's prosperity are implied to have been easier to attain, and the task is tougher today. We are now hypothesized to be in a period of marginal, rather than transformative, technological advancement.

The relationship between technology and household finances is complicated. It is conceivable that technology ultimately hurts the lot of regular Americans. However, it somehow seems more likely that future generations will see today's anxieties about technology as akin to that of Blackburn's spinners.

Sociodemographic Changes

In addition to these larger political-economic factors, society itself has changed in ways that may have affected personal finances. We focus on three: an aging population, the decline of marriage, and immigration.

An Aging Population

Yet another important long-term change that has contributed to souring household finances is an aging population. Figure 4.5 illustrates the scope of this change in a depiction of the changing elderly dependency ratio (the ratio of workers to elderly people).

In 1960, those 65 years of age or older made up 9.1 percent of society, and there were about 6.6 members of the working-age population for every elderly person. That was a period in which the typical 65-year-old man was expected to live an additional 13 years, and women were expected to live 16 additional years.[24] Today, about 14 percent of society is age 65 or older, there are 4.6 members of the working-age population for every elderly person, and the typical 65-year-old male and female is expected to live an

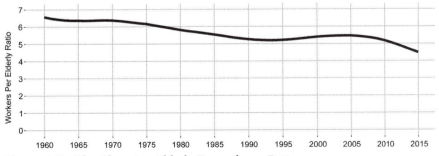

Figure 4.5 The Changing Elderly Dependency Ratio.
Source: World Bank (2016).

additional 18 and 20 years, respectively.[25] There are more older Americans, and they live longer, and there are fewer members of the working-age population in proportion to their members.

As we saw in Chapters Two and Three, households are more likely to have trouble earning incomes if they have not accrued much wealth in their working years (and most have not done so). Some of this difficulty is a product of ageism—older people face many age-related prejudices that discourage their employment.[26] Some of the difficulty is a matter of remaining cost-competitive in today's tough markets—young people are often well-trained and willing to work more for less. Some of it is a matter of health, which is sometimes a decisive factor in older people departing from the workforce. Whatever the cause, older, nonwealthy households have demonstrable challenges finding ways to secure the livelihood they enjoyed in their working years. The rising presence of elderly households seems like a probable contributor to the general deterioration of U.S. households. These problems can be compounded by the costs of medical care, therapeutic goods and services, and assisted living products, any of which can weigh heavily on household budgets.

In addition to the fact that more elderly households means a rising prevalence of households that often face personal earnings problems and health-related costs, an aging population can also weigh on the personal finances of the working-age population. The most straightforward example of such costs occur when an elderly parent becomes dependent on their children, either financially or through direct personal care. A 2015 study commissioned by TD Ameritrade suggests that about one-tenth of working-age households support a mother, and about half that number support a father.[27] Moreover, many of them provide care in addition to financial assistance. Such expenses—both in money and time—weigh on an adult child's ability to accumulate wealth for their own retirement, and, in cases where the demands to give care are high, may even hinder their ability to work and earn.

Even those without dependent parents still indirectly bear the costs of the country's growing elderly population through the costs of its elderly directed safety net programs, Social Security and Medicare, whose costs stood around 8.5 percent of the GDP in 2015, up from 2.1 percent in 1960 and 5.4 percent in 1980.[28] These rising costs are financed by payroll taxes, which are covered by a shrinking proportion of the population who is of working age.

Decline of Marriage and Rise of Living Single

In 1967, about 70 percent of U.S. adults lived with a spouse.[29] By 2015, that figure dropped to 50 percent. Some of this drop has been offset by the rise of those living with partners to whom they are not married, which went from 0.4 percent to 7.5 percent of U.S. households from 1967 to 2015, as well as slight increases in other living arrangements (e.g., living with relatives or nonrelated roommates) over that same period. However, the percentage of adults living alone has doubled, from 7.6 percent to 14.4 percent of all U.S. adults. These changes are depicted in Figure 4.6.

These changes are the product of several forces. Over the past several decades, young people have been delaying marriage. Divorce and cohabitation have become more accepted socially. Traditional barriers to women's access to education, gainful employment and an independent livelihood, and the ability to leave a marriage have been falling.

As with age, the data presented in Chapters Two and Three make it clear that single-adult households earn less, accumulate less wealth, and are more economically vulnerable. Living arrangements with multiple adults give a household multiple income streams and the capacity to split major living costs (e.g., housing, food, transportation). Even if the second adult in a union does not work, their ability to perform family and household work represents a considerable savings over commercial alternatives, which can be considerable in a household with children. Some estimates maintain that a stay-at-home mother renders household services whose commercial substitutes would run well over $110,000 per year.[30] A paired-adult household is better positioned economically.

Some researchers believe that causality also runs in reverse—that marriage is increasingly being confined to those at the top of the income scale.

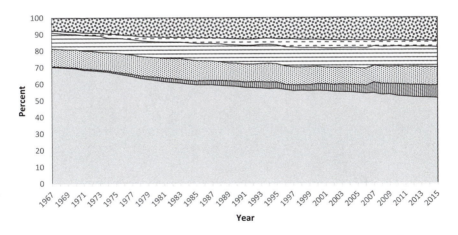

□ Married   ▥ Cohabiting   ▨ with Parents   ▤ with Relatives   ▤ with Non-Relatives   ▧ Alone

Figure 4.6   Living Arrangements, 1967–2015.
Source: U.S. Census Bureau (2016).

A 2010 report by the Pew Research Center[31] found that while marriage rates were broadly declining, marriage remained substantially more prevalent among the college-educated than lower education populations. The study found that lower education groups want to marry but often make economic stability a priority. In an era in which marriage is more frequently within economic classes instead of across class lines, those in the economy's lower ranks might face more challenges finding economically stable partners, if that is what they prioritize.

Immigration

Immigration is a perennially contentious issue, which always seems to attract the ire of some segment of society. Today, anti-immigration attitudes appear to be prevalent and strong. About half of Americans believe that immigration should be decreased and see immigration as having negative effects on the economy.[32] Figure 4.7 depicts changes in the foreign-born population as a percent of the total U.S. population.[33] The graph shows how the U.S. immigration policy was comparatively restrictive from the 1950s through the 1970s, the period in which the U.S. middle class seemed to prosper.

One might presume that immigration—particularly illegal immigration—damages the middle class by undercutting wages and pricing the native-born, citizens, and legal residents out of jobs. There is some evidence that such pressures may exist on low-skill workers in high immigration areas.

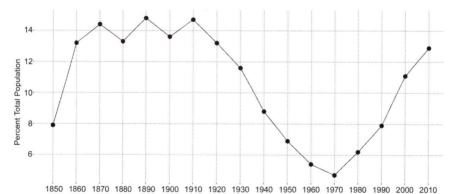

Figure 4.7   Foreign-Born Population (% Total Population), 1850–2010.
Source: U.S. Census Bureau. (1999). Table 1: Nativity of the Population and Place of Birth of the Native Population: 1850 to 1990 [Online data table]. Retrieved from https://www.census.gov/population/www/documentation/twps0029/tab01.html

Some economists have argued that immigration has resulted in a large, negative effect on the incomes of low-skill Americans.[34] A 2007 study by UC Berkeley economist David Card found that cities with large immigration inflows see a modest rise in the gap between high- and low-skill native-born workers, implying that immigration raises the gap between the lower and higher economic classes.[35] Moreover, he argues that a rising immigrant population may affect rents and general housing prices. Illegal immigration is also said to damage state and local government finances,[36] with some estimates running as high as more than $14,000 per family.[37]

On the other hand, it is often said that many of these immigrants—particularly illegal ones—do work that most Americans do not want to do, at least at the prevailing rates of pay (which may be influenced by immigration). Illegal immigration probably plays some role in keeping prices low, although there is reason to believe that these cost savings are limited to the extent that labor makes up the cost of producing and delivering goods.[38] In labor-intensive industries, they may have more impact on prices. For example, illegal immigrants are said to constitute one-fifth of the country's cooks and more than a quarter of its dishwashers, and their absence has been speculated to threaten the failure of restaurants and rising dining costs.[39] It may help make personal services less expensive—for example, as maids, drivers, grounds maintenance, janitorial staff, or moving workers—though these cost benefits seem more likely to accrue to better-heeled households.

It is important to remember that immigrants are disproportionately very low-skill or very high-skill workers. Immigrants compete not only at the lower-paid tiers of the labor market but also its highest. Many immigrants are economic high performers. The foreign-born population is more likely to have a graduate degree,[40] more likely to be entrepreneurs,[41] and less likely to be unemployed.[42] Immigrants who are participating in the formal economy are contributing both to the economy and public finances like any other American, and their presence helps spur consumer demand, investment, and other activities that ultimately result in more businesses and jobs. Immigration has helped the United States maintain a large working-age population as its natural birthrate has been falling. Moreover, as someone who lives and teaches in what is perhaps the United States' largest immigration community (Queens, New York), it is my personal view that immigration allows the United States to skim talent and energy from the rest of the world, regardless of whether those people are highly educated or not. The United States gets other countries' smart, ambitious, and determined people, while those who are dull, lazy, and unambitious are more likely to stay at home.

The Neoliberal Revolution

Earlier, it was noted that many of the long-term forces that weigh on household finances are either very difficult—if not practically impossible—to reverse or are changes that are probably things that we do not want to reverse. In contrast, economic policy is malleable—it can be willed to change much more easily than an aging population or technological advancement. Moreover, it is harder to find compelling reasons to cling to economic policies that do not serve regular Americans well.

Throughout this long deterioration of household finances, U.S. economic policies have followed a steady course toward embracing ideals that many commentators characterize as "neoliberal." *Neoliberalism* is a political and economic ideology that advocates for the dismantlement of Great Depression-era and postwar-era reforms that led to the dramatic growth and empowerment of the government. This ideology holds that individual freedom, economic prosperity, and societal betterment are achieved by pushing the country toward a more faithful emulation of free market principles, and replacing the influence of government policy-makers with that of investors and businesspeople. Neoliberalism's relationship with household finances will be a running theme over the remainder of this book. The following section introduces some background on neoliberalism and its basic tenets.[43]

Background

The neoliberal movement was rooted in early opposition to the mid-century government expansion. Some of this opposition was intellectual, part of a movement that disagreed with the economics of John Maynard Keynes and the policies of the Depression and wartime-era Roosevelt administration. Perhaps the best-known member of this movement was the Austrian economist Friedrich Hayek. He believed that the growth of government left the United States vulnerable to the kind of dictatorships seen in Germany or France.[44] He questioned the effectiveness and responsiveness of central planners, and he advocated for the superiority of economic decisions made by entrepreneurs.[45]

During the 1950s and 1960s, such notions were more marginal in the field of economics. Society maintained its faith that economic policy-makers were capable of controlling the economy in ways that could produce a regular, stable prosperity that benefitted society. Such promises were delivered in those decades, but, as noted earlier, this system broke down in the 1970s. There are several ways in which this crisis—and its then-unforeseen combination of high inflation, output recession, and high unemployment—hurt postwar "big government" policy strategies. First, it shook confidence in economic experts, and it sowed frustration with economic planners' seeming inability to resolve the country's economic problems. These macroeconomic problems produced a lot of labor conflict and strikes, laying the groundwork for an eventual backlash against unions. It was a crisis that defied conventional policy-making wisdom and shook economists' belief in their ability to fully control what goes on in the economy.

This set the stage for the ascendancy of Ronald Reagan, whose economic agenda had great affinities with this burgeoning antigovernment sentiment on economic issues. "Government is not the solution to our problem," he argued in his 1981 State of the Union address, "government is the problem."[46] Reagan led a movement to fundamentally depart from the policies and strategies of mid-century U.S. capitalism in several ways. First, he made substantial cuts to income taxes, most of which were targeted toward high-income earners—between 1981 and 1982, the top tax bracket for married people fell from 70 percent on incomes over $215,000 (about $560,000 in today's dollars) to 50 percent on incomes over $85,000 (about $221,000).[47] Second, he continued a broad initiative to deregulate the economy (which began under Carter) that ultimately reshaped credit markets, transportation markets, utility markets, and many others. Third, he altered the tenor of union-employer relations by firing striking air traffic controllers, a move that is widely believed to have led businesses to adopt hard postures toward the unions with which they dealt. These changes, coupled with a Federal Reserve that aggressively sought to control inflation, ultimately saw the stagflation crisis subside under his watch. Reagan's approach to economic policy was lionized and has served as a template for every subsequent administration until the 2008 crisis. Eventually, Democrats embraced deregulation, opposition to social services, tax cuts, and a range of other policies that would have been considered archconservative just two decades earlier.

Basic Principles

Neoliberalism is generally considered to be motivated by the principles of laissez-faire ("leave alone"), as in "the government should leave the economy alone." This view maintains that society's interests—however defined—are best served when the government refrains from interfering in economic affairs and more readily acquiesces to whatever outcomes stem from private decision-making and transacting. Neoliberalism's position on limited government should not be exaggerated. Adherents of this view do see some role for government in economic affairs but maintain that those functions should be more narrowly restricted to providing the social or legal infrastructure upon which a market system depends. For example, the government's role in providing a working money system, enforcing contracts, or maintaining public order garner little to no dispute. Exceptions are taken where governments are seen as overriding choices that belong to the province of business owners, managers, and consumers. These kinds of reforms include tax cuts, spending cutbacks, deregulation, the sale of government-owned property, the replacement of public sector employees with private contractors, free trade, free international capital movement, increased migration, and cuts to social programs. Such reforms were implemented in a variety of ways by the Reagan, Clinton, and both Bush administrations.

Although neoliberalism is strongly identified with a laissez-faire approach to economic governance, it is not a pure libertarian ideology. For example, many neoliberal era policies sought to actively encourage financial investments by giving special tax incentives for finance-related income. Governments developed programs to subsidize home ownership. States and localities often granted special tax breaks and regulation exemptions to businesses who promised to invest and create jobs locally. These types of policies are hardly hands-off—they privilege people or activities favored by economic planners and effectively channel resources to them. This is the second side of neoliberalism: trickle-down or supply-side economics. The two concepts are somewhat distinct, but they have a common core. *Trickle-down* economics is a doctrine that prioritizes channeling resources to those at the top of society's economic hierarchy, on the premise that their enrichment will spur spending, investment, and job creation that will ultimately raise everyone's living standards. Supply-side economics advocates for economic rules that channel income and decision-making power to investors and business managers—who are also those at the top of society's economic hierarchy—on the grounds that they make better decisions and are best positioned to create or expand businesses and jobs. The tie that binds is this view that channeling economic resources and power to investors, business owners, and managers serves society's best interests.

Effects on Household Finances

Neoliberalism's broad effects on people's economic and overall well-being is the subject of endless debate. On one hand, many see neoliberalism as a vehicle for redistributing resources toward the rich, which is presumed to have resulted in the impoverishment of the nonrich. By cutting taxes on the wealthy, undercutting laborers' bargaining power, or reigning in social programs, the government is thought to have tipped the scales against regular people, and put them in a weaker position to earn and save money. On the other hand, some see neoliberalism as having helped households in the face of other headwinds they face. Many of the aforementioned pressures facing regular households took root in the 1970s—before Reagan—if not earlier. If one accepts that neoliberal policies helped end the stagflation crisis and helped spur nearly two decades of prosperity and reasonable stability, then neoliberal policies can be seen as something that helped regular people.

It is very difficult to pass a clear, unhedged judgment on neoliberalism's effect on household finances. On one hand, it played a role in creating the social forces that pressure middle-class finances. It underwrote the free trade accords that propelled globalization. Its damage to unions and deinstitutionalization of labor market protections made the rise of today's "gig economy" of precarious, temporary work more viable. It championed cuts to redistribution and social programs. The list could go on. The main point is that one can mount a credible argument that neoliberalism damaged people's ability to sustain a livelihood.

Before wholly embracing the proposition that neoliberalism was a detrimental development, it is worth keeping two caveats in mind. The first is that the pressures of globalization, technology, and so on are not *only*—or even necessarily primarily—caused by neoliberalism. Globalization was arguably just as much a politically minded enterprise designed to integrate other countries into a shared, peaceful, rule-bound world order. There is good reason to believe that the computing revolution would have occurred without Reaganomics and that millions of cashiers, tax accountants, bank tellers, typists, and so on would still be facing increasing difficulty finding jobs. Many of the aforementioned demographic changes were well underway before 1980. One could mount a credible argument that neoliberalism was in fact a strategy that saved jobs in the face of these mounting pressures. Such an argument might ultimately prove false, but it is credible enough to take seriously.

Second, neoliberalism is widely argued to have helped drive down costs. In part, Chinese imports, automated production, small retail-crushing big box and online retail may have cost jobs, but they have also helped contain prices. It may have cost jobs or made it harder for people to get higher wages, but lower prices have the same effect as rising incomes. The absence of these price-containing effects might have made it harder for families to manage the nonpolicy headwinds that have made it harder to earn money.

This discussion proceeds with the view that neoliberalism's effects on household finances is complicated. It has helped in some ways and hurt in others. While there are clearly ways in which this movement resulted in policies that weakened workers' hands in dealing with employers, and clearly failed to produce a bounty of good jobs, it is difficult to say that such a bounty would have emerged under policies that prevailed in the 1960s or 1970s.

U.S. household finances have deteriorated over decades. During this long deterioration, the United States has experienced a range of concurrent changes. The country has had to contend with foreign competition and adjust to technological change. Regular Americans' money situation has been affected by an aging population and an increasing number of single-person households. There is considerable disagreement about whether economic policy has helped alleviate or exacerbate these problems. What is clear is that it is hard to see how household finances will simply self-resolve after the economy recovers fully. Household financial problems appear to be a long-term phenomenon with long-term causes. Absent any profound change to U.S. capitalism, it is hard to see why we should expect family finances to come roaring back, especially because they haven't done so since at least the 1990s.

CHAPTER FIVE

Runaway Spending

When contemplating the causes of U.S. households' financial problems, attentions often turn to the topic of real income stagnation. Although income problems are often the focus of discussions about households' financial difficulties, they are only part of the puzzle. Income stagnation means that incomes aren't growing quickly—not that they are falling. As long as people's spending also stagnates, their savings, debt, wealth, and financial security need not deteriorate.

The problem is that Americans do not seem to be reigning in their spending. This observation provides an important basis for opposition to the implementation of public assistance programs in response to household financial problems. Cheap imports, razor-thin-margin retailers, and technological advancement have made many products—including essentials such as food and clothes—very affordable. The idea that people have not seized on our era's immense opportunities to save money lends credence to the belief that people are causing their own problems.

More broadly, the idea that runaway spending is causing financial ruin feeds a very prevalent—and unflattering—narrative depicting U.S. culture as materialistic, frivolous, gluttonous, wasteful, and consumeristic. Americans are said to have been brainwashed by marketing. They are said to live in malls. Their capacity to control their consumption impulses is questioned. In essence, they are portrayed as consumption addicts. People's purported failure to manage money well suggests that extending aid to the financially distressed is tantamount to pouring money down a black hole. There are no limits to the amount of money that people can waste. Critics of social assistance programs argue that people need to learn self-discipline and that shielding them from the natural consequences of their excesses prevents them from learning necessary lessons about thrift.

While there may be some kernels of truth in this line of argument, it misses some important aspects of Americans' runaway spending and sows misunderstanding that might ultimately prevent us from developing effective responses to household financial problems. This chapter presents an analysis of how household spending has changed during this long deterioration in household finances. Since the early 1980s, households appear to be spending less on the kinds of frivolities that we often associate with consumerism, such as restaurant meals, clothes, cars, beauty products, or entertainment, in proportion to incomes. Instead, four types of products—healthcare, child care, education, and housing—seem to be driving rising household spending. These are not frivolous things. People's basic well-being is affected by their access to these kinds of products. Moreover, it is not so clearly the case that rising spending is the product of people buying quantitatively more of these things. Prices have also gone up, both in relation to incomes and general prices.

These results are reminiscent of earlier arguments advanced by Elizabeth Warren,[1] whose earlier work on household bankruptcy found that the financial burden of select products that are, arguably, essential to well-being—such as housing, education, healthcare, or child care—were reported to have weighed on family finances. These findings suggest that households' failure to tighten their belts may not be a product of wasteful consumerism but may instead be a product of the rising personal burden of securing access to products that are essential to well-being. The economy is failing to contain the cost of products that households cannot easily—or even advisably—forgo. We examine Warren and her colleagues' view in greater detail in the following section.

Spending Is Part of the Problem

During this long deterioration in household finances, the growth in household spending has slightly, but steadily, outpaced that of incomes. This slow change led to the creeping deterioration in household savings described in Chapter One. Figure 5.1 shows changes in per capita disposable income and consumption expenditures, adjusted for inflation, from 1970 to 2013. The gap between the blue and red lines—between income and consumption—roughly represents household savings. Note that the space between these lines has been steadily shrinking over time.

Over the 33-year period depicted in the figure, per capita expenditures generally grew about one-half of a percentage point faster than incomes. During the boom years, households would collectively raise their spending by slightly more than their incomes rose. During bad years, they often

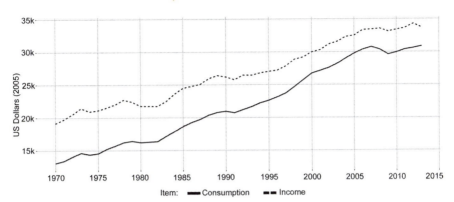

Figure 5.1 Real per Capita Household Disposable Income and Consumption
Spending over Time, United States, 1970–2013.
Sources: Bureau of Labor Statistics (2015). Consumer Price Index—All Urban
Consumers [Online database]. Retrieved from http://www.bls.gov/data/; U.S.
Census Bureau. (2015). Table H-6: Regions—by Median and Mean Income [Data
table]. Retrieved from https://www2.census.gov/programs-surveys/cps/tables/time
-series/historical-income-households/h06w.xls

collectively maintained their consumption levels, even when their incomes
were falling. Rising spending left households with less money to save, and
lower savings made it harder for households to accumulate wealth. This suggests that household finances may be strengthened by initiatives that
encourage households to cut spending.

Spending is likely part of what is causing people to save less and accumulate less wealth. In and of itself, this observation does not tell us enough to
make sense of the problem. The character of this rise in spending has important implications on the means by which we try to encourage spending cuts.
If spending is being fueled by wasteful or nonessential endeavors, then
containing spending probably involves finding ways to press people to
stop wasting money. Voters and taxpayers are bound to have little pity for
someone who has gotten into financial trouble for overspending on hedonism, impulse, social jockeying, gluttony, or some other ignoble motive.
They might see the pains of financial problems as justified—perhaps even
necessary—to impress the value of thrift.

However, if people's budgets are pressured by essentials, then the situation might seem different. This suggests that the economy is failing to make
basic essentials accessible and is forcing people to choose between the risk
of personal financial distress and the risks of forgoing health insurance,
medical treatment, quality child care, education, quality emergency services,
and other things that probably affect a family's well-being. Under these

circumstances, the morality and practicality of public programs to help defray people's living costs looks more like a corrective measure to a failure in the system. In general, U.S. households' rising spending is presumed to be motivated by ignoble purposes. The most prominent perspective of this sort might be characterized as the "culture of consumerism" narrative. We examine that narrative next.

The "Culture of Consumerism" Narrative

Why might U.S. families overspend on products, even if it damages their long-term financial well-being? Many scholars explain household over-spending as the product of *consumerism*, a cultural mind-set or ideology that hyper-valorizes the acquisition and accumulation of consumer prod-ucts. Collectively, Americans are said to equate the acquisition of consumer goods with well-being, personal fulfillment, or moral rectitude.[2] We are said to forge our personal identity through products we acquire.[3] We shop recreationally, and sometimes knowingly bury ourselves in unmanageable debt.[4] Our daily lives are described as bombarded by advertising, and public spaces have become replete with opportunities to consume. Technological innovations such as the credit card[5] or online shopping are said to have made it easier to buy on impulse without fully contemplating the wider implica-tions of our spending.

Consumerism is often described as an ideology cultivated to service capi-talism and the economic interests of businesses by encouraging perpetual streams of unnecessary sales. It is said to cement the political economy's conformity to capitalist ideals by pushing people to fetishize consumer products and sacrifice things of true value in order to get them. This mind-set is said to be propagated through the tools of modern marketing and media,[6] fostered through a distorted, product-centric worldview. This cul-ture of consumerism is linked to rising anxiety, poor health, distress and other ailments, or other forms of malaise.[7] Some argue that it helps perpetu-ate the impoverishment or disempowerment of middle and lower classes.[8]

The Narrative's Implications

The culture of consumerism argument imparts a particular diagnosis of overconsumption: a culture-wide inability or unwillingness to restrain spending on frivolous, nonessential purchases. It sees overspending as the product of cultural pressures that press people to fetishize the acquisition of goods and services. Often, those who subscribe to this narrative propose resolving consumerism's ills by reshaping this cultural mind-set to displace pro-consumerism with anti-consumerism cultural traits (e.g., schema, values, habits, worldviews, etc.). This can be broadly characterized as an attempt to inculcate enlightened asceticism. Interestingly, their solution shares common premises with arguments from popular conservative politics, which stress the utility of allowing market forces to whip people into shape.

Those who advocate for the inculcation of nonmaterialist worldviews and austere lifestyles as a solution offer many proposals to address high spending. Most of these proposals involve some form of reverse-cultural engineering, which tries to help people unlearn their product-centric worldviews, value systems, and practical habits. For some religious scholars, society's emancipation from consumerism can be achieved by fortifying the sway of traditional religious values, such as self-restraint, self-mastery, temperance, and so on.[9] Secular movements offer similar remedies. For example, there is the "voluntary simplicity" movement, a social movement that stresses the free-will choice "to cultivate nonmaterialistic sources of satisfaction and meaning."[10] There is also the "culture jamming" movement, which seeks to debase brand icons and marketing campaigns with the intent of sullying their luster and influence.[11] Noted consumption scholar Juliet Schor argued that resolving the strains of consumerism might involve inculcating a sense that time has value that is lost in the cycle of working and spending, so that people realize exactly what they are sacrificing when they make their trip to the mall.[12] There are many other concrete programmatic lists of potential initiatives, including educational programs, organized public movements to repudiate materialism and consumerism, and policy-based disincentives such as consumption taxes.[13] The main point of these redresses is to try to engineer culture to deemphasize the materialistic, acquisitive mind-sets that are thought to lead to overspending.

Interestingly, these types of correctives draw from a perspective that shares much common ground with more politically conservative views, which are more amenable the use of "market discipline" to press the financially imprudent to develop better financial habits. This group also sees people as gluttons for products that they do not need and cannot afford, but they see this gluttony as the result of a failure of self-restraint that people must cultivate to resist their natural acquisitiveness. Such views see it is as natural for people to want mountains of products, and see the basic mathematics of personal finance as providing the ultimate constraint on people's consuming impulses. Where people's impulse control fails, the market is supposed to impose natural consequences: people go bankrupt. The fear of bankruptcy is assumed to push people toward frugality. If fear of bankruptcy is not sufficient to contain imprudent spending, then the pains of personal bankruptcy and being cut from consumer credit is expected to press the point. Thus, the market "disciplines" people to exert the self-control that economic realities require. Insulating people from these threats is taken to sow immoderation, enabling people's consuming ways.

Although they may at first appear as opposing diagnoses and solutions, both views share common premises. Both viewpoints' underlying premise that rising spending is principally fueled by the acquisition of nonessential goods is important. If households are wasting their money on McMansions, "extra VCRs, cashmere sweaters and an SUV,"[14] then it seems entirely reasonable to expect them to exercise restraint. Through this lens, consumerism seems like an addiction, and it seems reasonable to demand that families exert more willpower.

Criticisms of the Perspective

The culture of consumerism narrative has many proponents but also its critics. One point of criticism questions whether this diagnosis is really capturing a definitive societal change that feeds into households' recent financial problems, as opposed to being just another reincarnation of an old, generic genre of social criticism. Complaints about people's shallow materialism and lack of virtue have been a mainstay of social criticism for centuries. Lest the vintage of these arguments be questioned, consider the following quote from Adam Smith, well over two centuries ago:

> The poor man's son, whom heaven in its anger has visited with ambition, when he begins to look around him, admires the condition of the rich. He finds the cottage of his father too small for his accommodation, and fancies he should be lodged more at his ease in a palace. He is displeased with being obliged to walk a-foot, or to endure the fatigue of riding on horseback. He feels himself naturally indolent, and willing to serve himself with his own hands as little as possible; and judges, that a numerous retinue of servants would save him from a great deal of trouble. He thinks if he had attained all these, he would sit still contentedly, and be quiet, enjoying himself in the thought of the happiness and tranquility of his situation. Through the whole of his life he pursues the idea of a certain artificial and elegant repose which he may never arrive at, for which he sacrifices a real tranquility that is at all times in his power, and which, if in the extremity of old age he should at last attain to it, he will find to be in no respect preferable to that humble security and contentment which he had abandoned for it. It is then, in the last dregs of life that he begins at last to find that wealth and greatness are mere trinkets of frivolous utility, no more adapted for procuring ease of body or tranquility of mind than the tweezer-cases of the lover of toys. (Adam Smith (*Theory of Moral Sentiments* IV.I.8, 1792))

There is a long history of argument bemoaning the shallow, materialistic acquisitiveness of popular culture. Are those who attribute rising household spending to such a culture of consumerism reaching these conclusions based on a deeply contemplated diagnosis of contemporary U.S. culture, or are they merely pulling out an old, tried-and-true generic line?

A second issue with the culture of consumerism narrative is that it examines the issue of consumption in a strongly negative, moralistic way. The British anthropologist Daniel Miller argues that many analysts see consumerism through strong "anti-materialism ideologies" that paint a particularly unflattering picture of consumers.[15] Consumption is broadly portrayed as wasteful and frivolous, divorced from "'true' needs" and "bound to express negative values such as status competition or insatiable greed."[16] These analysts characterize present-day popular consumption as quite similar to how Thorstein Veblen saw society's *nouveaux riches* at the turn of the century: "Consumption is still conspicuous consumption, and vicarious consumption based on emulation and the desire to deny labour. It's just that the examples used to illustrate the arguments have shifted by a century." A core part of Miller's critique, and one upon which this study follows up, is the notion that some forms of consumption are integral to people's well-being. Paying for a child's day care or college education, buying a car with important safety features, getting medical diagnostic tests and treatments, hiring a nurse or senior care facility to take care of an aging parent, or eating a diet with more fresh fruit and vegetables all register as consumption in official statistics. These things are not frivolities, rooted in the "negative values" Miller describes, are they?

We can quibble about the genuine novelty or value-influenced nature of this narrative, but perhaps the more compelling—and researchable—question is whether this narrative accurately portrays household spending behavior. If the character of household spending does not resemble the narrative, then the preceding questions are of little consequence. While the overall growth in household spending attests to the idea that overconsumption could be a problem, the types of products that Americans are buying are not those featured in the culture of consumerism literature.

A Look at the Data

The culture of consumerism narrative casts a particular light on household financial issues. Does the view faithfully characterize the reasons that households have failed to tighten their belts? This question can be probed empirically by looking at data from the Bureau of Labor Statistics (BLS) Consumer Expenditure Survey, a nationally representative survey that tracks people's spending behavior.[17] A closer look at these data suggests that household budgets are being principally strained by four types of products: healthcare, child care, education, and housing. These types of expenditures are not so easily identified as being as frivolous as those typically featured in the culture of consumerism literature.

Changes in Household Spending, 1984–2014

Figure 5.2 depicts changes in mean household expenditures from 1984 to 2013, both overall and across six product categories that exemplify many others in the data. Each figure expresses average spending levels in proportion to their 1984 levels. Note that the y-axis differs across individual figures.

These data suggest that, over this 30-year period, overall household spending has risen by about 6 percent in inflation-adjusted terms.[18] This is hardly the kind of spending boom suggested earlier. Some of this stability is the product of post-2008 spending cutbacks. Right before the crisis, in 2007, household spending was up 13 percent from its 1984 levels. Moreover, some of this appearance of stability is a result of the fact that the data in Figure 5.2 are different from the data of Figure 5.1, and the former data are taken to have difficulty capturing the spending behavior of society's wealthier households.[19] We have many indications that the boom in household spending is substantially a result of higher spending at the top of the income pyramid.

If we unpack average spending levels by income levels, differences emerge. For example, spending among the bottom 20 percent of income earners was about 5 percent lower than in 1984. In fact, household spending among the country's bottom quintile was lower during most of this 30-year period. While the country as a whole may have been spending more, society's lowest earners were spending less. In contrast, the data suggest that most of this rise in household spending has been fueled by rising spending among the top 20 percent, whose spending was up 16 percent in 2007. These households on average consume about four times as much as a bottom-quintile household and about three times as much as a middle-quintile household, so their rising spending disproportionately affects overall average spending levels. This boom in household spending seems to have been fueled by those at the top of the pyramid. By 2014, it was the only group that continued to spend more (+9 percent) than its 1984 inflation-adjusted levels. The middle 60 percent spent about as much as it did in 1984. Their spending levels had also risen during the 1980s through early 2000s but had since reverted to levels maintained thirty-some years ago.

Areas of Falling Spending

Figure 5.2 depicts two spending areas where Americans have made substantial cuts. By 2014, food expenditures had fallen by 10 percent, a substantial savings on the third-largest item on household spending budget (after housing and transportation). The spending cuts to apparel are even more remarkable: down over 40 percent from 1984 levels. The magnitudes of these changes are roughly similar across income groups.

This pattern of falling spending was seen across many other product categories, including home furnishings, home appliances, personal care goods and services, alcohol and tobacco, and reading materials. In addition, household spending was roughly unchanged for utilities, medical supplies, and entertainment products. Again, these cuts occurred across the income scale.

These falling expenditures stand as examples of the economically beneficial effects of globalization and technological advancement. They are not so much a product of the fact that people are consuming less food, clothing, appliances, so on, but rather that the cost of these goods is lower. These price changes are illustrated in Table 5.1, which describes the average annual inflation rate overall and across product categories. The table divides historical inflation rates into three columns. The first column represents a period of generally higher inflation, when inflation was coming down from its stagflation era highs and the world economy was transitioning out of the Cold War. The mid-1990s to 2007 represents a period in which globalization and the information technology revolution were underway. The post-2008 era gives us a sense of what happened after the crisis.

The table demonstrates not only how much inflation has come down over the past several decades but also which products have generally not risen in price. Falling spending in apparel, recreational products, personal care products, purchased (as opposed to leased) motor vehicles, home furnishing and utilities, and intercity transportation are all examples of products that have become cheaper, and household spending on these products have generally fallen relative to wages. These low prices have helped many households weather the effects of their slow income growth. However, not all products have become less expensive.

In many corners of the economy, economic production and distribution has been driven down by ultrafast productivity gains and fast-falling profit margins. Presumably, these declining prices give people the opportunity to save money that can be spent elsewhere. The problem is that spending has

Figure 5.2   Mean Household Spending, 1984–2014.

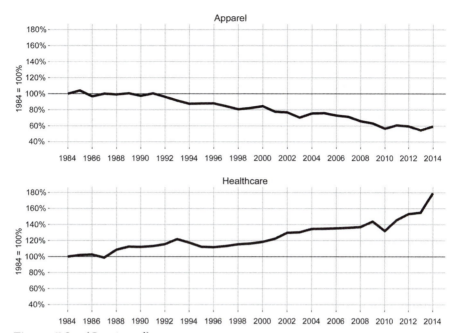

Figure 5.2 (Continued)
Source: Bureau of Labor Statistics (2015).

been buoyed by very rapidly escalating prices in other markets. The momentum of these rising prices are crowding out the benefits of these price cuts, and it seems likely that there may come a point at which clothing, food, and so on cannot keep falling fast enough to contain overall spending.

Areas of Rising Expenditures

While the prices of consumer products generally fell in proportion to incomes, spending rose in a selected set of product categories. For example, educational and healthcare have risen considerably. These expenditures, which are depicted in the middle of Figure 5.2, rose by almost 80 percent. By comparison, these surveys suggest that real disposable income has risen by about 20 percent during the same period. In addition, these data suggest that housing costs have outpaced income growth. While this difference is less striking than in education and healthcare, the housing expenditure is the largest item in household budgets, so it has an outsized impact on households' overall spending levels. We will discuss these spending areas in greater detail below.

One tie that binds these three spending areas is that the primary engines of living cost containment—importation and automation—have not

succeeded in driving down costs in these markets. The effects of these primary engines of spending may have been compounded by economic
policy changes. As we will see in Chapter Seven, the public sector's presence
in U.S. higher education and healthcare is comparatively light relative to
other highly developed countries.

Education Costs

Although education costs have risen substantially, their direct impact
on the average U.S. household's overall living costs is limited. The BLS
assumes that education costs on average about 3 percent of U.S. households'
overall living costs.[20] This is due to the fact that only part of society incurs
these costs, and only a minority incurs heavy costs. To develop a clearer
sense of the education costs borne by households, we have to drill down
past overall inflation figures presented in Figure 5.2 and examine the
microdata. We can do so using the BLS Survey of Consumer Finances.[21]
Unfortunately, high-quality publicly accessible microdata only goes back
to 1996, so we are unable to take a close look at the 1980s and early 1990s.
However, we can use the data to get a view of what has happened to living
costs since the mid-1990s.

The data suggest that, in 2014, only 18 percent of U.S. households incurred
educational costs. Most of them incurred limited expenses. Usually, these
expenditures involve materials, supplies, or lessons that supplemented the
fully socialized primary and secondary educational system in the United
States. Among households with any education expenditures, median spending was $750, or about 1.4 percent of their disposable income. Mean spend-
ing figures from Figure 5.2 suggest that education costs have been escalating
rapidly. This is not the result of a broad-based rise in education spending.
The heavy costs were borne by childless households and households with
adult children—those who are more likely to be pursuing postsecondary
training, where educational costs are not socialized.

The cost of college is considerable, and, as suggested previously in
Table 5.1, it has been rising quickly—more than double the rate of overall
prices or median wages. In 2015, the average published tuition for in-state
students at public universities was $9,410, and the total cost (including sup-
plies, room and board, books, etc.) net of tax credits and aid stood at
$24,061.[22] This is a considerable sum, particularly in comparison to other
highly developed countries (see Chapter Seven). At private schools, the net
total cost stood at $30,300 per year;[23] the public system's average costs are
not altogether different. In addition, college attendance rates are increasing,[24]
meaning more people will be exposed to these potential costs. A degree is

Table 5.1 Mean Inflation Rates, Overall and by Product Class, 1984–2013

Product Category	1980–1995	1995–2007	2007–2013	Overall
General Prices	3.5%	2.6%	1.9%	2.9%
Education	NA	5.7%	4.6%	NA
Child Care and Nursery School	NA	4.7%	3.2%	NA
College Tuition and Fees	9.2%	6.1%	5.3%	7.3%
K–12 Tuition and Fees	8.9%	6.3%	4.3%	7.1%
Tuition, Fees, and Child Care	8.8%	5.7%	4.5%	6.9%
Educational Books and Supplies	7.6%	5.8%	6.0%	6.6%
Medical Care	7.5%	4.0%	3.2%	5.4%
Hospital and Related Services	9.2%	5.7%	5.8%	7.3%
Prescription Drugs	8.2%	3.8%	3.1%	5.6%
Dental Services	6.6%	4.7%	3.2%	5.3%
Physicians' Services	6.9%	3.2%	2.6%	4.8%
Eyeglasses and Eye Care	NA	1.9%	0.9%	NA
Housing	4.1%	2.9%	1.4%	3.2%
Shelter	4.9%	3.2%	1.5%	3.6%
Fuels and Utilities	3.4%	4.1%	1.9%	3.4%
Furnishings and Operations	2.4%	0.3%	−0.3%	1.1%
Food and Beverages	3.7%	2.6%	2.6%	3.1%
Transportation	3.5%	2.4%	2.8%	3.0%
New and Used Motor Vehicles	NA	−0.4%	1.1%	NA
Motor Vehicle Parts and Equipment	0.5%	1.5%	3.2%	1.3%
Motor Fuel	0.2%	7.5%	4.1%	3.5%
Maintenance and Repair	4.3%	3.1%	2.7%	3.6%
Public Transportation	6.4%	2.3%	3.3%	4.3%
Airline Fare	7.1%	2.4%	3.7%	4.7%
Intercity Transportation	5.1%	0.0%	0.0%	2.3%
Intracity Transportation	5.6%	3.2%	4.1%	4.5%
Personal Care	4.0%	2.4%	1.6%	3.0%
Recreation	NA	1.4%	0.6%	NA
Apparel	2.5%	−0.9%	1.2%	1.0%

NA = Data not available during 1980–1995 period.

Sources: Bureau of Labor Statistics. (2015). Consumer Price Index—All Urban Consumers [Online database]. Retrieved from http://www.bls.gov/data/; U.S. Census Bureau. (2015). Table H-6: Regions—by Median and Mean Income [Data table]. Retrieved from https://www2.census.gov/programs-surveys/cps/tables/time-series/historical-income-households/h06w.xls

becoming less exclusively the domain of the wealthy over time, in part because college is seen as increasingly critical to remaining employed and out of poverty.[25] Those without advanced training face greater difficulty finding a place in the U.S.'s increasingly high-skill economy (see Chapter Four). Advanced training is becoming more of a necessity in finding a role in the economy.

Increasingly, college is being financed by student debt. The proportion of households with student debts is small (about 2.8 percent of households), in part because not everyone goes to college, and those who do incur debt for college often manage to pay it off while they are relatively young (so it does not appear in their balance sheets later in life). Nevertheless, these obligations can be considerable. In 2014, the median student debt obligation was $20,000, and about 10 percent owed $90,000 or more. Despite stories about people graduating with $200,000 in debt, the event is quite rare—only 1 percent of student debtors owe this much or more. This debt may lead to problems for those who incur it. For example, it is often argued that the need to service student debt pushes student to take work that is more immediately rewarding but less beneficial in the long term. Student debts may also interfere with students' ability to start saving for retirement or a home down payment early. Nevertheless, many—though by no means all—of those with debt are relatively well off. Student debtors earn considerably more than the general population (with a median income of $64,000, and one-quarter earning more than $107,000)—a situation in which someone seems capable of servicing the typical education debt. The six-figure student debts that are often described in stories about the crushing effects of student debt are rare.

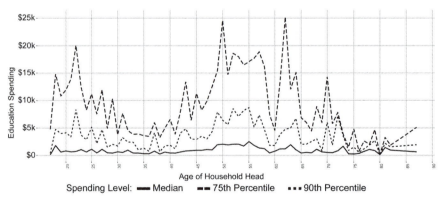

Figure 5.3 Education over the Life Cycle, Education Expenses, and Age of Household Head, 2014.
Source: Bureau of Labor Statistics (2015).

Even if we grant that postsecondary education is expensive, its negative impact on household finances is time-limited. Households generally incur substantial education costs in two waves, depicted in Figure 5.3. These two waves seem to occur in households' college years—either their own or that of their children.

Heavier costs materialize when people pursue a university degree, college diploma, or job training certificate, but these expenditures are temporary and are generally expected to result in higher earnings (things are more complicated than this, as discussed in Chapter Six). Most households do not precipitously fall into financial ruin from devastating education expenditures. Instead, it is probably fairer to characterize the effects of higher education as a temporary, nontrivial financial hit that occurs once or twice in a lifetime. The effects are temporarily damaging, but the cumulative effects of these and similar temporary shocks may be larger.

Perhaps more serious are the college expenditures that never materialize in spending data, for example, those who forgo postsecondary training that would benefit their future employability and personal finances. This might involve someone failing to enroll in or complete advanced training, or someone settling on inferior training, for financial reasons. We engage that issue in the next chapter.

Child Care

Child care is often treated as a personal household service, rather than an educational expenditure. This is probably a legacy of the days in which child care was a luxury—people with nannies probably also had maids, drivers, or other servants. Today, child care is economically critical for parents. A large majority of the country's children are parented by a single parent or working couple. Many of these households do not have the benefit of a relative who is able to babysit, so they need commercial child care. Some other highly developed countries have socialized child care, making it akin to K–12 education here.[26]

In 2014, about 6 percent of households reported child care costs, including 20 percent of households with children aged 2 to 15 and 30 percent of those with children aged 2 or less. These figures seem like low estimates that may exclude things such as "black market" child care, periodic babysitting, or interpersonal payments associated with unpaid care done by a relative, but we will not detain ourselves on these issues.[27] Among families reporting child care expenses, the average family spends $2,812 annually. The typical household that incurs these costs generally dedicates about 2 percent of their disposable income to child care, although a tenth dedicate 7 percent of their income or more. Many households keep these costs down by limiting one parent's work time, relying on relatives for free child care, or by relying on black market care providers. For those who want to place their children in regulated, institutional care, these prices can be considerable. State averages for institutionalized infant care range from an average of $22,000 in Washington, DC, to just under $5,000 in Mississippi.[28] Typically, child care costs are lower where people earn less money and poverty is higher. These are nontrivial sums of money, which can weigh heavily on a household's financials.

Do these expenses represent an increase over historical levels? Unfortunately, our microdata only goes back to 1996, when society's transition from stay-at-home married parents to divorce and dual incomes was taking place in the 1970s and 1980s. The data suggest that the proportion of households with child care expenditures is roughly the same since 1996.

Like education, child care costs generally weigh on family finances over a limited part of a household's life cycle. Typically, people will weather these costs from their late twenties through mid-forties—the period in which they tend to have children who are in need of care. They are burdensome when they occur but are presumed to pass eventually, leaving households to make up for lost ground.

Healthcare

Like education, healthcare expenditures are mostly borne by only part of the population. While most households (79 percent) incur *some* healthcare costs, healthcare is a minor budget item for many of them. About one-quarter of all households spent about $130—or just over $10 a month—on healthcare during 2014. The median household spent about $100 a month out-of-pocket. About 10 percent spent more than $400 a month—roughly what an apartment rental costs in much of the country. Finally, 1 in 10 households are spending the equivalent of a second (modest) home on healthcare.

The biggest ticket item in healthcare budgets is insurance. About 67 percent of households spent money on health insurance, and the median outlay was $1,475. This is not the total cost. Many of these expenses are in addition to employer-sponsored plans, which are reported to be absorbing a smaller proportion of fast-rising insurance costs.[29] This represents a considerable increase from 1996, when only 61 percent of households paid for health insurance out of pocket, and median costs were about half as much in inflation-adjusted terms. Health insurance costs have doubled at a minimum, and more people have had to bear these costs.

A similar story can be told of expenditures on prescription drugs. Although slightly fewer people spend on prescription drugs compared to 1996 (45 percent of households in 1996, compared to 39 percent in 2014), the costs faced by those who did spend on pharmaceuticals rose. In 1996, the median outlay on prescription drugs was $165, compared to $204 in 2014—a rise of almost one-third. These are roughly the costs of prescriptions for minor maladies or a temporary illness. For those who spend a lot on drugs—people with chronic or major conditions—the rise was similar (about one-third), but the bills were considerable. About 10 percent of those with drug expenditures spent almost $1,000 or more.

Health expenditures vary by age. Figure 5.4 describes how these expenditures change over the life course.

The median household headed by someone under 30 spends about $90 a year on healthcare. During the head of households' thirties and forties median expenditures rise to the $1,000 range and then slowly escalate to nearly $2,000 from their mid-sixties onward. Not only does the typical family have lower healthcare costs when it is younger, but also a larger proportion of households are able to avoid healthcare costs almost entirely. Nearly a quarter of all households spends $100 a year or less on healthcare until its heads reach their mid-forties. From age 65 onward, the 25th percentile household spends $1,000 a year on healthcare, even with socialized medicine for the elderly.

Households whose heads reach middle age and onward are more likely to experience considerable healthcare costs exceeding $5,000 or more. For middle-age households, these elevated costs are partly a matter of there being more people in the household, resulting in a higher probability that

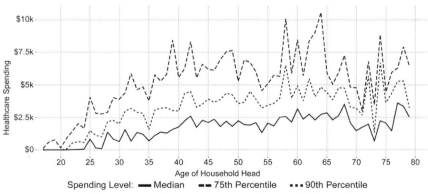

Figure 5.4 Healthcare Spending across Age of Household Head, 2014.
Source: Bureau of Labor Statistics (2015).

someone in the household will incur costs. As the heads age and the household empties, these elevated costs are more a matter of individuals facing higher prospects of encountering an expensive health-related issue. These costs rise somewhat as people enter their late fifties, but the financial impact of health problems is also buffered by the fact that the United States offers socialized health insurance to its elderly through the Medicare program.

As we will see in Chapters Six and Seven, healthcare is extraordinarily expensive in the United States. These expenses are the result of several problems, including the absence of cost controls, administrative bloat, and possible overuse of medical services.

Housing Costs

For much of the country, housing expenditures seem manageable. In 2014, the median household spent $6,596 on housing annually (about $550 a month). About one-quarter of the country's households spent less than $344 a month, and one-quarter spent more than $850. About 10 percent spent more than $1,312 a month.

These figures might strike many readers as extraordinarily low. The average is pulled down by households with unmortgaged homes, subsidized shelter costs (e.g., those receiving housing vouchers, or households whose shelter is covered by family members), and those who live in areas in which shelter is inexpensive. It is also important to remember that money paid on the principal of a mortgage is not considered an expense, but rather a form of saving—so the consumption part of people's mortgage service bills is smaller than the overall money paid out.

Since 1996, overall housing costs have risen by about 12 percent at the median, though it is slightly down from where it stood in 2007. This seemingly modest rate of increasing spending is a result of offsetting factors. For example, many types of housing costs, including home furnishings and appliances, utilities, maintenance, and operations, have not risen rapidly. In contrast, shelter costs have risen more quickly, particularly among renters of lower-cost quarters. In 2007, shelter costs were up 22 percent from 1996, but these costs have fallen 7 percent since then.

For homeowners, property taxes have risen by about 33 percent, but mortgage service costs have fallen with interest rates. Loose credit has also pushed up housing costs, as depicted in the Case-Shiller index shown in Figure 5.5. It suggests that home prices have multiplied several times in value, even while household incomes have not.

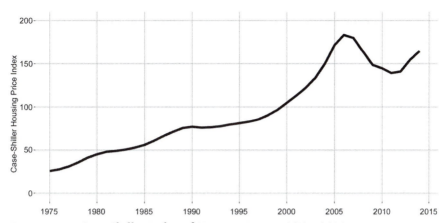

Figure 5.5   Case-Shiller Index of Housing Prices, 1975–2014.
Source: Federal Reserve Board (2015). S&P/Case-Shiller U.S. National Home Price Index©. Data series CSUSHPISA. Retrieved from https://research.stlouisfed.org /fred2/series/CSUSHPISA

The broader implications of appreciating home values are complex. For those who have owned homes over the past several decades, rising housing costs mean increased wealth. The situation is different for those acquiring homes. Cheap debt has made debt service cheaper and borrowing easier, which has in turn helped bid up housing costs. It may benefit those who own homes, but it locks new home buyers into more and longer-lasting debt, and rising home prices press people to invest more heavily in their homes.

Are we overconsuming on housing? Many observers cite the growing square footage of new home constructions to suggest that Americans have become greedy for bigger homes. Elizabeth Warren offers several pieces of data questioning this argument.[30] Data on new home constructions gloss over the fact that wealthier people may both tend to buy new homes and have larger homes. The proportion of people living in older homes jumped by nearly 50 percent, with roughly 60 percent of the country living in a home older than 25 years, and 25 percent living in homes older than 50 years. The median owner-occupied home grew from 5.7 to 6.1 rooms, which is hardly a dramatic expansion of living space. Even if Americans purchased more living space, they paid a greater premium for it; although square footage rose on new home constructions by roughly 40 percent between 1985 and 2007, home values rose approximately 250 percent.

Square footage costs, and in turn overall shelter costs, have grown as a percentage of household income, despite the rising incidence of dual-earning families.

Healthcare, child care, and education costs have clear implications on people's well-being and are thus easier to imagine as essential. The well-being implications of housing are less clear and are discussed at greater length in Chapter Six. In brief, the main well-being effect of housing—and a primary driver of housing costs—is the availability of public services that residency affords its residents. In areas with quality public services, particularly schools, housing is expensive. In places where housing is cheap, these public services fall well below first world standards.

A Series of Temporary Financial Hits

Each of these cost pressures afflict only part of the population at any given point in time for what seems like a limited time. These are economic rites of passage whose time will pass as a household progresses through its financial life cycle. The problem may be that these seemingly unrelated costs may have cumulative effects over their life cycles; that is, U.S. households are hit with a set of discrete financial shocks that cause temporary disruption but generally pass. Students weather the shock of higher education but (theoretically) eventually find work, pay down their debts and move on. Perhaps the cost delays saving money for that home down payment or birth of a child, but it eventually passes. Soon, parenthood arrives, along with the costs of childbirth, child care, and a home in a nondistressed school district. The costs can be sizable and may delay saving for college and retirement, but these costs too eventually pass. Next comes college, which parents might hope to help finance to protect their children from the potentially large burden of financing the kind of training thought to be necessary to find a meaningful role in the economy. These expenses also eventually pass. At this point, a household is probably somewhere in their mid-fifties and comes to realize that they have not saved enough to weather the costs of retirement and old age, which, even with the U.S.'s comparatively generous public pension and socialized health insurance for the elderly, can be considerable.

This loosely describes the process by which intelligent, self-aware, and nonfrivolous people find themselves under-saved and financially vulnerable. Individually, these costs seem life-cycle-specific and temporary. However, these expenditures occur across the life cycle, producing a lifetime of under-savings.

Concluding Thoughts

The idea that financial problems are caused by wasteful frivolities res-onates with many people. All of us can remember that time we spent too much on a coffee or ate at a restaurant instead of eating at home. We might recall buying something new when we could have bought it used from Craigslist or a garage sale. Maybe we drove when we could have taken the bus.

In this sense, there is some kernel of truth to the idea that people's waste-fulness is partly to blame for their money problems. However, these types of splurges are not as consequential in the grand scheme of things. In the words of the finance journalist Helaine Olen, "it's our Lipitor," not the lattes.[31] Even if people were to be more vigilant with their spending on clothes, food, cars, and such, the sheer momentum of education, health, and housing inflation seem likely to eventually wipe out household budgets.

The possible misinterpretation of rising household spending can lay the groundwork for ineffective policy responses. Campaigns to encourage belt-tightening—whether by market discipline or enlightenment—seem unlikely solutions. People seem willing to sacrifice financial well-being to ensure their access to basic essentials, and doing so is not an altogether senseless choice. Even worse is the possibility that such campaigns suc-ceed, and Americans start forgoing education or healthcare to balance their books.

These observations bring to mind an insightful quote from an audience member when I presented earlier research on this topic: "America is a place where the luxuries are cheap, but the necessities are expensive." This rings very true to me. Before moving to the United States, I would marvel at the low cost of consumer products. Clothes, electronics, toys, and just about anything at a U.S. shopping mall or supermarket were much cheaper than in my native Canada (not to mention the lower sales taxes). I would imagine how, were I to live in the United States, I would be able to afford so much more *stuff*.

The ways that Americans could save money were immediately obvious as soon as you step into a Walmart or Costco. However, after living in the United States for some time, I have realized that the money saved at Walmart is more than offset by bills that a Canadian does not really con-sider. Being out thousands of dollars for an emergency visit—even if you have health insurance—is not something that entered my imagination when thinking about the personal finances of living in the United States. Canadians do not consider the kind of furious saving that is necessary to send one's children to college because college degree costs are more similar to buying a car than a house.

That being said, there are always questions about whether this money is being spent wisely or foolishly. Do our children's economic fortunes hinge on us overspending on housing to get a foothold in a good school district? Does it matter if our children go to an expensive or cheap college, or even college versus junior college? Are all of these spending on "necessities" really so necessary? We turn to that question next.

CHAPTER SIX

Necessary "Necessities"?

Critics might argue that much of this "essential" spending is not really necessary. One might maintain that homes are growing more luxurious, colleges seem to resemble deluxe resorts, and a lot of healthcare is servicing people's hypochondria and their inability to accept mortality. Without denying that some basic levels of healthcare, education, or housing are undeniably important to people's well-being, one could argue that at least some—if not much—of these expenses are more reminiscent of the hedonism, status jockeying, vanity, and other base motives typically ascribed to household spending by those who subscribe to the "culture of consumerism" perspective. So how much of this spending is really necessary, and how much is dressed-up consumerism?

While there are almost certainly many examples of wasteful "essential" spending, stories about McMansions, private colleges, or unnecessary medical procedures obscure the fact that the costs of basic products are rising. Health insurance costs are the key driver of healthcare spending, there are strong rationales for arguing that everyone should have health insurance, and (at least until the Affordable Care Act [ACA]) quality basic health insurance was highly unaffordable. The vast majority of college-bound Americans go to public colleges and universities, whose admissions costs are increasingly hard to distinguish from their private counterparts. Housing costs are mainly driven by location, and, in the United States, your place of residence determines your access to schools, jobs, infrastructure, distance from social and environment problems, and a range of other nontrivial opportunities and amenities.

Many of these pressures have mounted in a broader context in which economic policy-makers have increasingly embraced neoliberal reforms.

Until recently, government had done very little to contain the spiraling cost of health insurance, and even its comparatively modest efforts to do so under Obamacare have attracted massive, sustained opposition. The burden of higher education has risen while government subsidies for public schools have fallen. The pressure to gain a foothold in a "good neighborhood" developed during a period in which policy-makers largely eschewed economic redistribution and sought to transfer responsibilities for public services down to local-level governments. Rather than taking a proactive role in containing the cost of these essentials—as is done in other developed countries—the United States relied on the "invisible hand" to contain costs, and the scheme failed.

One nagging question in this line of argumentation involves questions about the degree to which all of this "essential" spending is really essential. Although there is little doubt that some level of education, healthcare, and housing is essential to maintaining basic well-being, there comes a point past which spending on these "basics" is excessive. Purchasing a backyard pool or big screen TV also registers as housing expenditures in the data. Plastic surgery or tuition at a swanky private school count as healthcare and education costs, respectively. These are more obviously problematic miscategorizations of nonessentials as basic needs. However, what about people's sense that they need to send their children to good schools or cover their children's costs of college? What about their need to live closer to work or in a pricier area such as New York or San Francisco because the "good" jobs are there? What about their need for a pricey health insurance plan because their preferred doctor doesn't accept the cheaper ones? The line between what is necessary and what is optional can get fuzzy.

This is one of the more complicated issues facing the development of this argument, and we touched on similar issues in Chapter Three. To make some determination about a product's "essentiality," we must develop some definition about what people need or do not need, and our choices will influence our findings. An expansive definition of people's needs pushes an analysis to see more deprivation because fewer people are going to meet our high standards for an acceptable quality of life. Conversely, if we restrict our definition of a basic livelihood to bare minimums—food, shelter, and a library card—then our analysis will be more disposed to see deprivation rarer. The necessity of these types of costs are debatable, and arguments about what constitutes a need or a want can go on interminably. At some point, we need to develop some set of reasonable criteria that can allow our discussion to proceed.

There are many criteria by which to gauge people's quality of life, and thus many criteria by which to judge the true necessity of these "essentials."[1]

One way to make such a determination is to develop a sense of the degree to which the acquisition of a product has a likely impact on people's health, safety, and capacity to find gainful work. This third criterion—influence over a personal's capacity to find gainful work—is important because the ability to work provides people with a basis for earning money, living with independence and autonomy, and covering the costs of other basic products. To the extent that education, healthcare, and housing expenditures help people secure their health, safety, and capacity to work, then they are deemed to be essential. To the extent that such expenditures do not appreciably affect someone's health, safety, or basic employability, they are taken to be nonessential.

Explanations of Rising Prices

If society is to engage the rising cost of these basic products, it should consider why out-of-pocket costs are spiraling upward. Our explanations influence our interpretation of the problems and solutions that drive up spending.

Two generic explanations of rising costs are that they are a by-product of rising living standards, which we might term the "quality" and "quantity" explanations. The *quality* argument maintains that costs have risen because products are better, which presumably cost more to make, and these increased costs are passed on to consumers. For example, high pharmaceutical costs are often attributed to high research and development costs, we pay more for drugs to cover these costs, but these increased costs are covering drugs that are better. The *quantity* argument maintains that costs have risen because people purchase more. People spend more in healthcare and education because they purchase quantitatively more education and healthcare. Housing is more expensive because people are said to be buying bigger homes with more appliances and amenities. Both quality and quantity explanations of rising costs suggest a situation in which the costs of essentials are rising because our living standards are rising. We are spending more because we are getting better stuff and/or more of it.

A third argument—*profit taking*—maintains that living costs are being driven up by suppliers who take bigger markups on the sale of essentials. People are paying more, and the increased cost goes to those who work for, do business with, or invest in these industries. Unlike the previous two arguments, this scenario does not imply that the public is benefiting from the broader process that drives up the cost of necessities. Instead, it represents a failure of the market system, which allows people to profit at the expense of society at large. Under these circumstances, a society might question the benefit of leaving product markets in the hands of unfettered markets, as opposed to regulating them, socializing them, or fielding government alternatives to compete with the private sector.

This kind of profit taking may be facilitated by the privatization of the delivery of these essentials. *Privatization* is used here in the sense of converting a publicly owned or publicly administered operation or enterprise into a private, nongovernmental one. It can happen when, for example, a government goes from taking responsibility for delivering higher education or healthcare to one in which private markets are left to deliver these services. The government may continue to fund the enterprise but not administer it—for example, when it goes from directly running prisons to a system in which businesses are subcontracted to run them. Alternatively, it can simply stop funding or delivering services, for example, by simply shuttering public health mental treatment centers, and leaving families or the criminal justice system to deal with the mentally ill. High out-of-pocket prices are the result of governments' failure to subsidize, directly deliver, or price-regulate these products. The businesses who fill the void left by government upcharge the rest of society. In essence, such a view frames the rising cost of necessities as a result of neoliberalism and the market mechanism's failure to deliver a bounty of cheap, high-quality essentials. This perspective may see privatization as enabling unproductive profit taking.

Healthcare

In Chapter Five, we saw that healthcare expenditures rose by nearly 80 percent between 1980 and recent years. This rise has been substantially driven by rising prices; healthcare inflation has nearly doubled the rise in both general prices and incomes. Under normal circumstances, healthcare tends to be a minor budgetary item for most households. Healthcare costs materialize as shocks, which households experience as extraordinary and unpredictable. However, these shocks are quite common and widespread. Although relatively fewer households are hit with major medical expenses in any given year, the chances of a given household experiencing one or more such shocks over their lifetime is reasonably good.

Insurance Is the Fastest Rising Healthcare Expenditure

The primary driver of rising healthcare spending is rising expenditures on insurance. Table 6.1 compares healthcare spending in 1996 and 2014.[2] The table gives an overview of median total spending relative to posttax income, the proportion of households that spend money on major subcategories

Table 6.1   Healthcare Spending by Households (% Disposable Income), 1996 versus 2014

	1996	2014	Change
Total Spending			
Median Spending	1.72%	2.53%	+47%
Percent Spending over 5%	25%	32%	+28%
Percent Spending over 10%	13%	17%	+31%
Percent Spending over 25%	5%	7%	+40%
Health Insurance			
Percent Any Outlays	62%	69%	+11%
Median Outlays	1.3%	2.0%	+52%
90th Percentile Outlays	7.0%	11.6%	+67%
95th Percentile Outlays	20.8%	33.3%	+60%
Medical Services			
Percent Any Outlays	48%	42%	−13%
Median Outlays	0.5%	0.5%	−12%
90th Percentile Outlays	4.6%	4.3%	−7%
95th Percentile Outlays	10.5%	10.0%	−5%
Drugs			
Percent Any Outlays	46%	42%	−9%
Median Outlays	0.3%	0.3%	+7%
90th Percentile Outlays	3.2%	2.9%	−11%
95th Percentile Outlays	6.9%	6.8%	−1%
Medical Supplies			
Percent Any Outlays	12%	10%	−17%
Median Outlays	0.4%	0.4%	−19%
90th Percentile Outlays	2.5%	2.5%	+2%
95th Percentile Outlays	4.7%	6.5%	+38%

Source: Bureau of Labor Statistics (2015).

of healthcare expenditures, and the incidence of high expenditures (relative to incomes) overall and across major subcategories.

The typical household does not spend a lot on healthcare from year to year. Spending at the median is low in proportion to disposable incomes, at about 2.5 percent of take-home pay. Costs can rise quickly when a household is afflicted by a medical event (e.g., an injury or illness) or temporarily loses coverage (e.g., someone loses a job with insurance). In 1996, about one-quarter of U.S. households spent more than 5 percent of their disposable income (about 2.5 weeks of annual income) on healthcare, compared to one-third by 2015. The proportion spending more than 10 percent (or just over one month's net pay) rose from 13 percent to 17 percent, and those spending over 25 percent rose from 5 percent to 7 percent.

The table shows that health insurance has been the primary driver of these increased expenditures. Other types of expenditures have generally declined, both in terms of the percentage of households incurring any costs and the outlays of households that spend comparatively more on these products. Insurance has been the focus of discussions about healthcare for several years now, in no small part because it is the most obvious cost and in part because it was the focus of politically charged reforms under the ACA. Often, popular explanations of rising insurance costs focus on two appealingly simple explanations: insurance company or employer profiteering. Both probably draw attention away from the core drivers of rising healthcare costs.

One problem with insurance company profiteering explanations is the fact that these companies do not seem to be particularly profitable. Table 6.2 shows estimates of the profit margins taken in by the health insurance industry, along with other major healthcare industries and other major economic sectors.[3] Here, *profit margin* is the ratio of profit to sales—how much profit is made on every dollar of sold goods or services. The "Healthcare Plan" industry, including many of the country's largest publicly traded health insurance companies, registered relatively low profit margins in comparison to other healthcare industries or major economic sectors.

Although profits fluctuate from year to year and among companies within the same industry, the profit margins in 2015 appear to be quite typical. While health insurance may not be highly profitable relative to other healthcare subsectors, in the next chapter, we will see it is very expensive compared to other countries' health insurance and delivery systems. The private health insurance sector consumes more resources than public systems such as Medicare or foreign countries' highly regulated and/or socialized insurance systems. For example, a 2011 study found that the average U.S. physician spent $82,975 per year dealing with private insurers, just under 4 times the cost borne by Canadian physicians in their single-payer system ($22,205).[4] The time demands of negotiating this system were 10 times that borne by Canadians.[5] Insurance companies may be part of the problem, but it seems unlikely that the rising burden of healthcare can be fully reduced to insurance company salaries and profits.

A second commonly heard argument maintains that employers have capitalized on the tumult of healthcare reform to cut employee health

Table 6.2   Profit Margins in the Healthcare Industry, Publicly Traded Companies, 2015

Sectors/*Industry*	Market Capitalization (Billions)	Profit Margin
Drug Manufacturers—Major	50,131	21.4
Biotechnology	16,616	19.7
Drug Manufacturers—Other	252	18.5
Technology	*180,488*	*17.7*
Financial	*97,685,646*	*17.6*
Healthcare	*83,019*	*17.2*
Diagnostic Substances	15	11.7
Medical Instruments and Supplies	413	11.4
Medical Appliances and Equipment	3,601	10.6
Utilities	*32,370*	*9.9*
Drug Delivery	256	8.3
Consumer Goods	*249,515*	*7.7*
Medical Laboratories and Research	378	6.7
Services	*93,968*	*6.4*
Specialized Health Services	80	6.2
Industrial Goods	*56,515*	*4.8*
Hospitals	1,039	4.3
Healthcare Plans	2,569	3.2
Home Healthcare	11	2.6
Basic Materials	*332,353*	*1.9*
Drug-Related Products	21	–1.2
Conglomerates	*1,728*	*–2.3*
Long-Term Care Facilities	49	–2.9
Drugs—Generic	7,582	–4.8

Source: Yahoo! (2016).

insurance benefits. There is reason to believe that, over time, slightly fewer employers offer health insurance and that employers have been transitioning to insurance plans with higher co-pays, higher deductibles, or narrower coverage. This argument ignores the fact that insurance costs have been spiraling for employers as well. While larger firms have generally maintained coverage for their employees, smaller employers have steadily cut employee coverage since 2000.[6] In 2000, 68 percent of employers with fewer than 200 workers offered coverage, and 57 percent of those with fewer than 10 workers offered coverage. By 2015, these numbers fell to 56 percent and 47 percent, respectively. During that time, the cost of insurance premiums has nearly tripled. Larger employers (more than 200 workers) have overwhelmingly maintained employee coverage. All of this suggests that employers have generally maintained coverage and done so while employer payments for insurance have also been rising. Rising insurance costs are not clearly the result of employer cutbacks.

What seems more likely is that insurance premiums are rising mainly because payouts are rising, and payouts are rising because everyone is either consuming more or charging more. As Table 6.2 demonstrates, the healthcare sector is replete with highly profitable noninsurance businesses. Drug manufacturers and biotechnology firms do tremendous volume at very high markups, and many drug-related expenses are going to be channeled through hospital bills, doctor bills, and insurance premiums. Diagnostic equipment, supplies, and services are sold at much higher markups than most consumer goods and services, which also helps to drive up hospital, doctor, and insurance costs.

In sum, there appears to be a very broad-based rise in healthcare expenditures. The pressures of these expenditures are experienced by households in the form of faster-rising health insurance premium, cuts in the degree to which employer-sponsored health insurance absorbs medical costs, and perhaps some disappearance of jobs that offer health insurance. All of these pressures appear to be a result of a broader-based rise in healthcare costs across the entire sector, which affects households, employers, and insurance companies. In other words, the burden of healthcare spending is growing everywhere.

More and Better Healthcare (to Some Extent)

So expenses are widely rising across the healthcare sector. What is driving up these outlays? Are Americans consuming quantitatively more or better healthcare, or is the healthcare industry profiting at the expense of society at large?

We have some indication that the quality of healthcare is increasing. Perhaps the most basic metric of healthcare system performance is life expectancy, which has risen by roughly 12.5 years for men (a 20 percent rise) and 4 years (+5 percent) for women since 1970. Not all of this change can be attributed to medical care; for example, better safety conditions, healthier work environments, and declines in unhealthy behaviors (e.g., smoking) play an important role in lengthening lives (substantial reasons that men's life spans have lengthened so much). Estimates of the direct role of medical care are not abundant, but some analyses suggest that between one and two years of this rise come from medical advancements.[7] Improved healthcare can claim some credit for these improved outcomes in detection and survival rates for a wide range of diseases—from cancer to heart disease to diabetes—but successful public health and safety campaigns deserve a great deal of credit as well.[8]

There is some indication that people utilize more healthcare, but the overall record gives a mixed picture. For example, prescription drug use has risen. Between 1999 and 2012, the proportion of Americans taking prescription drugs rose from 51 percent to 59 percent, and the proportion taking five or more prescriptions rose from about 8 percent to 15 percent.[9] In other respects, usage has been stable or fallen. Rates of hospital use were relatively stable during the 1990s and 2000s (though lengths of stay shortened), but this rate has been declining since 2010.[10] Outpatient doctor visits did not rise considerably either.[11] Some areas and periods witnessed increases in the use of healthcare, and there are indications of decreased utilization as well. Moreover, any discernible growth is very modest in comparison to the rate at which outlays have grown.

Profit Taking

Although it is possible that improved quality and more utilization pushes up society-wide healthcare spending, other highly developed countries have experienced similar changes, but their healthcare costs are nowhere near as high as in the United States. For example, the French healthcare system has also had to bear the burden of financing investment in MRI machines, but an MRI diagnosis in France costs roughly a quarter of what it costs in the United States.[12] Price are high in the United States, despite the fact that MRIs are more abundant there (see the next chapter).

Many observers believe that healthcare costs are driven mostly by massive profit taking. In his widely acclaimed investigative report, *Time* journalist Stephen Brill found that hospitals charge huge markups on privately insured, and especially uninsured, procedures. These markups can be on the order of hundreds of times cost, even for commonplace low-tech items such as aspirin or latex gloves. Likewise, pharmaceuticals are very expensive in the United States in part because, unlike Canada, for example, governments do not wrest price concessions from pharma companies. These high prices are often justified on the grounds that drugs are expensive to develop, though critics often argue that these R&D costs are exaggerated and that drug companies spend more on marketing than research.[13] Doctors also fare quite well. According to the Bureau of Labor Statistics, the average general practitioner earns $192,120.[14] Reports maintain that average specialist salaries range from $158,597 for medical geneticists to $609,639 for neurosurgeons.[15] In comparison, the average British general practitioner earns the equivalent of $81,139 and, among all British specialists, the average salary is $146,741. Million-dollar hospital administrators are much less common abroad.

Money Wasted or Well-Spent?

Very few would argue with the notion that some basic level of healthcare is essential to people's well-being and is therefore a necessary investment. There is much room to debate how much medical care is necessary and where to draw the line between necessary and unnecessary healthcare. Perhaps the only kind of care that is firmly treated as essential in the United States is the provision of emergency care, which hospitals are legally mandated to provide. Health insurance for the elderly is also treated as essential, and the United States provides a federal system of socialized insurance for older Americans with Medicare. In conjunction with its states, the country has a patchwork of programs designed to provide health insurance to children through the Children's Health Insurance Program (CHIP) and to the poor through the Medicaid program. However, insurance for the working-age population is widely treated as optional, and a sizable part of the population are left uninsured (about 17 percent in 2013, half of whom said they did not have insurance because it is too expensive[16]).

Is not having insurance such a big problem? Although people will not necessarily die young without the perquisites of (quality) insurance—such as preventative healthcare or costlier therapeutic services—many studies suggest that life expectancy is lower among the uninsured.[17] Without insurance, people are exposed to the risks of not having access to proper therapeutic or preventative care. They are also exposed to potentially crippling debts if they experience an adverse medical event. Many other highly developed countries treat insurance as a necessity. Most healthcare spending is driven by insurance costs, and it seems quite reasonable to consider insurance a necessity, because it both affects access to healthcare and protects a household's finances from the shock of adverse medical events.

This is not to imply that no waste is involved. Many observers argue that Americans consume too much medical diagnosis and treatment. They maintain that Americans overuse healthcare,[18] and much of their spending is incurred in their last year of life[19] (implying that people are being kept alive artificially[20]). Without dismissing these very important questions, the fact remains that the U.S. healthcare system is very expensive. Far more is spent on the system than its resources, technology, availability, and success warrants. As we will see in the next chapter, both the private and public cost of U.S. medicine is far higher than any other highly developed country, and yet the system is decidedly typical, and in some respects lacking, compared to the systems of other rich countries. It seems a perversion to ask whether or not we should let people die earlier or deny them diagnostics and treatments that some (nontreating physicians) view as unnecessary *before* asking whether or not we should tackle what seems to be unproductive profit taking. A lot of healthcare spending may be unnecessary, but the spending is not being driven by consumer largesse. Instead, the drivers of these costs appear to be captured by this industry's suppliers in high costs.

Education

Primary and secondary education (kindergarten through 12th grade [K–12]) is fully socialized and universally accessible in the United States, but child care, preschool, and postsecondary training are not, and their out-of-pocket costs can be substantial. Although not all households incur these kinds of costs, those with children often face heavy costs for some part of their financial life cycles. These costs may be temporary, but they may have lasting consequences. There are clear rationales for treating both expenses as necessary, but there are also questions about whether people overspend on these things.

Child Care

In the United States, child care is widely considered to be a household service, akin to housekeeping or yard work—a household chore that parents pay someone else to complete. In many other highly developed societies, early childhood care is seen as a formative, educational endeavor, and societies create institutions to care and educate the very young in the same way that the United States does for its K–12 students. Education-oriented, institutionalized care is more strictly the province of wealthier parents in the United States compared to many other developed societies, although there are nascent—and very modest—efforts to expand publicly provided child care.

There are several reasons to see child care as a nontrivial service. Insofar as children are concerned, high-quality child care—center-based care with more and better-trained staff, higher-quality amenities, and more stringent structure and supervision—is thought to substantively impact young children's scholastic performance, behavioral skills, and social skills.[21] Perhaps more importantly, child care can play a critical role in allowing parents to work and earn money. The United States does not have system of mandated, funded parental leave or child care, and—as we saw in Chapter Two—many families lack the accumulated wealth or high incomes to sustain years of lost income involved in having a parent care for a child until the child is eligible for primary school. Single parents don't even have the option. Many families—especially young ones—rely on two incomes to sustain a livelihood. Single-adult households are much more vulnerable to poverty in no small part because they only have one income. Child care enables people to work.

At present, policy expands access to child care through income tax reductions and more local initiatives.[22] Tax reduction generally does not benefit lower-income households substantially because payroll taxes—not income taxes—are the mechanism by which their incomes are taxed. Moreover, the savings generated by these mechanisms are generally paltry relative to the costs of this care. Public child care aid is most forthcoming to the very poor, but more limited to families whose parents work but receive lower incomes. Studies suggests that poorer people are priced out of professionalized, center-based child care, and thus they generally receive poorer child care than their wealthier counterparts.[23] This low prioritization has left the provision of child care to be financed more exclusively by parents, and it can be expensive. According to U.S. Department of Education estimates, it costs an average of $12,401 to provide schooling for the country's average primary or secondary student.[24] Parents don't see this final bill because the cost is socialized. Child care costs, which are not socialized, are roughly similar.

Table 6.3 shows the 10 high- and low-cost child care states, along with a middle-cost state (Iowa).[25] It depicts the annual costs of infant and four-year-old care, both in terms of absolute costs and in relation to the states' median wages for single- and married-parent families. The table is sorted by the cost of infant care relative to median single-parent household income. The table shows how the cost of institutional child care can be staggering, especially for single-parent families. In 2015, market rates in the 10 most expensive states amounted to half or more of the median single-parent household income. Even married couples would have to bear considerable costs of about 15 percent of their household income. The cost of care for pre-school children can be just as high. These costs are even more staggering when we consider the fact that younger parents tend to have young children,

Table 6.3   Cost of Child Care in Selected States, 2015

Rank	State	Infant Care	% Single Income	% Married Income	Four-Year-Old Care	% Single Income	% Married Income
1	District of Columbia	$22,631	88.5%	14.4%	$17,842	69.7%	11.3%
2	Massachusetts	$17,062	62.8%	15.1%	$12,781	47.1%	11.3%
3	New York	$14,144	54.5%	15.2%	$11,700	45.1%	12.6%
4	Illinois	$12,964	54.0%	14.7%	$9,567	39.8%	10.8%
5	Minnesota	$14,366	53.6%	15.2%	$11,119	41.5%	11.8%
6	Oregon	$11,322	50.7%	15.2%	$8,767	39.3%	11.8%
7	Rhode Island	$12,867	49.2%	13.3%	$10,040	38.4%	10.4%
8	Wisconsin	$11,579	48.9%	13.7%	$9,469	40.0%	11.2%
9	Michigan	$9,882	48.6%	12.2%	$6,764	33.2%	8.3%
10	Kansas	$11,201	46.9%	14.1%	$7,951	33.3%	10.0%
25	Iowa	$9,485	39.4%	11.6%	$8,216	34.1%	10.1%
41	Nebraska	$7,926	32.7%	9.9%	$6,843	28.2%	8.6%
42	Utah	$8,641	32.3%	11.7%	$6,612	24.7%	8.9%
43	Arkansas	$5,995	32.1%	9.2%	$4,995	26.7%	7.7%
44	South Carolina	$6,475	31.9%	8.8%	$4,651	22.9%	6.3%
45	Alabama	$5,637	30.5%	7.7%	$4,871	26.3%	6.6%
46	Hawaii	$8,280	29.9%	9.5%	$9,312	33.6%	10.6%
47	Louisiana	$5,747	29.8%	6.9%	$4,914	25.5%	5.9%
48	Tennessee	$5,857	29.3%	8.2%	$4,515	22.6%	6.3%
49	Wyoming	$6,541	27.9%	7.8%	$5,833	24.9%	6.9%
50	Mississippi	$4,822	26.3%	7.1%	$3,997	21.8%	5.9%
51	South Dakota	$5,661	24.1%	7.3%	$4,804	20.5%	6.2%

Source: Child Care Aware (2015).

and their incomes are more likely to be below median than a household headed by middle-aged people.

Child care is clearly not a frivolity and can be critical to a family's ability to earn money. Without systems to help give parents the financial leeway to parent their own children, they are often pressed into a market where the out-of-pocket costs can be considerable. Of course, there are other alternatives. If they have enough money to hire their own nannies, parents often resort to the "black market" for child care and often while breaking tax laws that mandate the payment of payroll taxes. Some are able to rely on family members to provide free care, and there are programs to help poor families with the costs of child care. For those who cannot or do not want to avail of these options, they are left with staggering costs, which are commensurate with the purchase of a new car or an additional apartment.

Higher Education

The economic benefits of higher education are quite clear. As we saw in Chapter Two, more educated people tend to earn more and accumulate more wealth. They are also less likely to be unemployed and poor.[26] Educated people generally fare well in a range of well-being metrics: they live longer,[27] they are less obese,[28] their marriages last longer,[29] and some studies suggest they have higher levels of subjective well-being.[30] The list could go on. The main point is that there are many reasons to believe that higher education has a substantial positive impact on people's well-being. Moreover, as we noted in Chapter Four, higher-skilled laborers are probably not under as much pressure from foreign competition and automation as their low-skill counterparts, making education important to a households' (and perhaps larger workforce's) long-term economic viability.

Given these implied benefits, it should come as no surprise that more Americans are pursuing a postsecondary education. The proportion of Americans aged 25 to 34 with a college degree rose from 24 percent in 1980 to 35 percent in 2014.[31] This change was driven by a dramatic rise in college attainment by women, alongside a much more modest rise in male attainment. The proportion of people in this age range who completed some college or an associate's degree rose from 20 percent to 28 percent. More people are pursuing higher education; that is, they are consuming (or investing in) quantitatively more higher education.

The cost of education has also been rising. Since 1980, college tuition has more than tripled in cost, becoming far more expensive relative to stagnant household incomes.[32] In part, these rising prices are fueled by rising costs incurred by schools. At public four-year colleges, spending on student services rose by about 45 percent from 1990 to 2008, instructional support by 34 percent, academic support by 33 percent, and instruction itself by 19 percent.[33] Universities do not appear to be hiring considerably more employees, and in some respects they have been transitioning away from more expensive full-time teaching staff to cheaper, part-time instructors.[34] Along with increasing numbers of part-time instructors, colleges seem to be channeling more resources to noninstructional professional staff (the types that work in areas such as information technology, admissions, human resources, athletics, and student health).[35] According to Robert Hiltonsmith of the think tank Demos, healthcare coverage for these employees has played an important role in driving up the cost of employees.[36] Many analysts (including Hiltonsmith) maintain that the primary driver of rising out-of-pocket tuition costs is reduced state funding for higher education. Over recent decades, public funding for higher education has transitioned away from the direct subsidy and control of tuition costs to one that focuses more on subsidizing student loans.[37] An estimated 80 percent of rising tuition costs are attributed to falling state subsidies.[38]

The consequences of expensive higher education are wide-ranging. Children from high-income families are six times more likely to graduate college than those of low-income families.[39] Research suggests that student debt can depress graduation rates, damage postcollege financial health, and press students to forgo college to avoid debt or enroll in junior or nonselective colleges when they could otherwise qualify for four-year or more selective ones.[40] Moreover, heavy student debts may ultimately damage young people's long-term wealth accumulation. Student debt makes it more difficult to put together an emergency fund, save for retirement, or put money aside for a home down payment.

What about education at a high-price, prestigious institution? Many media stories lamenting the burden of student debt feature someone who graduated from an expensive elite private school. While we may sympathize with the pains of financing a basic education, fewer would shed a tear for someone who incurred massive debts hoping to purchase a spot among the U.S. elites. First, it is important to remember that this group is an exception, rather than the rule. Those attending Ivy League schools comprise a fraction of a percent of the country's college students. The vast majority of students (an estimated 73 percent in 2011) attend public schools, and only 9 percent attended flagship research schools.[41] The minority that do attend private schools may be wasting their money. Some data suggests that a student's choice in majors is a much stronger determinant of their incomes than the selectivity of their school.[42] While students may receive a very small bump in the average annual return on investment in education by attending competitive schools, the decisive differences are between those with engineering, math, or computer science degrees and those who major in the arts or humanities. Still, questions about super-expensive schools seem to be a side show. The bulk of the middle class is being affected by the rising cost of local public schools.

Housing

Many analysts maintain that rising housing costs are the result of people buying larger homes, perhaps noting that the square footage of a new home has risen considerably over past decades.[43] The implication is that housing prices are driven up by quantitative increases in housing acquired, which could be considered an increase in living standards and perhaps a by-product of America's consumerism. Such a viewpoint misses the point that *new* housing may be getting bigger, but the U.S. housing construction market generally serves wealthier families, while relying on a trickle-down of older homes to supply the middle class and lower class with housing.[44] As Ohio State sociologist Rachel Dwyer explains, the rising size of *new* homes is an artifact of the construction industry's orientation toward serving the more affluent.[45]

Most American households are not moving into these big, new homes. Elizabeth Warren notes that the proportion of people living in older homes jumped by nearly 50 percent, with roughly 60 percent of the country living in a home older than 25 years, and 25 percent living in one older than 50 years.[46] The median owner-occupied home grew from 5.7 to 6.1 rooms, which is hardly a dramatic expansion of living space. Even if Americans purchased more living space, they paid a greater premium for it; although square footage rose on new home constructions by roughly 40 percent between 1985 and 2007, home values rose approximately 250 percent. Square footage costs and, in turn, overall shelter costs, have grown as a percentage of household income, despite the rising incidence of dual-earning families.

Those who see rising housing prices as a result of bigger or better housing structures are missing the key driver of home values: location and the central role that location plays in the disbursement of essential services. The cost of housing is primarily driven up by the cost of shelter (the physical property) and property taxes. Other housing-related costs have been stable, if they haven't been falling. These costs are about location. People have been spending more to get a foothold in particular communities. Cheap housing is available in the United States, but households have not collectively addressed their money problems by moving into low-cost areas.

People have strong incentives to live in "better" or more privileged communities, and communities have incentives to exclude those who are poorer than the typical resident. Spatial inequality and socioeconomic segregation interact with the U.S.'s decentralized system of financing and disbursing public services to create massive incentives for people to spend to the limits of their finances when choosing where to live, particularly if they have children. This is not simply a matter of the very rich excluding the riffraff. The rich exclude the upper-middle class, who exclude the middle-middle class, who exclude the lower-middle class, and so on. This is not just a matter of accessing better services and insulating one's family from social problems, but it is also a defensive measure that protects what is generally a family's most valuable asset. Housing prices have a record of being more secure in more expensive communities. While it is possible to find inexpensive housing in the United States, that housing can be in distressed communities, in places with little access to work, and in areas that can have infrastructure and essential services reminiscent of developing countries.

Housing, Community, and Essentials

What are people buying when they buy a home? They are not just buying the physical structure and the amenities of its property—a view from the front porch, number of cars that can fit in the garage, number of bathrooms, and so on—but also a foothold into a community, and with it the benefits and burdens of being part of that community. In the United States, public goods and services are often financed and administered at a local level, and being in a better-heeled community means sharing a better-financed system of public and communal resources with people who are less dependent on public and communal resources. Spatial inequality is very high, so the rich, moderately rich, middling, slightly poor, and very poor are all relatively unlikely to live together, as opposed to mixing more. The country allows serious social problems to fester in its more impoverished communities, while the public goods of wealthy communities can be genuinely outstanding by just about any society's standards. When people pay up for housing, they are purchasing access to public services and infrastructure. Housing in a pricier neighborhood *promises* better essentials.

There is some degree of uncertainty as to whether better-funded localities actually deliver higher-quality public schools and policing, or whether those who live in pricier places are more inclined to achieve educationally or avoid crime. In either case, the degree of spatial inequality among U.S. localities creates communities of haves and have-nots. Those who see housing spending as a matter of people wanting McMansions may be over-looking these motives when making home purchasing decisions.

K–12 Schools

While K–12 schooling is fully socialized insofar as people do not directly pay for primary or secondary school tuition, households do indirectly purchase access to it through their choices about where to live. School quality can vary considerably between districts. For example, a recent analysis of math and reading scores suggest that sixth-grade students in places such as Los Altos (California), Mendham (New Jersey), or Westford (Massachusetts) were more than three grades ahead of an average district (e.g., New York City) and more than five grades ahead of poor districts such as Detroit, Cleveland, or Camden (New Jersey).[47] Econometric analysis finds that home values are significantly related to school performance.[48] School quality varies widely across neighborhoods, and wealthier neighborhoods tend to have better schools.

To the extent that people are purchasing access to a quality school district, they are purchasing education, and education has a well-documented relationship with earnings and well-being. Is the relationship causal? Is it that poor school districts fail their children or that poorer school districts are more populated by children who are disposed to do poorly in school? Some analyses suggest that school district plays a very minor role in a student's success. One recent study concluded that school districts accounted for 1.1 percent of variation in achievement, school-level factors for 1.7 percent, and teacher-level factors about 6.7 percent,[49] implying that more than 90 percent of a student's performance seems attributable to non-school factors. About 32 percent is attributed to demographic factors, such as age, race/ethnicity, cognitive disability, poverty, nativity, and English fluency. The remaining 59 percent is attributed to student-level factors—some of them personal (e.g., a student's intelligence, drive, work habits, perseverance, attitude toward school) and others social (e.g., the influence of family, peers, or neighbors).

These kinds of findings suggest that people are overpaying on housing because they are situated in "good districts." The idea that district and school could *collectively* shape about 4 percent of a student's performance portrays the neighborhood school as a potential minor factor in shaping a child's success. It seems far more important that children get good teachers, a good home influence, positive peer influences, good genetics, and a productive disposition. But the influence of social factors also provides a case for overspending. Even if we accept the proposition that schools themselves aren't decisive in shaping young people's academic achievement, parents might opt to raise their children in a community in which academic achievement and college ambitions are the norm. Put differently, people might overspend on housing to raise their children among other college-bound or higher socioeconomic status children. Many studies find that peers exert a substantial influence over children's academic achievement.[50] Raising one's child in a community where achievement is prevalent may give a child a better chance of being in a higher-achievement peer group. Conversely, raising children in a community in which distress is prevalent may make it more likely that one's own child grows up in peer groups that are adversely affected by distress.

Perceptions of school quality also affect a household's finances through its impact on home values. Perhaps the most compelling reason to value perceived "good" school districts is that other people believe them to be important, and these beliefs will affect the salability and market value of a person's home, which is typically the largest asset on a household's balance sheet. Even if the school district is wholly irrelevant to children's educational development and future employability, the home buyers' belief in its importance may help a family home retain or appreciate in value.

Access to Transportation and Work Opportunities

A second issue is access to work. This access can manifest itself in multiple ways. Affordable housing seems to prevail in places with high unemployment or little population—areas that are remote or wrestle with serious economic problems. While a family could save on shelter by moving to downtown Detroit or rural Mississippi, where employment opportunities (particularly well-paid ones) may be more scarce, and the move could result in a net loss after the forgone income of a weak job market is factored into the equation. Home values are also shaped by the length of commute and access to the transportation infrastructure.[51] Those who live in larger metro areas may have an opportunity to live in more affordable communities near job centers, but they will have to pay more for shorter commutes and access to public transit. It may be possible to find affordable housing in a large metro area, but it may involve hours of commuting. Someone has to watch the kids or take care of household business during the extended drive to and from work.

So while it is true that there are American communities in which houses can be bought for prices that might strike foreigners as absurdly low, many families cannot afford to live in them because it is hard to earn a living in the locales in which they are set. There may not be jobs that are available nearby, and the jobs that can be found involve very long commutes. Commuting also involves costs, both in terms of transportation outlays and in terms of time. A single parent with two hours of daily commuting time must find someone to care for his or her children during the trip.

Public Safety and Emergency Services

Safety is another common motivator of housing choices. Many studies find a relationship between crime rates or factors that could affect the perceived risk of crime (e.g., a sex offender moving nearby, a local homicide).[52] While there is an abundant supply of homes that cost less than $100,000 in cities such as Detroit, New Orleans, St. Louis, Baltimore, or Newark, these locations have city-wide murder rates that are four or five times the national average, and violent crime rates reach nearly 1 percent of the population per year.[53] Media stories maintain that cities such as Detroit and New Orleans can have police response times that run several hours.[54]

On one hand, a closer consideration of the data suggests that fears about the true risk of crime and slow police response in low-cost neighborhoods may be exaggerated. The literature on the determinants of police response is scant, but one study of Houston-area response times suggests that police response tends to be faster in disadvantaged areas.[55] At the very least, there is a possibility that police response is not necessarily bad in poor neighborhoods. In terms of people's risk of crime, many observers believe that we tend to exaggerate our risk of being victimized, particularly by a stranger. Even in high-crime localities, the likelihood of being murdered is often a fraction of a percent, and two-thirds of murders are committed by victims' personal relations.[56]

Still, perception of crime risk affects home prices and, in turn, household wealth accumulation, much like perceptions of local school quality. Even if people see crime risk as minimal in just about any locality, they may still opt to live in a low crime area to ensure that their home maintains and accrues value.

Insulation from Housing Market Shocks

One of the biggest shocks of the 2008 crisis (both in emotional and financial terms) was the damage done to home values. People invest heavily in their homes and expect those investment to retain their values. The collapse in home values left many households "underwater"—with mortgage debts that were bigger than the value of the home itself. The crisis brought an epidemic of foreclosures. Observers found that these foreclosures were more prevalent in lower-income communities,[57] and local foreclosures can have negative effects on home values.[58] In the years that followed the crash, housing in low-value neighborhoods widely failed to recover, even while those in higher-value places have done so.[59] These findings suggest that down-market homes are more exposed to losses in value during economic downturns and may be less likely to appreciate in tough economic environments. It might be a financially defensive play to invest in a home that is in as affluent a community as possible.

Potential to Purchase Access and Insulation

Money spent on housing can conceivably purchase access to many services and amenities that help improve living standards, and can help purchase insulation from society's problems. A better-financed community has the capacity to offer better libraries, recreational facilities, and other community services. Housing money can also be used to insulate a household from societal problems. For example, housing can be purchased that is far from the hundreds of hazardous waste sites in the United States, unlike the 4 percent of Americans who live within one mile of an EPA-designated superfund site, and the 13 percent who live within three miles.[60] To the extent that people benefit from being surrounded by others in better financial circumstances, who have higher education, or have more intact families, then people may benefit from living and raising their children in these types of social environments as well. The list of potential benefits could go on. The main point is that money people spend cannot easily be reduced to the frivolous consumption of oversized McMansions. In the United States, a place where socioeconomic segregation is high and intercommunity redistribution is low, gaining a foothold in a wealthier community means accessing better-financed goods and services that are essential to well-being, and perhaps safeguarding families' tremendous investment in their homes.

At the same time, Americans' collective struggle to "move on up" to a "better" neighborhood may involve some status consciousness or snobbery. While few of us would argue that people are getting their money's worth when they spend their way out of genuinely distressed communities, it is not entirely clear whether the value added in moving from a middling to high-end community offers much contribution to a person's health or economic prospects, net of their genes, job, family situation, personal habits and choices, luck, or other circumstances not related to membership in a community. The main rationale becomes financial, related to the presumption that buying up in a housing market is a more secure investment.

Still, there is little doubt that Americans collectively reject what would seem like the financially sensible strategy of purchasing a home that is below their means. It is hard to say whether this reluctance has objective merit or exists more purely as a result of our collective prejudices favoring those who are richer.

Market Failures to Deliver Value

Proponents of laissez-faire often believe that the free market is the socially optimal way of organizing a society's economic activities. Presumably, such an organizational scheme would make it easy for people to obtain things that they really need. In a free market, we might suppose that this comes from innovation, efficiency enhancements, and a willingness to cut profit margins in the face of both competitive and consumer pressures.

This scheme has worked very well in many sectors: apparel, consumer electronics, entertainment, home furnishings, appliances, cars, reading materials, and many other product markets. It has not succeeded as well in healthcare, child care, higher education, and housing. It isn't for lack of trying—the major mechanisms for lowering costs, such as foreign out-sourcing, automation, or deskilling jobs, have certainly been attempted in healthcare and higher education but they just haven't succeeded (yet). Child care relies heavily on undocumented work arrangements, but the burden of even a low-paid worker is a lot to bear for the typical family. Private developers aren't collectively rushing to build residential developments to serve the bulk of society that lives at the middle or bottom of the economic pyramid. The free market simply has not succeeded in creating a bounty in these sectors.

What is interesting is that the United States has been particularly committed to the privatization of these markets, compared to other highly developed societies. A look abroad can be instructive, so we turn to international comparisons next.

CHAPTER SEVEN

A Look Abroad

If the cost of essential products is hurting household finances, could policy-makers fix the problem by regulating or socializing these costs? These types of policy responses can be a hard sell in U.S. politics, where many argue that they are impractical, self-defeating strategies that ultimately lead to higher prices, lower quality, more limited supplies, and ultimately runaway taxes and economic stagnation. For the most part, Americans have relied on neo-liberal policy strategies to improve consumers' access to products.

Does this neoliberal approach work? Chapter Five argued that such strategies have a reasonably good track record of making consumer products better, cheaper, and more plentiful. The U.S.'s relatively fervent embrace of neoliberalism has largely paid off in its promise of material bounty across many product markets and has delivered high living standards insofar as material consumption opportunities are concerned. However, Chapter Six argued that although neoliberalism may have proven to be a useful guide to economic policy in many product markets, it has not clearly succeeded in education, healthcare, child care, or housing markets—products that are argued to be pressing households to overspend and under-save.

Can socialism, price regulations, social policies, and other such "govern-ment interventions" in economic markets succeed in easing the cost pres-sures of these essential products, or are these policies as counterproductive as critics claim? One way to probe this question is to look abroad to see how these policies have worked in other countries. It isn't hard to find cases to study—most other developing countries actively use socialization and price regulation to defray the costs of these basic products. The U.S.'s aversion to them is the exception among highly developed countries.

This chapter compares the U.S.'s and other highly developed countries' social and economic policies' success in ensuring that quality child care, education, healthcare, and housing are accessible in their societies. The data suggest that the cost of child care, healthcare, and higher education are high in the United States, and the average cost of housing is middling. Despite these high out-of-pocket costs, none of these product markets appear to do a remarkably good job of delivering quality products to consumers. The quality that we presume to be characteristic of ultrahigh-end educational or healthcare institutions—such as Harvard or the Mayo Clinic—are not representative of its mass markets, where quality is more or less average compared to other developed countries.

It is often argued that the U.S.'s proclivity for free markets ultimately benefits the average American by spurring prosperity, containing promises, sowing innovation, and ultimately raising general living standards. While there may be some merit to this view, this macroeconomic prosperity's benefit to regular people's finances and overall well-being has clear limits. The observations that follow ultimately suggest that stronger social programs could contain the burdens that essential products place on household budgets. The strategy is possible and can plausibly work, given that it does work in other countries.

A Snapshot of U.S. Capitalism

Over the course of this chapter, we will compare U.S. policies, household finances, and well-being with those of other highly developed countries (hereafter, HDCs). In comparison to other HDCs, the United States is a comparatively rich and reasonably prosperous country whose commitment to social programs can at times seem weak. Table 7.1 describes some of these differences.[1]

The United States Is Rich but Unequal

The United States is a wealthy country, even in comparison to other HDCs. On a per capita basis, its gross domestic product (GDP)[2] output registers at roughly 15 percent higher than that of the Dutch, 20 percent higher than Germany, 37 percent higher than the United Kingdom, and almost 50 percent higher than France or Japan. In comparison to Southern Europe's less wealthy countries—Portugal, Italy, Greece, and Spain—U.S. output is nearly double on a per capita basis. Of course, GDP measures are very crude, so these comparisons shouldn't be taken too literally. However, they do offer a clear suggestion that U.S. society has considerable resources at its disposal on a per person basis, even in comparison with other rich countries. This comparative wealth of resources should give the

Table 7.1 Macroeconomic Conditions of the United States vs. Other Highly Developed Countries

Metric	Per Capita GDP (PPP)	Median Household Income	GDP Growth	Unemplmt.	Inflation Rate	Total Tax Revenue (% GDP)
Period	2014	2013	2004–2014	2004–2014	2004–2014	2013
Norway	$64,856	$51,489	0.5	3.4	1.8	40.5
Switzerland	$57,235	NA	1.1	4.1	0.5	26.9
United States	**$54,630**	**$43,535**	**0.9**	**6.8**	**2.3**	**25.4**
Ireland	$48,755	$25,085	0.9	9.4	1.5	29.0
Netherlands	$47,663	$38,584	0.7	4.6	1.7	36.7
Austria	$46,222	$34,991	1.0	5.1	2.1	42.5
Germany	$45,802	$33,333	1.5	7.7	1.6	36.5
Sweden	$45,183	$50,514	1.2	7.5	1.1	42.8
Denmark	$44,916	$44,360	0.2	5.8	1.8	47.6
Canada	$44,057	$41,280	0.9	7.1	1.8	30.5
Australia	$43,930	$46,555	1.4	5.2	2.7	27.5
Belgium	$42,578	$26,730	0.7	7.9	2.1	44.7
Finland	$39,981	$34,615	0.6	8.1	1.7	43.7
United Kingdom	$39,762	$31,617	0.7	6.4	2.6	32.9
France	$38,847	$31,112	0.5	9.0	1.5	45.0
Japan	$36,426	$33,822	0.8	4.2	0.2	30.3
New Zealand	$36,390	$35,562	1.0	5.2	2.5	31.4
Italy	$34,706	NA	-0.9	8.7	1.9	43.9
Spain	$33,211	NA	-0.1	16.6	2.3	32.7
Portugal	$28,393	NA	0.0	10.5	1.8	34.5
Greece	$25,877	NA	-1.3	14.9	2.3	34.4

NA = Not Available.

Sources: Gallup (2013, December 16); OECD (2016); World Bank (2016).

country more latitude to deliver more income, social programs, or essential products for its people. Given this wealth, we might expect U.S. household finances and living standards to also lead the developed world. To the extent that it does not, one might question whether the society is using its resources to its people's benefit.

Inequality is one possible explanation of that fact that the U.S.'s comparatively high output does not seem to directly translate into world-leading overall living standards. Among the Organisation for Economic Co-Operation and Development (OECD) countries, only markedly poorer countries—such as Mexico, Chile, and Turkey—register higher Gini coefficients.[3] Although the aggregate economy is highly productive, the typical household appears to take in about as much money as those in households with considerably lower per capita GDPs. Even though the U.S. per capita GDP is considerably higher (~20 percent) than Canada or Australia, the median households in these countries are roughly the same. That excess does not trickle down as much as one might presume.

Reasonably Prosperous

Macroeconomic prosperity is a nontrivial factor affecting household finances in that it can affect the job market, it can depress asset prices, and it can tighten the availability of credit. In discussions comparing the United States and other HDCs, it is often presumed that the United States is a model of economic dynamism, while "Old Man Europe" hobbles along. There is some merit to the claim when comparing the United States to genuinely distressed countries (e.g., Greece), but such comparisons are not altogether different from comparing Germany to a poor U.S. state, such as Mississippi. On the whole, the U.S.'s purportedly superior macroeconomic performance is partly an exaggeration. Compared to other HDCs, the overall U.S. economy has been reasonably prosperous: its growth rate has been middling, its unemployment rate has traditionally been slightly lower than most major European economies, and its inflation rates have been very low, like most wealthy countries.

Neoliberal Governance

The United States differs from much of the highly developed world in its dedication to neoliberalism. One facet of this commitment to free markets and limited government is depicted in the rightmost column of Table 7.1, which presents the ratio of general government revenue[4] relative to GDP. Despite much internal rhetoric about runaway taxes, the U.S. public sector is comparatively small, relative to the overall size of the economy, in terms of how much revenue it draws from society. The U.S. government is an enormous enterprise in absolute size, but this size is the product of a moderately light investment in the public sector by a massive, highly productive economy.

Social Spending in the United States

This penchant for limited government extends to social programs, although the U.S.'s collective unwillingness to field large social programs can also be exaggerated. Table 7.2 describes per capita social spending in the United States and 18 other HDCs.[5] Overall, U.S. per capita spending on social programs is roughly middling. It ranks 12th among the 18 HDCs described in the table. In proportion to the overall size of its economy, it ranks near the bottom, alongside other English-speaking wealthy countries. This means that the United States does not invest heavily in social programs in general. Its expenditures are middling, but that is a product of the fact that the United States is comparatively wealthy, so its modest social spending levels look impressive in comparison to poorer countries that invest in social programs more heavily.

It might surprise some readers to see that overall social spending levels are higher in the United States than in Canada or the United Kingdom, which Americans generally understand to be more socialist. That view makes particular sense from the viewpoint of a younger person because U.S. social programs are not geared toward them. The United States has some rather generous social programs, but they are mainly directed to the elderly. For example, the United States offers socialized healthcare to the elderly, which in its expensive healthcare markets results in high per capita spending levels. The United States spends far more on healthcare than many other developed countries that offer universal socialized coverage, while the system leaves about 14 percent of the population—mostly of working age—uncovered.[6] Likewise, its spending on old age pensions handily exceeds that of Canada and roughly equals levels seen in wealthy continental European countries. Social Security payments can be very generous compared to other elderly pension systems. In 2014, the maximum payment from the Canada Pension Plan was C\$1,065 (U.S. \$905 at a 0.80 exchange rate) per month, compared to \$2,663 per month in the U.S. Social Security program.

In contrast, active labor market programs, which include things such as public job centers, training and apprenticeship programs, or employment subsidies, are far more extensive elsewhere. Family-oriented

Table 7.2 Social Spending in the Highly Developed World, 2010

	Total	Total (% GDP per capita)	Active Labor Market Programs	Family	Health	Housing	Incapacity Related	Old Age	Survivors	Unemployment	Other Areas
Luxembourg	$16,150	16.5	$378	$2,726	$4,130	$208	$2,400	$3,943	$1,223	$802	$341
Norway	$11,024	17.0	$295	$1,462	$2,663	$76	$2,554	$3,260	$135	$233	$345
Austria	$10,392	22.5	$298	$1,027	$2,411	$39	$1,156	$4,281	$700	$365	$114
Switzerland	$9,965	17.4	$250	$546	$2,500	$45	$1,392	$4,195	$403	$369	$266
Denmark	$9,722	21.6	$646	$1,301	$2,194	$224	$1,637	$2,665	$3	$738	$314
Sweden	$9,630	21.3	$400	$1,240	$2,270	$156	$1,679	$3,274	$166	$204	$241
France	$9,491	24.4	$337	$884	$2,574	$244	$556	$3,674	$544	$490	$187
Belgium	$9,483	22.3	$259	$922	$2,604	$73	$828	$2,659	$672	$1,199	$266
Germany	$9,394	20.5	$317	$766	$2,762	$228	$1,075	$2,979	$709	$509	$49
Netherlands	$8,978	18.8	$455	$610	$2,951	$141	$1,463	$2,272	$78	$577	$431
Finland	$8,974	22.4	$328	$1,023	$1,739	$162	$1,279	$3,287	$292	$636	$228
United States	**$8,550**	**15.6**	**$56**	**$327**	**$3,562**	**$147**	**$687**	**$2,592**	**$319**	**$477**	**$383**
Ireland	$8,263	16.9	$329	$1,465	$2,179	$147	$851	$1,635	$389	$1,054	$214
Italy	$7,907	22.8	$116	$395	$1,942	$7	$605	$3,903	$699	$226	$13
United Kingdom	$7,836	19.7	$134	$1,322	$2,570	$484	$824	$2,224	$29	$180	$70
Spain	$7,181	21.6	$253	$407	$1,868	$59	$727	$2,316	$603	$886	$62
Japan	$7,076	19.4	$89	$398	$2,277	$33	$297	$3,364	$442	$94	$82
Canada	$6,535	14.8	$109	$463	$2,653	$153	$321	$1,431	$138	$289	$978
Australia	$6,439	14.7	$112	$969	$2,105	$119	$902	$1,895	$61	$185	$92

Source: OECD (2016).

programs—such as parental leave or child care (discussed a bit later)—are very modest. Although U.S. unemployment programs look middling, these figures were buoyed by an emergency extension of the U.S. Unemployment Insurance program in the wake of the Great Recession. In essence, the United States spends considerable amounts of money on its Social Security and Medicare programs, but spending on those at other points in the life cycle—youth, young adults, and the middle-aged—is much lighter.

A Source of American Prosperity?

In many circles, the more austere state of nonelderly-directed social spending is considered to be part of the U.S.'s larger recipe for economic success. Many commentators maintain that the United States is a rich country precisely because its social safety net is weak, and, more broadly, its government is more inclined to maintain a hands-off approach to economic governance. This market-driven prosperity may allow the United States to maintain its extensive social programs without investing heavily in them. Moreover, while social programs could conceivably deliver essential products at a lower out-of-pocket cost, it is often argued that socialism and other sorts of government interference results in the types of programs that plagued communist societies in the Cold War era, such as supply shortages, rationing, and second-rate products.

The Need for a Closer Look

Presumably, greater social spending and a stronger social safety net would defray the out-of-pocket costs involved in securing these essential products. How do other countries organize these markets? Are products much more affordable there? Does this affordability come at the cost of access or quality? We turn to these questions next.

Social Policies and Access to Essentials

Ideally, a society is able to make access to high-quality essential products universal. *Universal access* means everyone can obtain a good or service, be it education, healthcare, housing, or any other product. Access is not universal to the extent that people are denied products for lack of money, adequate supply, or some other impediment. The stipulation that these essentials be of *high quality* is used to differentiate the nominal provision of an essential product from one that makes an adequate contribution to well-being. It is the difference between getting some kind of education or healthcare and receiving a *good* education or healthcare.

While all highly developed societies maintain some commitment to the idea that people should not be denied access to necessities, they differ on what products are considered "necessary." For example, many countries consider preventative healthcare, higher education, and child care to be sufficiently necessary as to warrant legal guarantees that people will not be denied these services. The United States maintains some of these commitments— for example, with emergency medical care, primary schools, or emergency services such as policing or firefighters—but the principle of universal access broadly appears to be applied to a narrower range of products than in other highly developed societies. Next, we compare how these commitments differ with respects to child care, higher education, healthcare, and housing.

Child Care

Many developed countries treat child care as an essential service and have developed systems of regulations and public investments that are designed to blunt the economically disruptive effects of having young children. Some of them treat child care as a right that is possessed by the child, and they have sought to develop early childhood education and care systems that help edify young children. In contrast, the United States broadly treats child care as nonessential. For the most part, its investment in access is generally relegated to state and local initiatives designed to ensure that the poor have child care that enables them to work. Although recent regulatory changes have given some new mothers the latitude to take time off after childbirth without losing their job, maternity and parental leave is weaker than elsewhere.

Between a child's birth and the age at which they are eligible to participate in the public school system, parents face a practical problem of deciding who will care for their child. For two-parent families, one parent can exit the workforce and provide care, provided that they can afford the loss of an income. For single-parent households, which constitute a considerable plurality of households with younger children, such an option is unavailable. If a stay-at-home parent is not an option, and a family does not have the good fortune of a relative with the opportunity and latitude to provide free care, then they need outside child care. Both the need and cost of outside care vary across countries.

Parental Leave

Parental leave affects the financial demands of having children by mitigating the income losses associated with taking time off to care for one's children. Under some circumstances, parental leave is paid, which means that parents will receive payments that offset some, or even all, of the income lost by taking time off work. Even when parental leave is not paid, unpaid leave can mitigate the damage to lifetime earnings that might have occurred if the parent of a new child were forced to quit, lose seniority, and be forced to restart their career later and perhaps elsewhere.

Table 7.3 describes differences in maternity and parental leave among the world's most economically developed societies.[7] *Maternity leave* is given to a new mother upon childbirth, while *parental leave* can be shared between father and mother. *Weeks of paid leave* include the typical amount of leave time that offers payment to the parent, usually through a social insurance fund administered through the government. The *average payment rate* is the amount of a parent's income that is estimated to be covered by leave payments. The table is sorted by total weeks of paid leave.

In just about any society, women face professional and economic costs for having children, but these costs weigh much more heavily on U.S. women. It is not just that they have less paid leave, but proportionally fewer women qualify for leave.[8] For those women who do have the good fortune of working in a job that entitles them to leave—they have an enduring, full-time job at an organization that is not exempt from leave requirements, and their job is not deliberately structured to avoid these requirements (e.g., an independent contractor)—there is the question of whether her household is able to weather the strain of losing her income. Unlike most other highly developed societies, there is no society-wide program to provide new parents with financial aid to offset the income they may lose by leaving the workforce to parent full time. As we saw in earlier chapters, most American families are ill-equipped to weather such a shock.

Without parental leave, questions about care come down to questions about whether or not a household has the economic latitude to weather either a parent's departure from the workforce or the heavy financial costs of commercial child care, be it through a supervised institution or through a black market relationship forged on Craigslist. If they are fortunate enough to live near relatives, they may be willing and able to provide free child care. Not all parents have the latitude to step out of the labor market themselves and continue to live near their working children (living costs are lower in places with fewer jobs for younger people).

Care for Young Children

In places such as Finland or France, government programs purposively harmonize maternal/parental leave, preschool, and primary schooling in

Table 7.3 Maternity and Parental Leave across the World's Most Developed Countries, 2009

	Weeks of Paid Maternity Leave	Average Payment Rate (%)	Weeks of Paid Parental Leave	Average Payment Rate (%)	Total Length of Leave (weeks)	Average Payment Rate (%)
United States	0.0	0.0	0.0	0.0	0.0	0.0
Switzerland	14.0	56.8	0.0	0.0	14.0	56.8
Netherlands	16.0	100.0	0.0	0.0	16.0	100.0
New Zealand	16.0	47.9	0.0	0.0	16.0	47.9
Australia	6.0	42.0	12.0	42.0	18.0	42.0
Portugal	6.0	100.0	24.2	57.6	30.2	66.1
Belgium	15.0	76.6	17.3	20.3	32.3	46.4
United Kingdom	39.0	31.3	0.0	0.0	39.0	31.3
France	16.0	93.5	26.0	14.6	42.0	44.7
Luxembourg	16.0	100.0	26.0	38.8	42.0	62.1
Italy	21.7	80.0	26.0	30.0	47.7	52.7
Denmark	18.0	54.1	32.0	54.1	50.0	54.1
Canada	17.0	48.3	35.0	54.7	52.0	52.6
Germany	14.0	100.0	44.0	65.0	58.0	73.4
Japan	14.0	67.0	44.0	59.9	58.0	61.6
Austria	16.0	100.0	44.0	80.0	60.0	85.3
Sweden	8.6	77.6	51.4	61.1	60.0	63.4
Norway	13.0	98.7	78.0	41.8	91.0	50.0
Finland	17.5	78.5	143.5	20.1	161.0	26.5

Source: OECD Family Database (2016).

ways that buffer young families from the impact of having children. In those countries, preschoolers are legally entitled to day care after their mother's maternity leave is exhausted. So the new French mother receives a funded four-month leave, after which heavily subsidized day care is provided to her until the child is old enough to start primary school. In contrast, the U.S. child care system is highly privatized and market-driven, such that there is not a designed system to blunt the financial impact of parenting young children. Governments are not totally absent—states and localities often extend child care subsidies to low-income households, but the remainder of society is left to fend for itself. In the context of the government's light presence in child care—and perhaps as a result of it—child care costs are comparatively expensive in the United States.

Table 7.4 provides an overview of public funding, private costs, and participation in child care across HDCs.[9] The U.S. system is costly, and formal care participation is low. *Public Expenditures (% GDP)* gives the amount of government spending on child care and early education services, relative to GDP. These expenditures are comparatively low in relation to the overall economy and in comparison to the stronger investments made in many Northern European countries. While spending alone does not fully determine the accessibility and quality of a child care and early childhood education system, it does give us a sense of the relative importance that policy-makers assign to it. U.S. figures are comparatively low.

The broader organization of early childhood care and education renders a system that incurs relatively high out-of-pocket costs. *Net cost (% income)* gives the cost of child care, net of public aid or subsidy, relative to household income. The United States ranks second of 17 in net costs for a two-parent family, behind the United Kingdom. That being said, British parents have paid leave at their disposal, as well as longer unpaid leave rights. Note that few countries—the United States, Canada, and Japan—have mechanisms for containing the costs borne by single-parent households, despite the fact that such households are particularly vulnerable financially and have fewer recourses for child care.

Unfortunately, the data on participation in formal and informal care is sketchy. The data do make it clear that formal care participation rates are comparatively low in the United States, particularly compared to near-universal enrollment rates in Europe. The data are not clear on what is happening to those children—informal care rates are roughly similar to other developed countries, though informal care appears to be used on a part-time basis in other countries.

Overall, child care is highly unaffordable in the United States. Other English-speaking OECD countries, such as the United Kingdom, Canada,

Table 7.4 Net Cost of Child Care (% Average Wages), OECD Countries, 2014

	Public Expenditure (% GDP)	Net Cost (% Income)		Formal Care Participation		Informal Care Participation				No Formal or Informal Care	
		Two-Parent	Single-Parent	Ages 0–2	Ages 3–5	Ages 0–2	Mean Hours	Ages 3–5	Mean Hours	Ages 0–2	Ages 3–5
Australia	0.6	15.7	13.6	NA	64.8	30.8	NA	29.3	NA	NA	NA
Austria	0.5	2.7	6.3	19.7	84.1	35.2	10.2	49.4	9.2	51.9	9.6
Belgium	0.7	10.2	7.4	49.3	98.7	23.6	18.5	21.4	10.3	39.5	4.6
Canada	NA	22.2	45.7	NA	45.9	NA	NA	NA	NA	NA	NA
Denmark	2.0	10.7	0.0	67.0	97.7	30.5	20.0	27.5	5.0	37.4	6.1
Finland	1.1	16.8	12.7	27.7	74.0	17.3	21.8	18.1	28.9	70.0	25.5
France	1.2	9.7	3.7	49.7	99.6	50.6	18.6	41.5	12.0	43.4	5.8
Germany	0.5	9.7	3.6	29.3	94.6	28.1	NA	33.2	NA	NA	NA
Italy	0.6	NA	NA	23.1	95.1	42.3	19.0	40.4	13.0	47.0	6.9
Japan	0.4	15.3	22.7	NA	88.8	NA	NA	NA	NA	NA	NA
Netherlands	0.9	19.9	10.0	54.6	94.1	48.1	9.8	50.6	7.0	29.3	4.7
Norway	1.2	11.2	11.9	54.3	96.5	7.4	14.7	3.5	7.8	42.5	10.7
Portugal	0.4	4.2	2.0	45.1	89.4	34.2	NA	33.6	NA	30.9	6.4
Spain	0.6	5.6	15.1	35.3	96.6	9.0	28.7	6.5	17.7	57.8	8.1
Sweden	1.6	4.4	3.6	47.3	94.0	0.6	10.0	1.7	11.5	48.2	4.0
Switzerland	NA	23.6	13.8	38.2	46.1	46.9	14.5	42.2	11.1	32.4	11.8
United Kingdom	1.1	33.8	8.0	35.1	96.3	35.0	15.1	39.6	15.0	46.4	33.9
United States	0.4	28.7	52.4	NA	65.7	32.4	NA	37.6	NA	NA	NA

NA = Data not available.

Source: OECD (2016).

Australia, and New Zealand, have expensive child care markets as well. Like the United States, these countries also eschew socialized, universal accessible child care in favor of programs that subsidize child care for poorer households, but they are less aggressive in defraying the costs for middle-class parents. However, those countries have more extensive parental leave programs, which can offset these costs. For those in continental Europe, the costs of child care are substantially less burdensome. U.S. costs are five to six times higher than those faced by Belgian or Swedish families.

Higher Education

The higher education system in the United States is widely celebrated as the best in the world. Reports gush about the country's representation in global rankings of top universities, its citations in leading journals, its market share of international students, and its stock of Nobel Prizes. The purported quality of U.S. universities, coupled with the country's comparatively high enrollment rates, can be used to justify the high costs of U.S. education. While it may be pricey, U.S. higher education is taken to be of stellar quality, and it does not seem to price people out of the market.

Table 7.5 compares U.S. higher education costs with those of other HDCs.[10] *Education costs* include tuition, mandatory fees, and the costs of books and study materials. Net total costs after taxes include education and estimated living costs, less grants and tax inducements for education.

Direct education costs in the United States are more than double that of other HDCs, except Japan. In many continental European countries, higher education is substantially more socialized, and its out-of-pocket costs are more limited to books, study materials, and other sundry expenses that might be borne by a U.S. high schooler. In part, total overall costs are defrayed by lower living costs (driven by low housing rents in many communities in which schools are set) and government grants and deductions; ultimately, however, the U.S. out-of-pocket costs of higher education, relative to incomes, appear to be roughly double those borne in continental Europe.

These high prices do not seem to price people out of the market. In terms of providing access, the U.S. system is quite good. Data from the World Bank suggest that the ratio of students enrolled in tertiary schooling to the tertiary school-aged population is almost 90 percent in the United States, which is considerably higher than the 60 percent to 70 percent range seen across Europe. These high enrollment rates are undoubtedly enabled by the U.S.'s burgeoning student loan industry, which is not heavily regulated, benefits from many public subsides, and is protected against debt discharge in personal bankruptcy.

Table 7.5 Four-Year University Costs, 2010

Country	Education Costs	% Median Income	Net Total Costs after Taxes	% Median Income	% Labor Force with Tertiary Education	Ranked Universities per 10M	Nobel Prizes per 10M
Japan	$11,865	52%	$24,376	107%	NA	0.3	1.8
Australia	$7,692	33%	$17,618	77%	NA	11.5	5.0
United States	**$13,856**	**51%**	**$19,369**	**68%**	**34%**	**2.4**	**11.0**
England & Wales*	$5,288	21%	$13,772	56%	40%	5.4	19.3
New Zealand	$3,118	16%	$9,328	48%	NA	4.4	6.6
Latvia	$3,299	24%	$5,258	39%	32%	0.0	5.0
Canada	$5,974	22%	$9,959	37%	52%	3.7	6.4
France	$585	3%	$6,395	31%	37%	1.2	9.4
Netherlands	$3,125	11%	$8,111	30%	34%	7.7	11.2
Sweden	$600	3%	$6,056	29%	37%	9.3	30.7
Finland	$1,243	6%	$5,641	27%	41%	1.8	7.2
Norway	$596	2%	$6,276	24%	42%	3.9	24.9
Denmark	$530	2%	$5,229	23%	32%	8.9	24.6
Germany	$933	4%	$3,352	15%	27%	3.3	13.0

*Enrollment and quality metrics for all of the United Kingdom.

Sources: Usher & Medow (2010); World Bank (2016); Times Higher Education (2016); BBC (2010, October 8).

People are enrolling at higher rates, though not necessarily finishing. The proportion of the labor force that actually *completes* higher education is considerably lower, as the figures describing the proportion of the labor force with higher education degrees in Table 7.5 notes. U.S. schools appear to be enrolling a lot of people, but the labor force is not more highly educated. This failure brings up the question of quality. Are Americans getting a better-quality education? While there can be little doubt that the United States houses top-notch universities with endowments that most foreign schools would have difficulty imagining, most U.S. college students do not attend these kinds of schools. The *average* student pays comparatively high costs, but does he or she receive a commensurately high-quality education?

One problem with the aforementioned quality metrics of university system quality—number of ranked schools, number of Nobel Prizes, or share of the global student market—is that they deal in absolute counts. The United States is going to score well in part because it is a very large country. With 10 times the population of Canada, we would expect the country to have 10 times as many ranked universities and Nobel Prizes, or 10 times the global student market share. If we look at averages, or scale these metrics to population, the U.S. system looks less impressive. For example, although the United States has 77 of the world's top 250 universities, according to the Times Higher Education *World University Rankings*, this is about 0.33 per million population. This is a pretty middling ratio. Likewise, Americans are not disproportionately represented among Nobel Prize recipients. Their share of the international student market (an estimated 19 percent[11]) is only slightly higher than the United Kingdom (12 percent) and France (7 percent), even though the United States is several times larger than these countries.

It is not that the U.S. higher education system is bad. It has some excellent institutions, and the quality of education seem to be roughly that of a typical HDC. However, the very high out-of-pocket costs borne by U.S. students cannot be justified on the grounds that the average quality of U.S. schools are better than those abroad. Other countries are able to deliver excellent-quality schools with low out-of-pocket costs.

Healthcare

After years of political conflict over healthcare reform, most Americans are thoroughly aware that their healthcare system involves heavy out-of-pocket costs. One might infer that these heavy out-of-pocket costs are at least partly offset by lower taxes, due to the fact that the government is able to save money by not purchasing health insurance for everyone. The data

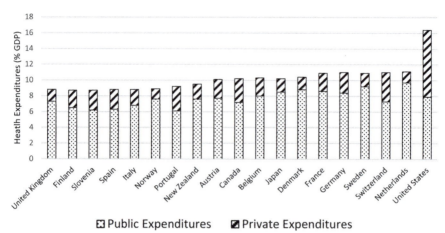

Figure 7.1 Healthcare Expenditures across Highly Developed Countries, 2013. *Source:* OECD (2016).

suggest that no such savings exist. Figure 7.1 shows spending on healthcare by both the government and private sector (relative to GDP) compared to 19 HDCs.

The United States spent 16.4 percent of its GDP on healthcare in 2013, about 46 percent more the second-biggest spenders (Switzerland and the Netherlands) and about 61 percent more than Canada. This included both considerable government and private sector expenditures. In 2013, the U.S. government spent slightly more on healthcare (7.9 percent of GDP) than the Canadian government (7.2 percent).

Why does the United States spend so much? How can the U.S. *government* spend about as much as the Canadian or British government, even though the latter two provide health insurance to everyone? One possibility is that Americans are buying quantitatively more healthcare or getting higher-quality care. However, international comparisons in healthcare resources suggest that Americans' general access to healthcare resources is quite average. Table 7.6 compares international differences in healthcare resources.[12]

The table suggests that the United States does not have extraordinarily high numbers of medical practitioners or hospital beds for its extraordinarily high spending. Its mental healthcare system is paltry and has broadly been replaced by its prison system. It does seem to have more capital equipment—at least insofar as MRIs, PET scanners, or gamma cameras are concerned. However, despite this abundance, reports suggest that access to this equipment has not necessarily improved. In the United States, MRI scans typically cost $1,080, versus $280 in France.[13] These

Table 7.6 Healthcare Resources by Country

	Per Thousand Population			Units per Million Population				
	Health and Social Workers	Active Physicians	Hospital Beds	MRIs	PET Scanners	Gamma Cameras	Radiation Therapy Equipment in Hospitals	Radiation Therapy in Ambulatory Sector
Australia	60.9	3.5	3.8	15.0		20.1		
Austria	46.9		7.7	19.1	1.9	12.1	4.9	0
Belgium	59.0		6.3		2.4		15.0	
Canada	61.4	2.5	2.7	8.8	1	20.6		
Denmark	88.9	3.9						
Finland	75.6	3.3	5.3	21.6	2.2		9.6	0
France	50.3	3.3	6.3	8.7	1.1	5.8	9.6	
Germany	61.7	4.3	8.3		1.6		5.0	
Italy	29.9	4.1	3.4	24.6	2.2	10.7	6.6	0.4
Japan	55.4	2.4	13.4					
Netherlands	82.4	3.3	2.8	11.8	3.1	10.4		
New Zealand	52.1	2.7	2.8	11.1		3.4		
Norway	108.6	4.9	4.0					
Portugal	35.7		3.4		0.8		3.9	
Spain	30.3	4.1	3.0	14.8	1.2	6.2	4.6	0.2
Sweden	75.4	4.2	2.6					
Switzerland		4.0	4.8		3.3	9.1	6.8	9.8
United Kingdom	60.2		2.8	6.0				
United States	**61.8**	**2.6**	**2.9**	**34.5**	**4.2**	**47.2**	**7.5**	**5.0**

Source: OECD (2016).

differences in costs create barriers to access: for those without the good fortune of having health insurance, or good health insurance, this kind of price difference can be substantial, regardless of how many MRIs are housed within the country's borders.

Presumably, these lower costs come at the cost of long wait times. A 2013 study by the Commonwealth Fund[14] suggests that wait times aren't particularly short in the United States, they just look good in comparison to Canada, but Canada fares poorly in international comparisons of health-care wait times. There are other countries with socialized systems that perform considerably better than the United States and Canada. For example, the study found that about 48 percent of U.S. respondents reported being able to see a primary care physician the same day or next day, worse than all other reported countries except Canada. By comparison, about 76 percent of Germans are able to secure fast primary care appointments. Likewise, about 35 percent of Americans report having access to after-hours primary care, as opposed to 95 percent of Dutch or Brits. Access to specialists seems comparatively good in the United States, with 76 percent of respondents reporting that they could see specialists within four weeks of making appointments, though this figure is higher in the socialized British system (80 percent).

So wait times are not particularly low and resources do not seem particularly abundant in the United States. But perhaps the clearest indicator that U.S. healthcare is not so much better than other, cheaper systems is life expectancy, a topic to which we will turn in our discussion about international differences in well-being later in this chapter. On the whole, U.S. healthcare is stronger in some areas and weaker in others, but in no way is the quality of care as remarkably high as the private and overall societal costs of its healthcare system.

Housing

U.S. living standards are high with respect to having access to cheap, large houses. Compared to many HDCs, there seems to be an abundance of cheap homes, along with a range of public incentives designed to help people buy homes. Many Western Europeans marvel at the possibility that one can buy a single family detached home for $50,000 in a major U.S. city. However, as discussed in Chapter Six, these houses are often in communities with weak job markets, strained social services, and social problems. In more affluent communities, which are generally those with stronger essential services and higher living standards, housing has gotten more expensive. These housing market dynamics occur across the world.

Overall, in strict cost terms, U.S. housing appears to be of middle expense. Figure 7.2 depicts the ratio of home values to income (top) and the ratio of home values to rents (bottom). The former gives us a sense of how cheap or expensive it is to buy a home. The latter gives us a sense of how much cheaper or expensive it is to rent, as opposed to own.

Overall, U.S. housing prices are average, as is the cost of renting relative to home ownership. In comparison to other countries, the United States appears to be a country of greater extremes. A 2015 study found that the United States has some of the most housing-affordable major metropolitan areas among the English-speaking OECD countries.[15] In communities in

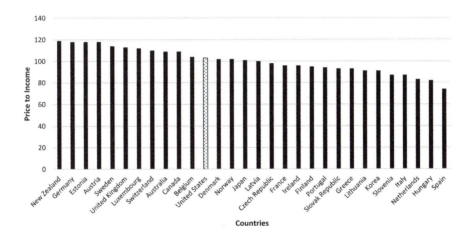

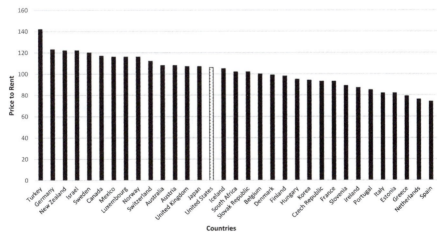

Figure 7.2   Home Ownership and Rental Affordability, 2015.
Source: OECD (2016).

upstate New York, the Midwestern states, or the Southern interior, housing can be as low as 2.5 to 3 times the value of median incomes. The study identified other countries with similar communities—such as Edmonton and Ottawa (Canada), Falkirk (Scotland), Leeds (United Kingdom), and Karratha and Kalgoorlie (Australia)—but low-cost communities of this sort are plentiful in the United States. At the same time, some of the English-speaking developed world's most expensive housing markets are in the United States—such as New York, Boston, and much of the West Coast—where housing can cost 5 to 10 times prevailing incomes. This is not unique to the United States: similar developments have occurred in London, Plymouth, Bristol, and Bath (United Kingdom); in Vancouver and Toronto (Canada); in Sydney (Australia); and in Auckland (New Zealand) as well.

The problem, as noted in the previous chapter, is that some of this very cheap housing is in highly distressed areas. Questions linger about the quality of cheap U.S. housing with respect to the basic services that are attached to housing—schools, infrastructure access, work opportunities, and myriad other essentials. While it is possible to get a cheap home in inner-city Detroit or rural Texas, are these quality homes in comparison to down-market European neighborhoods?

By several indications, distressed U.S. communities are in worse shape than their counterparts in other HDCs. The U.S.'s low-performing school districts register rock-bottom academic proficiency scores and would be considered bad in middle-income countries, let alone rich ones. High-crime U.S. cities have murder rates that approximate major Brazilian or Mexican murder centers, rather than French and British ones. The serious problems facing the U.S.'s poor neighborhoods could fill a book on their own, and listing these kinds of problems do not, on their own, render an airtight case that a person is better off growing up poor in Finland, Germany, or the Netherlands than in the United States. Still, it is hard to see the U.S.'s poor communities as delivering better schooling, better livelihoods, or more lifetime advantage than poor places in other very wealthy countries. The United States as a whole may be wealthy, but it is not altogether clear that the living standards and amenities of neighborhoods with cheap housing are what would be deemed minimally acceptable in other HDCs' standards.

Household Finances

Do these differences in essential product costs have a discernible effect on household finances? Answering this question is difficult because the cost of basic necessities is just one of several factors that will influence household finances. For example, household savings and debt aren't strictly a function of living costs. Tax breaks and penalties, financial regulation, monetary policy, interest rates, economic sentiments, market booms and busts, cultural attitudes, and any other number of factors can cause otherwise similar societies to have different prevailing savings rates, debt loads, and wealth accumulation. The complexity involved in disentangling these factors is very high, such that we are unlikely to reach a firm and final conclusion on the relationship between household finances and cost of living in today's HDCs here.

That being said, we have very good reason to expect that U.S. household finances would be among the strongest in the developed world. As noted at the outset of this chapter, U.S. incomes are high, and their taxes are low, compared to other HDCs. Its overall economy has been reasonably prosperous. Its tax system strongly incentivizes financial and real estate investment, and there is ample opportunity to make such investments. Its comparatively weak social safety net and the high stakes of being without money presumably create a pressure to accumulate and hold money. One might presume that Americans are well-positioned and well-incentivized to save money and accumulate wealth.

Figure 7.3 presents three metrics describing the household finances of other HDCs—household savings, debt, and wealth—all relative to household income. They suggest that U.S. household finances are—again—middling. U.S. households tend to have above-average wealth, but their savings are low. Indebtedness is average.

The country's savings rates have not been very high over the decade depicted in the figure. U.S. households appear to save more aggressively than Canadians, Japanese, Finns, Danes, and Brits, but less than the Swiss, Swedes, Germans, and French. These differences are not so clearly a function of social programs and living costs; there are high and low savings countries among those who aggressively contain the cost of essentials and those who maintain a more laissez-faire posture, such as that of the United States.

So why do savings rates differ?[16] Care must be taken in comparing national savings rates because countries assess these rates differently, and these estimates can be of varying quality. A 2015 analysis of European Union (EU) countries found that roughly half of the difference in savings rates is attributable to national wealth levels, the degree to which a population has aged, and consumer prices.[17] Additionally, government taxes and economic growth may have some impact. These factors suggest that the United States would have a savings rate that leads the developing world because it is very wealthy, its taxes are very low, and its population is not as old as many European ones. These factors, coupled with institutional

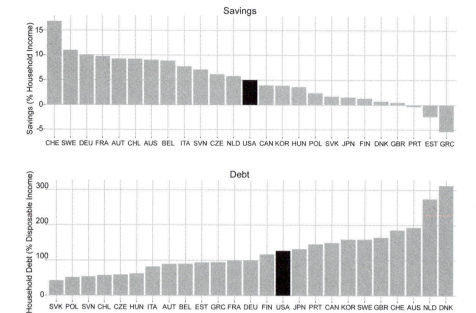

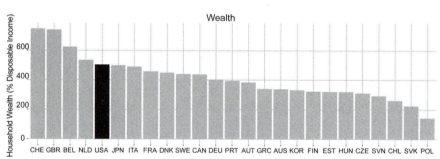

Figure 7.3 Household Finances, United States versus Other Highly Developed Economies, 2003–2013.
Source: OECD (2016).

factors that would presumably raise savings—tax incentives to save, a weak welfare state, a wide range of opportunities to invest—make the U.S.'s middling savings rate seem low, relative to what we might expect.

In and of itself, low savings relative to our expectations does not prove that the high cost of necessities are hurting household finances. Our expectations about what drives savings might be wrong. The United States might have an anti-savings cultural disposition that leads them to under-save. There are any number of possible explanations. Still, it seems quite clear that the United States has all the makings of a high savings country, yet it is in the bottom-half among HDCs. The Germans, Swedes, French, and others maintain stronger savings rates, despite higher taxes and a richer social safety net, which casts doubt on the idea that socialism damages household finances or that freer markets spur personal savings.

Debt is a similarly complicated issue. Again, the United States registers as a middling country, with household debt loads that are far smaller than the highly socialized Danes or Dutch, but much higher than in Finland, Germany, or France. As was the case with savings, care must be taken when interpreting debt figures. In many respects, the opportunity to acquire debt is a by-product of financial health. Recall from Chapter Three that poor people have difficulty getting loans, so being out of debt does not necessarily mean being in a position of financial strength. Compared to other HDCs, opportunities to borrow are comparatively plentiful in the United States, which might lead us to expect higher household debts. As was the case with savings, institutional factors play a very important role in shaping societies' savings rates. When policy restricts lending, or when it makes the terms of lending more onerous, people are likely to borrow less, apart from whatever is happening with the cost of basic essentials. Ultimately, U.S. households are reasonably wealthy in relation to their incomes. The United States ranks fifth in the countries depicted in Figure 7.3, with an average level of wealth that is five times that of incomes.

So household finances in the United States are middling, which at first glance seems fine until we return to the fact that people need more money to access basic necessities. For example, while Canadians and Americans seem to have similar incomes, savings rates, debt loads, and accumulated wealth, Canadians do not need as much money to ensure that they can get healthcare, a university education, or a home in a nondistressed community. It is similar to the difference between young people from rich families who live on minimum wage and those who earn that amount and have no family. Their incomes and perhaps general personal financial situations look similar on paper, but there can be little doubt that the former is in a much better economic position.

Well-Being across the Developed World

International comparisons of household finances are complicated by the fact that the causes and consequences of household savings, debt, and wealth accumulation differ across societies. For example, data in the previous section suggested that U.S. household finances were in considerably better shape than Danish or Finn ones. We might infer from these data that U.S. households are in a better economic situation, but Americans also need more money to secure a basic livelihood than Danes or Finns. The latter might not have as much access to money, but they arguably need less money to secure access to essentials. Financial security may be less of an issue for societies with socialized or otherwise cost-controlled markets for basic necessities because the effects of financial problems on well-being might be limited. For this reason, comparisons of general living standards can be instructive.

Ultimately, how does the U.S. system of market-driven essentials provision work out for American people in terms of overall well-being? The U.S. system involves trade-offs, in which it presumably sacrifices cost-controlled necessities in pursuit of market-driven prosperity, more jobs, higher incomes, lower taxes, (generally) lower consumer prices, and the many other purported benefits of laissez-faire economic systems. Ultimately, do these trade-offs result in higher or lower living standards?

Again, the answer is complicated. To some degree, the assessment of living standards requires value judgments, whereby the analyst decides what constitutes part of a "good" or "well" life. By some conceptions of well-being, U.S. living standards are very high. By others, living standards are middling to poor. The final assessment depends on what is valued the most. Figure 7.4 compares U.S. living standards to 18 other HDCs using data from the OECD's *Better Life Index*, a quantitative study of well-being across wealthy countries.[18] Dark dots depict the United States, and light dots represent others.

The general insight that comes across in these well-being comparisons is that U.S. living standards are very high in terms of money and goods consumption opportunities. For example, the second bar in Figure 7.4 shows that Americans have larger homes than most other developed countries, with 2.4 rooms per person. Over much of Europe, the average household has slightly less than 2 rooms per person. In general, U.S. homes are well-equipped. They are more universally equipped with basic facilities (e.g., plumbing, electricity), and appliance ownership is high even among society's poor.[19] These comparatively good housing conditions occur in a context in which housing costs are moderate (as suggested in Figure 7.2 above). All of this points to the success of the U.S. economy in delivering affordable housing in terms of the homes themselves. A similar story can be told of Americans' access to a range of consumer products, such as cars, clothing, personal beauty products, food, and much else. Overall, the U.S. system has been quite successful in delivering reasonably high household incomes (refer to Table 7.1), while consumer goods prices have widely fallen (Chapter 5).

By now, we have thoroughly established the U.S.'s prowess in creating opportunities to acquire consumer products, but how well does the system work in terms of delivering other commonly valued quality-of-life metrics?

In terms of job market quality, the market for jobs seems relatively weak in the United States. Although the severely deteriorated state of the Spanish and Italian job markets make Americans' situation look good by comparison, the U.S. job market is middling in its success creating jobs, and the jobs it does create seem to be precarious and demanding. Americans' risk of losing their job seems quite high, and workers typically dedicate much more of their week to work-oriented pursuits. The U.S. job market is not particularly good—it's average—and the terms of the jobs it offers can have considerable time demands.

This theme of middling to lower-ranking quality is apparent in many quality-of-life metrics. Earlier, we noted the middling quality of the typical U.S. higher education institution. Mediocrity appears to run through the system, with secondary school aptitude tests that register as average among HDCs. Americans are strongly disposed to see themselves as being healthy, although the country's extraordinarily low life expectancy raises questions about whether these positive self-reports have a strong basis in established fact. Despite these many challenges, Americans often sit near the top of rankings in terms of subjective satisfaction about their lives.

What are we to infer from these findings? To the extent that one equates well-being with raw consumption capacity—the opportunity to acquire and consume products in general—the U.S. system can be seen as very successful in delivering high living standards. However, to the extent that one values nonconsumption quality of life, the system is not highly successful. Jobs are comparatively precarious, work-life balance is poor, schools do not perform well, crime is high, and life expectancy is low. To their credit, Americans maintain a positive mental attitude and express high levels of satisfaction with their health and life. Readers can decide on their own whether they agree with such a rosy view or see it as a matter of diminished expectations.

Paying the Bills

Of course, expanding social programs costs money. Someone has to pay the bills, which means higher taxes. Many voters are probably reluctant to expand social programs because doing so would imply higher taxes. How much higher would taxes be if the United States were to adopt European-style social programming?

Table 7.7 compares the tax burdens taken by all levels of government among 19 HDCs. The table suggests that taxes are comparatively low in the United States. Overall taxes are about 20 percent higher in Canada, about 40 percent higher in Germany and the Netherlands, and roughly 80 percent higher in Denmark and France. Income taxes on individuals are

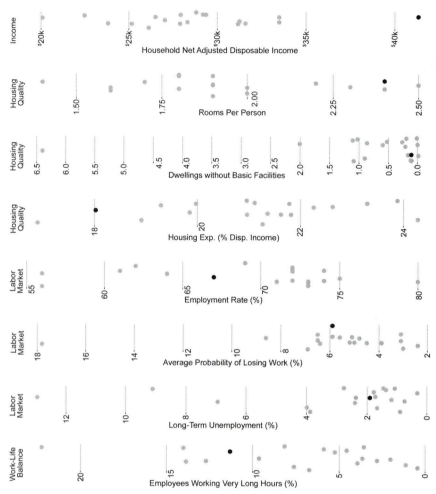

Figure 7.4   Selected Well-Being Metrics from the OECD Better Life Index.

not particularly low in the United States—they amount to about 10 percent of GDP, which is quite typical of HDCs. U.S. taxes are low mainly because its sales taxes, corporate income taxes, and payroll taxes are low. To the U.S.'s credit, sales and payroll taxes are much more progressive taxes, which means that their burden falls less heavily on poorer people. The net result is that the U.S. tax system is often cited as the most progressive in the developed world.[20] Still, after everyone has worked through the complexities of the tax code, the top 20 percent of U.S. society pays a lower share of taxes than their share of income, whereas the middle 60 percent slightly overpays.[21]

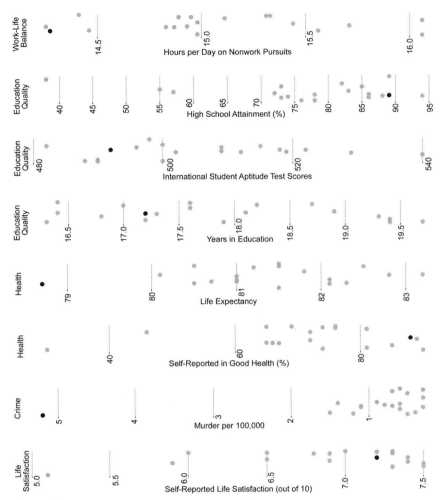

Figure 7.4 (Continued)
Note: Dark circles represent the United States, light circles represent other countries.
Source: OECD (2016).

Concretely, were the United States to emulate a European-style tax system to match European-style social programs, the net result might be something along the lines of a slight increase in income tax rates, raising or eliminating the cap that limits high-income earners' payroll taxes, and a sizable increase in sales taxes (perhaps partly through a national sales tax) that would render overall rates of 15 percent to 20 percent.

It is hard to see these types of tax changes as politically viable. Voters are generally hostile to tax increases, and this hostility is particularly strong in the United States. In part, however, it may be a product of Americans

Table 7.7 Consolidated Government Taxes (% GDP), 2014

Country	Total Taxes (%)	Income Taxes			Social Security Contributions (%)	Property (%)	Goods and Services (%)
		Total (%)	On Individuals (%)	On Businesses (%)			
Denmark	47.6	29.8	26.1	2.7	0.1	1.8	15.4
France	45.0	10.9	8.4	2.5	16.7	3.8	10.8
Belgium	44.7	15.9	12.8	3.1	14.2	3.5	10.8
Italy	43.9	14.5	11.7	3.2	13.1	2.7	11.5
Finland	43.7	15.2	12.8	2.4	12.6	1.3	14.5
Sweden	42.8	14.8	12.2	2.6	10.0	1.1	12.2
Austria	42.5	12.3	9.7	2.2	14.6	0.7	11.7
Norway	40.5	18.7	9.9	8.8	9.5	1.2	11.1
Netherlands	36.7	9.1	7.2	1.9	15.0	1.2	10.9
Germany	36.5	11.3	9.5	1.8	13.9	0.9	10.2
Portugal	34.5	11.2	7.8	3.4	8.9	1.1	12.9
United Kingdom	32.9	11.7	9.1	2.5	6.2	4.0	10.8
Spain	32.7	9.6	7.3	2.0	11.3	2.2	9.2
New Zealand	31.4	17.4	11.9	4.4	0.0	1.9	12.0
Canada	30.5	14.5	11.2	3.0	4.8	3.2	7.4
Japan	30.3	9.8	5.8	4.0	12.4	2.7	5.3
Australia	27.5	15.7	10.8	4.9	0.0	2.6	7.8
Switzerland	26.9	12.4	8.5	2.8	6.7	1.8	6.0
United States	25.4	12.0	9.8	2.2	6.1	2.9	4.4

Source: OECD (2016).

feeling like they are stretched to their financial limits and not having faith that they will get something in return for the taxes they spend. A lot of money simply isn't directed toward civilian purposes—U.S.'s government spends considerable amounts of money on its military. The money that is directed toward shoring up people's well-being seems widely wasted and ultimately fails to deliver value to taxpayers. As noted earlier, it gets very poor value for its public spending on healthcare due to its failure to control costs or curb profit. Many of its entitlements are given to people who don't need them. Things might be different if Americans saw value in the government services that their taxes finance and if they saw public programs as a lifeline that helps edify them economically.

Although a German or Swede may ultimately surrender more in taxes, the services they receive in return make them less dependent on accumulating money. The converse seems true in the United States, where access to money plays a more critical role in securing necessities.

Looking Abroad for Lessons, and Questioning the Orthodoxies of Home

What are the major takeaways from our discussion of how the U.S.'s basic essential prices, household finances, and overall well-being differ from that of other HDCs? First, people in other highly developed societies generally do not have to bear the burden of the U.S.'s pricey healthcare, child care, and education systems. Other governments appear to have succeeded in ensuring that these products are affordable, and they appear to have done so without diminishing their availability or quality. The United States is somewhat unique in the way that its government does so little to contain the out-of-pocket costs of these basics, and Americans do not enjoy a bounty of world-leading essentials for the world-leading prices they pay. In fact, it is hard to discern any clear benefit, perhaps aside from low overall taxes. While Europe has problems of its own, its wealthier countries have found ways to socialize the costs of essentials without destroying prosperity or economic progress.

Americans have many reasons to be proud of their country, and the United States has accomplished many great things. But no one is the best at everything, and Americans are clearly not the best at creating an environment in which household finances and general well-being thrive. The United States is great at creating consumption opportunities for its people, and consumption is an important part of people's living standards. However, these consumption opportunities materialize in a broader system that makes people's livelihood tenuous. Jobs are comparatively tenuous. People's reliance on money to secure access to necessities makes people's basic living standards tenuous. The depths to which the poor can sink in terms of being denied essential products or thrust into highly distressed communities arguably makes many people's hold on a first world quality-of-life tenuous. There is much to admire about the United States, but its system for delivering goods and services that are essential to well-being does not seem like one of them.

Americans have much to gain by looking abroad and considering ideas that other HDCs have devised to engage the kinds of pressures that harm household finances. These comparisons suggest that access to quality essentials, household finances, and overall living standards are quite mediocre in the United States, despite the fact that this country has unmatched resources to secure all three. Doing so may require that Americans reconsider their basic conceptions about what constitutes practical, productive policy, and reconsider the economic orthodoxies that seem to weigh down the finances and broader well-being of regular Americans. In the next chapter, we close by reconsidering these orthodoxies and imagining new possibilities.

CHAPTER EIGHT

The Choice

We conclude the study with a brief review of its findings and some reflection on their broader implications. These findings suggest that the middle class's struggles with money are at least partly driven by the U.S.'s market-oriented, neoliberal approach to organizing its education, healthcare, and housing markets. This organizational scheme is underwritten by a widespread presumption that laissez-faire, business-oriented policies are society's best bet for prosperity, jobs, and material enrichment. Whatever its merits in other spheres of economic life, the U.S.'s comparatively fervent embrace of neoliberal policies has failed to deliver an abundance of high-quality and affordable healthcare, child care, education, and housing. Other highly developed societies appear to have succeeded in organizing these markets in ways that make high-quality products affordable, if not universally accessible. Although emulating Europe might not ease all of the economic pressures that strain the middle class's finances, doing so might at least buffer families from the multitude of headwinds that exacerbate their personal economic hardships.

Could Americans enjoy British- or Canadian-style socialized medicine, German- or Dutch-style subsidized higher education, or French- or Swedish-style support for the care of young children? The United States certainly has the resources and expertise to develop and deploy such systems. There are clear reasons to believe that these kinds of programs are practically possible and could help staunch the spending pressures that press regular Americans into financial difficulty. The main question is whether the country truly wants to strengthen social policies and has the political will to see these kinds of reforms happen. If the years of political fallout that followed the passage of the Affordable Care Act—policies that probably strike people from other highly developed countries as quite modest—are any indication, there are powerful constituencies and cultural narratives that oppose strengthening social policies.

Absent a strong political push to strengthen social programs, U.S. households are probably left on their own to carry these heavy burdens. Maybe they can do so with conscientious budgeting, coupon-clipping, skipping restaurant meals, and similar efforts to cut corners. However, the rapid pace at which these essential costs are escalating suggests that these kinds of penny-wise saving tactics will only last for so long. To borrow from finance journalist Helaine Olen,[1] the system is pressing families into pound foolishness. They face a heavy—and, more importantly, fast-escalating—cost of purchasing access to basic necessities. Increasingly, middle-class people's ability to save, accrue wealth, and manage debt involves their willingness to forgo preventative and therapeutic healthcare, regulated and institutionalized child care, or advanced postsecondary training. It might involve a willingness to raise one's family in a community whose school quality, commuting time, crime levels, or social problems would be seen as patently unacceptable to people in northwestern Europe or Canada.

Major structural economic and social changes are probably needed to help U.S. households achieve firmer financial footing. These kinds of reforms require overcoming strong political opponents and deep-seated commitments to neoliberal policies and neoliberal thinking.

Review of Study's Key Findings

Let us begin with a review of the preceding study's key findings. We began with a discussion of U.S. households' long descent into their present state of financial precariousness. Overall, U.S. household finances look considerably worse than they did 30 or 40 years ago. People have stopped getting secure jobs with regular raises. They save much less, borrow much more, and go bankrupt more often. The majority of the country lives paycheck to paycheck, and only a minority of people have a demonstrated ability to accumulate enough money to sustain a livelihood into old age.

Debates over what to do about these deteriorating finances tend to gravitate toward one of three generic strategies: doing nothing, developing government initiatives to solidify household finances, or redoubling the U.S.'s forty-some-year-long commitment to neoliberal reform. Satisfaction with or belief in the ultimate benefit of the status quo is a good reason to advocate for doing nothing. Doing nothing often rests on faith that society's economic system is ultimately sound and that problems will eventually self-correct. Such a view seems difficult to maintain here because the deterioration of household finances seems to be an enduring problem that has festered for decades. This problem does not seem to be sorting itself out.

This leaves the United States with the latter two options. Disagreements over the benefit of government action versus pro-business and pro-investor "free market" policies are a major partisan dividing line in contemporary politics. Our appraisal of either side's merits is steered by our view of what is causing household finances to deteriorate, and our understanding of the practical strategies available to us to reverse or buffer the effects of these causes. Over the past several decades, policy-makers have leaned toward addressing economic problems with "free market" or neoliberal policies, but the continued importance of government programs should not be underestimated. In this age of neoliberalism, most Americans are either dependent on public aid in the present or seem poised to rely on public assistance in the future. U.S. living standards—and in fact all modern, highly developed capitalist countries' living standards—are highly reliant on government programs. The question is not whether or not to have extensive social welfare programs, but whether or not a country's portfolio of social programs renders desirable outcomes.

Analysts often cite income stagnation as having caused household finance problems. There is no doubt that income problems are a major part of the problem, but it is not the sole cause. People have to keep on spending more for a stagnant income to convert into falling savings and rising debt. People's failure to restrain spending is part of the problem. Many cultural critics cast rising spending through the prism of some type of deficient or nonadmirable quality ascribed to U.S. culture: unrestrained acquisitiveness, materialism, status obsession, vanity, and some other character flaw. Many of these criticisms are new incarnations of a generic, centuries-old criticism that always finds a market. However, a closer look at the data suggests that spending is buoyed by a process that was advanced by Elizabeth Warren and her colleagues over a decade ago, which maintained that households' overspending, and the financially damaging consequences of this overspending, are substantially driven by the spiraling cost of necessities.

More specifically, a closer look at household spending data suggests that, in proportion to incomes, spending on the types of products typically featured by proponents of such "culture of consumerism" explanations—such as clothing, cars, home appliances, home furnishings, personal care products, or food—have roughly paced incomes, if not fallen relative to incomes. It is not necessarily that people are purchasing less in these product categories, but rather that the twin engines of technology and foreign outsourcing have driven down costs in these areas. These costs savings are arguably one way in which neoliberal policies have succeeded in strengthening household finances. However, the data suggest that spending on education, healthcare, and shelter have exerted a strong and often growing strain on household budgets. In these product markets, prices have been escalating very rapidly, in comparison to both incomes and general consumer prices.

Arguably, healthcare, education, and housing are products that are, to some degree, essential for well-being. The relationship between healthcare and education may be straightforward, but perhaps not housing. In the United States, many essential public services—primary and secondary schooling, emergency services, transportation infrastructure, libraries, welfare services—are financed and disbursed by local-level governments. In a society with high levels of inequality and residential segregation, getting a foothold in as "good" a neighborhood as possible may mean spending to the limits of one's ability to afford housing. Moreover, the heavy cost of housing means that households have to channel inordinate amounts of their personal wealth into their housing, and housing in more expensive and exclusive neighborhoods may be more conservative investments.

The implications of seeing rising spending as a product of rising costs of necessary products, as opposed to unrestrained consumerism, are quite profound. We tend to blame people for their financial misfortune and may even see the pains of their financial failure as a form of productive justice, which teaches people lessons about their excesses. The problem with a system that makes healthcare, child care, or education expensive is that, at best, we are punishing people for spending money on things that they really need. In some respects, these people are acting as altruistic parents who sacrifice their own financial well-being to safeguard and edify their children's future. An even worse scenario would be that this kind of "market discipline" works, and people start to forgo these basics.

Rather than seeing household financial struggles as wholly the result of a personal failure, Warren's explanations point to systemic failure. Economic policy-makers have failed to create an environment that makes high-quality essentials easily available to everyone. They have presumed that an unregulated market would press those who produce and supply healthcare, education, and housing to innovate and raise productivity to compete with each other. Market forces were supposed to press suppliers to cut costs and profit margins, and/or deliver substantially better products, a scheme that has worked well in many product markets. They do not seem to work that way in these particular markets.

What is going on? In part, education, child care, and healthcare have not been amenable to two of the primary vehicles upon which modern business relies to cut costs: foreign outsourcing and automation. There are some efforts—think illegal foreign nannies, Massive Open Online Courses (MOOCs), or WebMD—but, for the most part, the standard strategies that have helped push down consumer prices have not succeeded in these markets. Other highly developed countries have resisted this impulse to privatize, deregulate, and/or underfund education or healthcare, or dismantle the economically redistributive programs that keep wealthy communities from monopolizing high-quality essentials. To a German, Dutch, Brit, Swede, or Canadian, it might make sense to make serious investments in public programs that make quality essentials universally accessible, or at least much more affordable. Yet Americans seem to say no.

Why? Part of the problem is that the problem is not clearly apparent to much of society. Another part involves deeply rooted beliefs about the relationship between governments, private enterprise, and living standards. In other words, they either do not see the problem, or they do not believe that strengthening government programs will solve the problem. These may not explain the totality of this resistance, but they are likely contributors.

A Process That Hides in Plain Sight

Part of the reason Americans do not confront the rising burden of basic necessities with a strong, concerted collective initiative is that they do not see household financial problems as a serious societal issue, or they do not see its links with weak social programs. Some believe that households' financial problems are temporary or simply a matter of people complaining because they have inflated lifestyle expectations, impulse control problems, or class envy. Some believe that society need not concern itself with people's personal problems or that no one has a right to complain if they are living indoors with basic heat, electricity, and plumbing; maintaining a subsistence diet; and enjoying access to a library, emergency room, and public school.

Over the previous chapters, this study tries to confront these presumptions. It shows how households save less, borrow more, and go bankrupt more often. It shows that these problems materialized over multiple economic cycles and continued to deteriorate instead of self-correcting during economic boom times. It finds that overspending is clearly part of what was hurting household finances, even though incomes were stagnating and becoming more precarious. While one can almost always find ways to shave a dollar here and there off of people's spending, and the idea that a dollar saved here and there eventually adds up to something, these folksy truths overlook the problem that much of this runaway spending is driven by the rapidly escalating costs of products so essential to well-being that people cannot—and arguably should not—forgo them.

These are the broad, macro-level machinations of the process driving household financial problems, but it may be difficult to develop a sense of how these more abstract trends manifest themselves concretely in everyday life. The process by which these strains damage finances may not be obvious at first glance, but they are not hard to grasp once pointed out. Households do not save enough money, and they do not accrue enough wealth to independently secure their access to (often costly) basics. Why don't they save enough? The process materialized in what seems like a serious of unrelated, temporary shocks, but they are all manifestations of a system that fails to make essentials cost-accessible.

The process may begin with the choice to attend college. One can choose to forgo college and sacrifice the employability and income benefits afforded by higher education. As the march of technology and global outsourcing advances, these sacrifices seem likely to rise. If one does decide to pursue advanced training and lacks the good fortune of either being in a community or coming from a family that subsidizes these costs, higher education may mean debt. The early career savings used to pay down educational debt is money that is not being saved for a home down payment, child's college fund, or retirement.

Presumably, children eventually come. This might be another person who needs food, clothes, and health insurance. It might necessitate child care, which "costs" a family in the form of either bigger expenses or lost income. It might also involve an eventual relocation to a community without substandard schools or other problems. Typically, communities with these resources fight to keep affordable housing out, so getting a foothold in these communities requires people to buy as much housing as they can afford. Purchasing an expensive home not only entails higher spending but perhaps also an aggressive channeling of one's savings into residential housing—a historically poor-performing asset.

If a family has the good fortune of weathering these storms without unforeseen calamity, the data suggest that they are likely to get a bit of a financial breather between the moment their youngest starts public school and their oldest starts postsecondary schooling (if they plan on helping their children). Of course, there are still some burdens. The public school day ends long before standard work hours end, and many parents are going to need some child care until their kids are old enough to watch themselves. By the time this breather arrives, any lost college or retirement savings will have forgone the benefit of compounded returns.

By the time a household hits its fifties, and children's higher education costs start to be incurred, healthcare costs can also start escalating. This is also typically the moment in which those who are under-saved for retirement begin their desperate struggle to catch up. These savings begin quite late and have missed much opportunity for compounded returns. Households may try to compensate by engaging in very aggressive (risky) investments, which is not what a person is supposed to do in the years leading up to retirement.

Much of the country will approach old age with little to nothing saved for retirement, and they will hope to work well into old age. Fortunately, they have the benefit of the Medicare, Medicaid, and Social Security social welfare programs to help prevent society from sinking into a massive problem with elderly poverty. This plan to work into old age can be sustained so long as health problems and ageism do not push people out of the workforce. Eventually, however, work stops, and health costs escalate. These costs can be staggering and can wipe out a person's accumulated wealth. If the costs of old age do not completely exhaust a household's assets, they may have something to leave to the next generation.

The process is slow. It unfolds over decades, through what looks like a serious of temporary, unrelated problems—college, child care, housing, children's college, healthcare, and retirement. It is not so readily apparent that these things produce circumstances that systematically lead to chronic under-savings and a delay in savings that forgoes compounded returns. Stronger social programs may help people save money and make their well-being less contingent on having enough money.

Questioning Neoliberal Orthodoxy

There are many sources of political or intellectual opposition to the development or expansion of public programs designed to socialize the cost of these necessities. Some of this opposition does not appear to be motivated by a principled dedication to capitalism and personal freedom, or a principled opposition to big government, regulationism, welfarism, and redistribution. For example, Skocpol and Williamson's study of the Tea Party in the United States found that, amid much of its anti-government rhetoric, there was considerable support for social welfare programs directed toward the movement's own demographics (e.g., Medicare, Social Security).[2] Indeed, many observers believe that some opposition to the Affordable Care Act was tied to older voters' concern that this new social program would water down the benefits they enjoy under Medicare.[3] There is much reason to believe that some opposition to welfare in general is often motivated by its often implicit attachment to racial minorities and a prevalent sense of racial animus.[4] These are the more facile sources of opposition to expanding government programs designed to socialize the costs of essentials. A more intellectually serious source of opposition comes from a widespread belief that, in principle, neoliberal policies build a better society.

Some argue that neoliberalism is a means of ensuring political freedom. An example of this argument might maintain that the concentration of economic power in the hands of government creates a tempting mechanism by which political elites can coerce the general population.[5] While there may be some merit to the idea that a Soviet-style command-and-control economy is a risk to democracy, good governance, and political freedom, the types of reforms being advanced here are more fairly characterized as a move away from contemporary U.S. capitalism and toward something that more closely resembles contemporary German, Dutch, British, or Canadian capitalism, or U.S. capitalism in the pre-Reagan era. We are talking about moving from a system in which the government spend about 15 percent of GDP to one in which it spends 20–25 percent. It is worth noting that international governance data suggest that northwestern Europeans and Canadians are less corrupt, more publicly accountable, more rule-bound, and generally better-governed than Americans.[6]

Another line of argumentation maintains that, in principle, government "intervention" in market forces harms prosperity and overall material well-being.[7] A nuanced application of this view might maintain that, as a rule of thumb, the economy performs better when governments leave more discretionary power to private actors and refrain from trying to draw or manipulate the resources being used in private sector activity. Private sector actors are presumed to be better informed than public officials about the businesses in which they operate. The private sector is presumed to be more responsive, nimble, industrious, and innovative. In leaving them alone, private enterprise is expected to compete with each other by creating perpetually more and better products at lower cost, all of which is supposed to enrich society materially. Government officials are presumed to know less, be less responsible, less interested in improving quality or lowering prices, and more disposed to be corrupt. While an even-handed proponent of neoliberalism might concede that, sometimes, these expectations do not materialize in fact, they are nevertheless a faithful generalization of how the economy works. As such, it seems safe to presume that free, unregulated markets are best able to sow prosperity, create jobs, and improve living standards, unless we have reason to believe that we are dealing with an exception to this rule.

Whatever the merits of these generalizations, these expectations have not materialized in U.S. housing, education, and healthcare markets. The United States maintains a strongly laissez-faire, business-oriented policy posture in these markets. The U.S.'s private healthcare sector is large and unregulated. The country has progressively privatized more of its higher educational system and has used public funds extensively to help develop a private, for-profit postsecondary schooling. There are no paid parental leave systems or serious public early educational systems to compete with its child care markets. Governments generally do not invest in the development of residential real estate for the lower- and middle classes. If there is any country that conforms to neoliberal ideals in the developed world, it is the United States. Yet the country does not enjoy that bounty of cheap, high-quality products in the areas of housing, education, and healthcare. The free market is not working as advertised. It hardly seems to make sense that doubling down on neoliberalism would improve these results.

The Choice

Prevailing long-term personal finance trends do not look promising for the U.S. middle class. Since at least the late 1990s—but perhaps as far back as the late 1960s—regular U.S. families' finances have slowly soured, during both the economy's booms and busts. To the casual observer of U.S. economic politics, it might seem like the electorate has tried every combination of Democratic and Republican federal administrations and congresses, and, regardless of whichever party occupies whichever office, these long-term negative trends do not seem to be seriously reversing course. To many, this persistent failure to reverse the U.S. middle-class's souring economic fortunes suggests that policy-makers, the broader economy, and perhaps the larger political system are fundamentally corrupt.

There is substance to the view that corruption and generally poor governance are part of the problem, but such a diagnosis only captures part of the problem. Household finances are being hurt in part by larger forces that policy-makers cannot so easily reverse or may not want to reverse because they are integral to other important agenda items. The population is aging, and technology is rendering old jobs and skill sets obsolete. To the extent that people are not able to find a niche in the "new economy," the march of technology may be making most people obsolete to economic production and distribution. While reversing globalization may seem much more doable, the practicality of this choice is not clear-cut. Reversing globalization may save old manufacturing jobs, but it also threatens jobs and investments in major economic sectors (e.g., U.S. exporters, finance, multinational enterprises), damages economic mechanisms that help contain consumer prices and the cost of credit, and may even damage the U.S.'s international relations and prospects for international peace. Moreover, it may be that the middle-class prosperity driven by the U.S.'s trade-protected mid-20th-century manufacturing sector was a historical anomaly, and the grinding, economic gray times confronting today's middle class are more the historical norm.

All of this is to say that all of the problems facing the U.S. middle class may not easily be erased with policy changes. That said, economic policy is not necessarily buffering the U.S. middle class from the pressures of technology, trade, demographic change, and so on. A strong welfare state might both safeguard people's access to basic necessities and help strengthen people's personal finances by loosening the heavy costs that keep them from saving money. Such systems already exist in countries that are just as wealthy, economically healthy, democratic, and politically free as the United States. The United States has the resources to create a quality educational system that serves children from birth to the moment they are ready to assume a meaningful role in the economy. It has the ability to ensure that everyone has access to quality healthcare and that healthcare does not threaten to bankrupt people. It has the resources to make every neighborhood—even the poor ones—completely acceptable places to maintain livelihoods and raise children. Perhaps the main barrier is that regular Americans do not see such policies as benefiting them, and they are not sufficiently motivated to demand these policies from their politicians.

Notes

Chapter 1

1. Pew Research Center. (2015, December 9). *The American middle class is losing ground: No longer the majority and falling behind financially.* Retrieved from http://www.pewsocialtrends.org/files/2015/12/2015-12-09_middle-class_FINAL-report.pdf

2. Kotkin, J. (2014, February 16). The U.S. middle class is turning proletarian. *Forbes.* Retrieved from http://www.forbes.com/sites/joelkotkin/2014/02/16/the-u-s-middle-class-is-turning-proletarian/#4937bd532f29

3. Pew Research Center. (2015, December 9). *The American middle class is losing ground: No longer the majority and falling behind financially.* Retrieved from http://www.pewsocialtrends.org/files/2015/12/2015-12-09_middle-class_FINAL-report.pdf

4. Kalleberg, A. (2009). Precarious work, insecure workers: Employment relations in transition. *American Sociological Review, 74,* 1–22.

5. Hacker, J. S. (2008). *The great risk shift: The new economic insecurity and the decline of the American dream.* New York, NY: Oxford University Press.

6. Hacker, J. S. (2008). *The great risk shift: The new economic insecurity and the decline of the American dream.* New York, NY: Oxford University Press; Gosselin, P. (2009). *High wire: The precarious lives of American families.* New York, NY: Basic Books.

7. Sullivan, T., Warren, E., & Westbrook, J. L. (1999). *As we forgive our debtors: Bankruptcy and consumer credit in America.* Washington, D.C.: Beard Books; Warren, E. (2005). The overconsumption myth and other tales of law, economics and morality. *Washington University Law Quarterly, 82,* 1485; Tyagi, A., & Warren, E. (2004). *The two-income trap: Why middle-class parents are broke.* New York, NY: Basic Books; Himmelstein, D. U., Warren, E., Thorne, D., & Woolhandler, S. (2005). Illness and injury as contributors to bankruptcy. *Health Affairs,* 63–71.

8. Hacker, J. (2008). *The great risk shift: The new economic insecurity and the decline of the American dream.* New York, NY: Oxford University Press.

9. Center for Budget and Policy Priorities. (2015, May 12). *Chart book: The legacy of the great recession.* Retrieved from http://www.cbpp.org/research/chart-book-the -legacy-of-the-great-recession

10. Kavoussi, B. (2012, July 25). Recession killed 170,000 small businesses between 2008 and 2010: report. *Huffington Post.* Retrieved from http://www .huffingtonpost.com/2012/07/25/us-lost-more-than-170000-small-businesses -2008-2010_n_1702358.html; Fox News. (2012, July 26). Economy lost more than 200,000 small businesses in recession, census shows. Retrieved from http://www .foxnews.com/politics/2012/07/26/economy-lost-more-than-200000-small -businesses-in-recession-census-shows

11. Cohen, J. N. (2015, June 11). Housing prices since 1975 [Blog post]. Retrieved from http://fragilefinances.org/2015/06/11/housing-prices-since-1975

12. National Bureau of Economic Research. (2010). U.S. Business Cycle Expansions and Contractions [Data table]. Retrieved from http://www.nber.org/cycles .html

13. Pew Research Center. (2012, August 22). *The lost decade of the middle class.* Retrieved from http://www.pewsocialtrends.org/files/2012/08/pew-social-trends -lost-decade-of-the-middle-class.pdf

14. Data from: (1) Census Bureau. (2014). Table F-5. Race and Hispanic origin of householder—families by median and mean income: 1947 to 2012 [Data set]. Retrieved from https://www.census.gov/data/tables/time-series/demo/income -poverty/historical-income-families.html; (2) Federal Reserve Bank. (2014). Personal saving rate, percent, annual, seasonally adjusted annual rate [Data set from Series PSAVERT of Federal Reserve Economic]. Retrieved from http://research .stlouisfed.org/fred2; (3) Federal Reserve Bank. (2014). CMDEBT/GDP, bil. of $/ bil. of $, annual [Data set from Series CMDEBT_GDP of Federal Reserve Economic]. Retrieved from http://research.stlouisfed.org/fred2; and (4) American Bankruptcy Institute. (2014). Annual business and non-business filings by year (1980–2013) [Data table]. Retrieved from http://www.abi.org/newsroom/bankruptcy-statistics

15. Cohen, J. N. (2016). Income growth across the income scale [Blog post]. Retrieved from http://fragilefinances.org/2016/08/26/income-growth-across-the -income-scale

16. Desilver, D. (2014, October 9). For most workers, real wages have barely budged for decades [Blog post]. Retrieved from http://www.pewresearch.org/fact -tank/2014/10/09/for-most-workers-real-wages-have-barely-budged-for-decades

17. Kalleberg, A. (2009). Precarious work, insecure workers: Employment relations in transition. *American Sociological Review, 74*, 1–22.

18. Butrica, B. A., Iams, H. M., Smith, K. E., and Tode, E. J. (2009). The disappearing defined benefit pension and its potential impact on the retirement incomes of baby boomers. *Social Security Bulletin, 69*(3). Retrieved from http://www.ssa.gov /policy/docs/ssb/v69n3/v69n3p1.html

19. Cohen, J. N. (2016, August 30). Financial income stagnation [Blog post]. Retrieved from http://fragilefinances.org/2016/08/30/financial-income-not -important

20. Cohen, J. N. (2016, September 12). Family businesses: In decline? [Blog post]. Retrieved from http://fragilefinances.org/2016/09/12/entrepreneurial-busi ness-formation-over-time

21. Notwithstanding temporary expansions to workers' programs after the 2008 crisis.

22. The past century's mean return on a conservative portfolio. See Chapter 3.

23. *Gross domestic product* (GDP) is an estimate of the value of all economic transacting in a country during some set period of time (usually a year). We use the GDP as a proxy for the overall size of the economy and scale other economic metrics to it as a means of gauging their size relative to the economy.

24. Balz, D. (2015, December 12). Charting Trump's rise through the decline of the middle class. *Washington Post*. Retrieved from https://www.washingtonpost .com/politics/charting-trumps-rise-in-the-decline-of-the-middle-class/2015/12 /12/0f5df1d8-a037-11e5-8728-1af6af208198_story.html

25. Butrica, B. A., Iams, H. M., Smith, K. E., & Tode, E. J. (2009). The disappearing defined benefit pension and its potential impact on the retirement incomes of baby boomers. *Social Security Bulletin, 69*(3). Retrieved from http://www.ssa.gov /policy/docs/ssb/v69n3/v69n3p1.html

26. Jones, R. P., Daniel, C., & Havarro-Rivera, J. (2015). Economic insecurity, rising inequality, and doubts about the future: Findings from the 2014 American Values Survey. Retrieved from http://publicreligion.org/site/wp-content/uploads /2014/09/AVS-web.pdf

27. Hahn, R. D., & Price, D. (2008). *Promise lost: College-qualified students who don't enroll in college*. Retrieved from http://files.eric.ed.gov/fulltext/ED503317 .pdf

28. Greenberg, M. H. (2007). Next steps for federal child care policy. *Next Generation of Antipoverty Policies, 17*(2), 73–96.

29. Zivin, K., Packowski, M., & Galea, S. (2011). Economic downturns and population mental health: research findings, gaps, challenges and priorities. *Psychological Medicine, 41*, 1343–1348.

30. Aber, J. L., Bennett, N. G., Conley, D. C., & Li, J. (1997). The effects of poverty on child health and development. *Annual Review of Public Health*, 18, 463–483; Lindstrom, M., Hansen, K., & Rosvall, M. (2012). Economic stress in childhood and adulthood, and self-rated health: A population-based study concerning risk accumulation, critical period, and social mobility. *BMC Public Health*, 12, 761–775.

31. Bob Tedeschi (2009, June 12). Beware of neighbor's home foreclosure. *New York Times*. Retrieved from http://www.nytimes.com/2009/06/14/realestate /mortgages/14mort.html

32. Himmelstein, D. U., Warren, E., Thorne, D., & Woolhandler, S. (2005). Illness and injury as contributors to bankruptcy. *Health Affairs*, 63–71.

33. For an extended discussion, see Scott, J. C. (1999). *Seeing like a state: How certain schemes to improve the human condition have failed*. New Haven, CT: Yale University Press.

34. Pew Research Center. (2010, May 4). "Socialism" not so negative, "capitalism" not so positive. Retrieved from http://www.people-press.org/files/legacy-pdf/610.pdf

35. Jacove, D. (2013). One in three Americans prepare a detailed households budget. Retrieved from http://www.gallup.com/poll/162872/one-three-americans-prepare-detailed-household-budget.aspx

36. Hastings, J., Madrian, B. C., & Skimmyhorn, W. L. (2013). Financial literacy, financial education, and economic outcomes. *Annual Review of Economics, 5,* 347–373; Lusardi, A., & Mitchell, O. S. (2014). The economic importance of financial literacy: Theory and evidence. *Journal of Economic Literature, 52*(1), 5–44.

37. For reviews, see Harvey, D. (2007). *A brief history of neoliberalism.* New York, NY: Oxford University Press; Centeno, M., & Cohen, J. N. (2010). *Global capitalism: A sociological perspective.* Cambridge, UK: Polity; Centeno, M., & Cohen, J. N. (2012). The arc of neoliberalism. *Annual Review of Sociology, 38,* 317–340; Peck, J. (2013). *Constructions of neoliberal reason* (New York, NY: Oxford University Press).

Chapter 2

1. Morin, R. & Motel, S. (2012, September 10). A third of Americans now say they are in the lower classes. Retrieved from http://www.pewsocialtrends.org/2012/09/10/a-third-of-americans-now-say-they-are-in-the-lower-classes/

2. U.S. Federal Reserve. (2014). *Survey of consumer finances.* Retrieved from http://www.federalreserve.gov/econresdata/scf/scfindex.htm

3. This figure and those that follow are derived from data from the Federal Reserve Bank's *Survey of Consumer Finances.* It is a different source than that used by the Census Bureau in its income calculations from Chapter One. Measurement and estimation mean that our analyses are dealing with gross, rather than fine, differences. Readers should assign less importance to distinctions amounting to a few hundred or even thousands of dollars. More meaning can be drawn from distinctions involving greater sums, for example in the tens of thousands of dollars.

4. Cohen, J. N. (2016, September 14). Family businesses: In decline? [Blog post]. Retrieved from http://fragilefinances.org/2016/09/14/family-business-decline

5. Cohen, J. N. (2016, August 31). Household income sources: Who gets welfare? [Blog post]. Retrieved from http://fragilefinances.org/2016/08/31/household-income-sources

6. Cohen, J. N. (2016, September 14). Who pays the federal government's bills? [Blog post]. Retrieved from http://fragilefinances.org/2016/09/14/who-pays-the-federal-governments-bills

7. Federal Reserve Board. (2015, December 28). Household debt service and financial obligations ratios [Data table]. Retrieved from http://www.federalreserve.gov/releases/housedebt

8. U.S. Federal Reserve. (2014). *Survey of consumer finances.* Retrieved from http://www.federalreserve.gov/econresdata/scf/scfindex.htm

9. A regression analysis is a statistical method for building predictive or explanatory models. It delivers formula used to predict variable values using other metrics ("predictors").

10. Piketty, T. (2014). *Capital in the twenty-first century.* Princeton, NJ: Belknap.

11. Seitz-Wald, A. (2011, September 19). Multi-millionaire rep. says he can't afford a tax hike because he only has $400k a year after feeding family [Blog post]. Retrieved from http://thinkprogress.org/economy/2011/09/19/322405/gop-rep-whines-400k

12. In financial parlance, we are pricing out a *perpetuity*, that is, a bond or security that is supposed to pay out forever. Such securities exist, although they are very rare. For example, the United Kingdom issued such bonds during World War I. Such bonds were retired by acts of British Parliament only recently. See Kollewe, J., & Farrell, S. (2014, October 31). UK bonds that financed First World War to be redeemed 100 years later. *Guardian*. Retrieved from http://www.theguardian.com/business/2014/oct/31/uk-first-world-war-bonds-redeemed

These types of securities are priced as

$$PV = \frac{A}{r}$$

where *PV* is the present-day value of the security, *A* is the periodic payout of the security, and *r* is the interest rate associated with the security.

13. In this exercise, we presume a perpetual income of $45,000 in 2013 dollars for the near-wealthy and $90,000 for the wealthy.

14. Our assumptions are to treat T-bills as cash equivalents, for example, if they were laddered. We treat Treasury bonds as an ultraconservative allocation of debt investments, and we consider the S&P 500 index as a reasonably conservative allocation of equity investments (the index is mostly composed of large, blue-chip firms).

15. Morningstar Investor Services. (2010). *Mutual fund portfolio allocation.* Retrieved from https://corporate.morningstar.com/us/documents/Marketing OneSheets/ADV_MPF_MutualFundPortfolioMap.pdf

16. Mean returns reported in this section were calculated using data inflation from Reinhardt, C., & Rogoff, K. (2011). From financial crisis to debt crisis. *American Economic Review, 101*(5), 1676–1706; and Damodara, A. (2015). Annual returns on stock, T.bonds and T.bills: 1928–current [Data table]. Retrieved from http://pages.stern.nyu.edu/~adamodar/New_Home_Page/datafile/histretSP.html

17. Of course, averages don't mean that someone will get these returns every year. There will be good years and bad years. For example, income investments did better in the 1990s and early 2000s than today. The good years are expected to be ones in which people save in anticipation of the bad ones.

18. Cohen, J. N. (2016, February 18). Family businesses: In decline? [Blog post]. Retrieved from http://fragilefinances.org/2016/02/18/family-business-decline

19. A rather colorful report by United for a Fair Economy suggests that about 21 percent of those in the 2012 *Forbes 500* richest Americans earned enough

wealth to rank in this group. An estimated 35 percent came from solidly middle-class or lower-class backgrounds, while the remainder enjoyed capital and opportunities from varying degrees of family affluence.

20. Piketty, T. (2014). *Capital in the twenty-first century.* Princeton, NJ: Belknap.

21. American Society of Civil Engineers. (2013). *2013 report card for America's infrastructure.* Retrieved from http://www.infrastructurereportcard.org/transit

22. The latter is a simplified version of the former. See Census Bureau. (2014). Poverty thresholds. Available for download at http://www.census.gov/data/tables /time-series/demo/income-poverty/historical-poverty-thresholds.html; Department of Health and Human Services. (2013). 2013 poverty guidelines. Retrieved from http://aspe.hhs.gov/poverty/13poverty.cfm

23. Along with consideration of the household head's age in single and two-person households, and special provisions for a higher poverty line in Hawaii and Alaska.

24. Short, K. (2014, October). *The supplemental poverty measure: 2013.* Current Population Reports. Retrieved from http://www.census.gov/content/dam/Census /library/publications/2014/demo/p60-251.pdf

25. Rector, R., & Sheffield, R. (2011). Understanding poverty in the United States: Surprising facts about America's poor. *Heritage Foundation Backgrounder #2607.* Retrieved from http://www.heritage.org/research/reports/2011/09/understanding -poverty-in-the-united-states-surprising-facts-about-americas-poor

26. Rector, R., & Sheffield, R. (2011). Understanding poverty in the United States: Surprising facts about America's poor. *Heritage Foundation Backgrounder #2607.* Retrieved from http://www.heritage.org/research/reports/2011/09/unders tanding-poverty-in-the-united-states-surprising-facts-about-americas-poor

27. Anderson, R. J. (2011). Dynamics of economic well-being: Poverty 2004–2006. *Current Population Reports, F70–123.* Retrieved from https://www.census.gov /prod/2011pubs/p70-123.pdf

28. Short, K. (2014, October). *The supplemental poverty measure: 2013.* Current Population Reports. Retrieved from http://www.census.gov/content/dam/Census /library/publications/2014/demo/p60-251.pdf

29. Pew Charitable Trusts. (2012). *Payday lending in America: Who borrows, where they borrow, and why.* Retrieved from http://www.pewtrusts.org/en/research-and -analysis/collections/2014/12/payday-lending-in-america

Chapter 3

1. Salkin, A. (2009, February 6). You try to live on 500k in this town. *New York Times.* Retrieved from http://www.nytimes.com/2009/02/08/fashion/08half mill.htm

2. For example, see Jones, R. P., Cox, D., & Navarro-Rivera, J. (2014). *Economic insecurity, rising inequality, and doubts about the future: Findings from the 2014 American values survey.* Washington, D.C.: Public Religion Research Institute. Retrieved from http://publicreligion.org/site/wp-content/uploads/2014/09/AVS-web.pdf; Financial Investor Education Foundation. (2013). Financial capability in the

United States: Report of findings from 2012 National Financial Capability Study. Retrieved from http://www.usfinancialcapability.org/downloads/NFCS_2012 _Report_Natl_Findings.pdf

3. U.S. Trust. (2014). Insights on Wealth and Worth: Annual survey of high-net-worth and ultra-high-net-worth Americans: Report. *Bank of America.*

4. Harris Poll. (2014). The 2014 Consumer Financial Literacy Survey: Report for National Foundation for Credit Counseling. Retrieved from https://www.nfcc .org/NewsRoom/FinancialLiteracy/files2013/NFCC_2014FinancialLiteracySurvey_datasheet_and_key_findings_031314%20FINAL.pdf

5. Lusardi, A., & Mitchell, O. S. (2014). The economic importance of financial literacy: Theory and evidence. *Journal of Economic Literature, 52*(1), 5–44.

6. Kahneman, D. (1999). Objective happiness. In D. Kahneman, E. Diener, and N. Schwartz (Eds.), *Well-being: foundations of hedonic psychology*. New York, NY: Russell Sage Foundation.

7. Gilbert, D. (2007). *Stumbling on happiness*. New York, NY: Vintage.

8. Short, K. (2013, November). *The research: Supplemental poverty measure 2012*. Current Population Reports. Retrieved from https://www.census.gov/prod /2013pubs/p60-247.pdf; Gould, E., Wething, H., Sabadish, N., & Finio, N. (2013, July 3). What families need to get by: The 2013 update of the EPI's family budget calculator (Issue Brief #368, Economic Policy Institute). Retrieved from http:// www.epi.org/publication/ib368-basic-family-budgets

9. McGregor, J. A., Camfield, L., & Woodcock, A. (2009). Needs, wants and goals: Well-being, quality of life and public policy. *Applied Research in Quality of Life,* 4, 135–154.

10. McGregor, J. A., Camfield, L., & Woodcock, A. (2009). Needs, wants and goals: Well-being, quality of life and public policy. *Applied Research in Quality of Life,* 4, 135–154.

11. Presuming a premium capped at 3 percent of an income at 133–150 percent of its corresponding poverty line income and national private child care tuition rates of $4,079; see Child Care Aware. (2013). *Parents and the high cost of child care: 2013 report*. Retrieved from http://www.usa.childcareaware.org/2013/11/parents -and-the-high-cost-of-child-care-a-report

12. College Board. (2013). *Trends in college pricing, 2013*. Retrieved from http:// trends.collegeboard.org/sites/default/files/college-pricing-2013-full-report .pdf

13. Minton, S. (2013). *Low-income families and the cost of child care*. Retrieved from http://www.urban.org/sites/default/files/alfresco/publication-pdfs/412982 -Low-Income-Families-and-the-Cost-of-Child-Care.pdf

14. Giving USA. (2015, June 29). Giving USA: Americans donated an estimated $358.8 billion to charity in 2014: Highest total in report's 60-year history [Blog post]. Retrieved from http://givingusa.org/giving-usa-2015-press-release-giving -usa-americans-donated-an-estimated-358-38-billion-to-charity-in-2014 -highest-total-in-reports-60-year-history

15. Hamilton, L. (2013). More is more or more is less? Parental financial investments during college. *American Sociological Review,* 78(1), 70–95.

16. Himmelstein, D. U., Warren, E., Thorne, D., & Woolhandler, S. (2005). Illness and injury as contributors to bankruptcy. *Health Affairs*, 63–71.

17. Short, K. (2013, November). *The research: Supplemental poverty measure 2012*. Current Population Reports. Retrieved from https://www.census.gov/prod /2013pubs/p60-247.pdf

18. Lusardi, A., Schneider, D., & Tufano, P. (2011, Spring). "Financially fragile households: evidence and implications." *Brookings Papers on Economic Activity*, 83–134.

19. Levy, J. (2015). In U.S., uninsured rate sinks to 12.9%. Retrieved from http://www.gallup.com/poll/180425/uninsured-rate-sinks.aspx

20. Insurance Information Institute. (2013). Uninsured motorists [Data table]. Retrieved from http://www.iii.org/fact-statistic/uninsured-motorists

21. LIMRA. (2013). Facts about life 2013 [Brochure]. Retrieved from http://www .limra.com/uploadedFiles/limracom/Posts/PR/LIAM/PDF/Facts-Life-2013.pdf

22. Palmer, K. (2013, October 9). Why you probably need more disability insurance [Blog post]. *U.S. News and World Report*. Retrieved from http://money .usnews.com/money/personal-finance/articles/2013/10/09/why-you-probably -need-more-disability-insurance

23. Leamy, E. (2013, March 11). Survey shows only a third of renters have insurance. ABC News. Retrieved from http://abcnews.go.com/Business/survey -shows-renters-insurance/story?id=18685618

24. Silver, D. (2014). Who's poor in America? 50 years into the "War on Poverty": A Data Portrait. Retrieved from http://www.pewresearch.org/fact-tank/2014 /01/13/whos-poor-in-america-50-years-into-the-war-on-poverty-a-data-portrait

25. Silver, D. (2014). Who's poor in America? 50 years into the "War on Poverty": A Data Portrait. Retrieved from http://www.pewresearch.org/fact-tank/2014 /01/13/whos-poor-in-america-50-years-into-the-war-on-poverty-a-data-portrait

26. Johnson, R. W., & Park, J. S. (2011). Can unemployed older workers find work. Retrieved from http://www.urban.org/sites/default/files/alfresco/publication -pdfs/412283-Can-Unemployed-Older-Workers-Find-Work-.pdf; U.S. Government Accounting Office. (2012). *Unemployed older workers: Many experience challenges regaining employment and face reduced retirement security*. Retrieved from http://www.gao.gov/assets/600/590408.pdf

27. Benz, J., Sedensky, M., Tompson, T. & Agiesta, J. (2013). *Working longer: Older Americans' attitudes on work and retirement*. Retrieved from http://www .apnorc.org/PDFs/Working%20Longer/AP-NORC%20Center_Working%20 Longer%20Report-FINAL.pdf

28. Helman, R., Adams, N., Copeland, C., & VanHerhei, J. (2014). The 2014 retirement confidence survey: Confidence rebounds—for those with retirement plans. Retrieved from http://www.ebri.org/pdf/briefspdf/ebri_ib_397_mar14.rcs.pdf

29. Parker, K., & Patten, E. (2013). The sandwich generation: Rising financial burdens for middle-aged Americans. Retrieved from http://www.pewsocialtrends .org/files/2013/01/Sandwich_Generation_Report_FINAL_1-29.pdf

30. Unfortunately, our BLC estimates are not easily applied here, as this analysis deals with a different data set—the Survey of Consumer Finances

(SCF)—which lacks the fine-grained geographic information required to develop anything more than the broadest estimates. Given the high degree of generalization involved in making such assumptions, and the false sense of certainty that such estimates might impart, we opt for a straightforward, inexact measure that is roughly commensurate with the official poverty-line of a two-person elderly household.

31. For a conservative portfolio with 25 percent invested in T-bills (with a long-term return of 3.6 percent), 50 percent in T-bonds (5.4 percent), and 25 percent in Fortune 500 equity (11.3 percent).

32. We use the average of male and female expectancies from the Social Security Administration's 2016 Actuarial Life Table published at https://www.ssa.gov/oact/STATS/table4c6.html

33. This is a presumed portfolio that is 40 percent S&P 500 shares, 40 percent Treasury bonds, and 20 percent Treasury bills. Many investment professionals would consider this to be a highly conservative portfolio for a young person and a very aggressive one for someone near retirement.

34. The present value of a target retirement nest egg is calculated as $PV = FV/(1+r)^n$, were P = present value, FV = future value, r = rate of return, and n = compounding periods. We discount the estimated value of future payments, presumed to be 10 percent of gross income, which is obtained by $PV = (INC*0.1)*[((1+r)^n - 1)/r]$, where INC = current gross income, and other terms are as in the previous formula.

Chapter 4

1. Reinhart, C., & Rogoff, K. (2011). *This time is different: Eight centuries of financial folly*. Cambridge, MA: Harvard University Press.

2. Helleiner, E. (1994). *States and the emergence of global finance: From Bretton Woods to the 1990s*. Ithaca, NY: Cornell University Press.

3. For more, see Gordon, R. J. (2016). *The rise and fall of American growth*. Princeton, NJ: Princeton University Press.

4. Cohen, J. N. (2015, September 28). The engines of economic growth [Blog post]. Retrieved from http://fragilefinances.org/2016/09/28/the-engines-of-economic-growth

5. Banks, A. S. (1976). Cross-National Time Series, 1815–1973. ICPSR07412-v1. Ann Arbor, MI: Inter-university Consortium for Political and Social Research. http://doi.org/10.3886/ICPSR07412.v1; World Bank. (2015). *World development indicators* [Online database]. Retrieved from http://databank.worldbank.org

6. Cohen, J. N. (2015, September 14). Who pays the federal government's bills? [Blog post]. Retrieved from http://fragilefinances.org/2016/09/14/who-pays-the-federal-governments-bills

7. For example, see Piketty, T., & Saez, E. (2003). Income inequality in the United States, 1913–1998. *Quarterly Journal of Economics, CXVII*(1), 1–39.

8. Matthews, D. (2012, July 11). Poverty in the 50 years since "The Other America," in five charts [Blog post]. *Washington Post*. Retrieved from https://www.washingtonpost.com/news/wonk/wp/2012/07/11/poverty-in-the-50-years-since

-the-other-america-in-five-charts; Sherman, A. (2013, September 13). Official poverty measure masks gains made over last 50 years. Retrieved from http://www .cbpp.org/research/official-poverty-measure-masks-gains-made-over-last-50 -years

9. Of course, these are broad generalities—the mid-20th century was not glorious for all Americans. Racial segregation was comparatively strong, unions often excluded blacks, and African Americans are said to have been pressed into poorly compensated, dirty, and dangerous work. Women may have benefited from household prosperity, but they were often marginalized personally and deprived of many of the rights and protections they enjoy today.

10. Cohen, J. N. (2015, September 27). Long-term trends in corporate profits [Blog post]. Retrieved from http://fragilefinances.org/2016/09/27/long-term-trends -in-corporate-profits

11. For more, see Block, F. (1977). *Origins of the international economic disorder: Study of the United States international monetary policy from World War II to present.* Oakland, CA: University of California Press.

12. Block, F. (1977). *Origins of the international economic disorder: Study of the United States international monetary policy from World War II to present.* Oakland, CA: University of California Press.

13. See Centeno, M., & Cohen, J. N. (2010). *Global capitalism: A sociological perspective.* Cambridge, UK: Polity.

14. Eichengreen, B., & Irwin, D. A. (2010, December). The slide to protectionism in the Great Depression: Who succumbed and why? *Journal of Economic History, 70*(4), 871–897.

15. Ruggie, J. G. (1982). International regimes, transactions, and change: Embedded liberalism in the postwar economic system. *International Organization, 36*(2), 379–415.

16. Sachs, J., & Warner, A. (1995). Economic reform and the process of global integration. *Brookings Papers on Economic Activity, 1,* 1–118. Retrieved from https://www.brookings.edu/wp-content/uploads/1995/01/1995a_bpea_sachs _warner_aslund_fischer.pdf

17. Data sources include Balke, N. S., & Gordon, R. J. (1989, February). The estimate of prewar GNP: Methodology and new evidence. *Journal of Political Economy, 97*(1), 38–92; Bureau of Economic Analysis. (2016). *National economic accounts* [Online database]. Retrieved from http://www.bea.gov/national/index.htm; National Bureau of Economic Research. (2008). NBER macrohistory database [Online database]. Retrieved from http://www.nber.org/databases/macrohistory /contents/; World Bank. (2016). World development indicators. Retrieved from http://databank.worldbank.org

18. Branson, W. H., & Junz, H. B. (1971). Trends in U.S. trade and comparative advantage. *Brookings Papers on Economic Activity,* 285–338.

19. The trade restrictionism that prevailed in the mid-20th century was strongly tied up with an international system governing money flows and exchange rates established after World War II at Bretton Woods. For excellent introductions, see

Cohen, B. (2001). Bretton Woods system. In R. J. Barry Jones (Ed.), *Routledge encyclopedia of international political economy* (pp. 95–102). London, England: Routledge; Bordo, M. (1991). The Bretton Woods international monetary system: An historical overview. In Michael D. Bordo and Barry Eichengreen (Eds.), *A retrospective on the Bretton Woods system: Lessons for international monetary reform* (pp. 3–108). Chicago, IL: University of Chicago Press. The details of this collapse are chronicled in Block, F. (1977). *Origins of the international economic disorder: Study of the United States international monetary policy from World War II to present.* Oakland, CA: University of California Press; and in Centeno, M., & Cohen, J. N. (2010). *Global capitalism: A sociological perspective.* Cambridge, UK: Polity.

20. For an extended overview of the emergency of this liberal order, see Centeno, M., & Cohen, J. N. (2010).

21. Brynjolfsson, E., & McAfee, A. (2012). *Race against the machine: How the digital revolution is accelerating innovation, driving productivity, and irreversibly transforming employment and the economy.* Available at http://raceagainstthemachine.com/

22. Cowan, T. (2011). *The great stagnation: How America ate all the low-hanging fruit, got sick, and will (eventually) feel better.* London, UK: Penguin.

23. Gordon, R. J. (2016). *The rise and fall of American growth.* Princeton, NJ: Princeton University Press.

24. Bell, F. C., & Miller, M. L. (2005). *Life tables for the United States Social Security area 1900–2100* (Actuarial Study No. 120, Social Security Administration). Retrieved from https://www.ssa.gov/oact/NOTES/pdf_studies/study120.pdf

25. Social Security Administration. (2012). Period life table, 2011 [Online table]. Retrieved from https://www.ssa.gov/oact/STATS/table4c6.html#ss

26. See Angus, J., & Reeve, P. (2006). Ageism: A threat to "ageing well" in the 21st century. *Journal of Applied Gerontology, 25,* 137–152; Neumark, D. (2008). The Age Discrimination in Employment Act and the challenge of population ageing (NBER Working Papers No. 14317). Retrieved from http://www.nber.org/papers/w14317.pdf

27. Based on the study's estimates that found that one-fifth of U.S. households support adult relatives, about 42 percent of which support a mother and 23 percent support a father. See TD Ameritrade. (2015). *Financial support study: Understanding financial obligations across generations.* Retrieved from https://s1.q4cdn.com/959385532/files/doc_downloads/research/TDA-Financial-Support-Study-2015.pdf

28. Office of Management and Budget. (2016). Table 14.5: Total government expenditures by major category of expenditure as percentage of GDP: 1948–2015 [Data table]. Retrieved from https://www.whitehouse.gov/sites/default/files/omb/budget/fy2017/assets/hist14z5.xls

29. Figures in the paragraph from U.S. Census Bureau. (2016). Table AD-3: Living arrangement of adults 18 and over, 1967 to present [Data table]. Retrieved from http://www.census.gov/hhes/families/data/adults.html

30. For example, see Goudreau, J. (2011, May 2). Why stay-at-home moms should earn a $115,000 salary. *Forbes.* Retrieved from http://www.forbes.com/sites

/jennagoudreau/2011/05/02/why-stay-at-home-moms-should-earn-a-115000
-salary/#26f377bec0ed

31. Pew Research Center. (2010, November 18). *The decline of marriage and the rise of new families.* Retrieved from http://www.pewsocialtrends.org/files/2010/11 /pew-social-trends-2010-families.pdf

32. Krogstad, J. M. (2015). On views of immigrants, Americans largely split along party lines [Blog post]. Retrieved from http://www.pewresearch.org/fact -tank/2015/09/30/on-views-of-immigrants-americans-largely-split-along-party -lines

33. Malone, N., Baluja, K. F., Costanzo, J. M., & Davis, C. J. (2003). The foreign-born population: 2000. Census 2000 Brief, US Census Bureau. Retrieved from https://www.census.gov/prod/2003pubs/c2kbr-34.pdf; Greico, E. M., Acosta, Y. D., de la Cruz, G. P., Gambino, C., Gryn, T., Larsen, L. J., Trevelyan, E. N., & Walters, N. P. (2012). The foreign-born population in the United States: 2010. American Community Survey Report ACS-19. Retrieved from https://www.census .gov/prod/2012pubs/acs-19.pdf

34. Borjas, G. J. (1995). The economic benefits of immigration. *Journal of Economic Perspectives, 9*(2), 3–22.

35. Card, D. (2007). *How immigration affects U.S. cities* (Center for Research and Analysis of Migration, CDP No 11/07). Retrieved from http://www.cream -migration.org/publ_uploads/CDP_11_07.pdf

36. Congressional Budget Office. (2007, December 6). *The impact of unauthorized immigrants on the budgets of state and local governments.* Retrieved from https:// www.cbo.gov/sites/default/files/110th-congress-2007-2008/reports/12-6 -immigration.pdf

37. Rector, R., & Richwine, J. (2013). *The fiscal cost of unlawful immigrants and amnesty to the U.S. taxpayer* (Heritage Foundation Special Report on Immigration #133). Retrieved from http://www.heritage.org/research/reports/2013/05/the -fiscal-cost-of-unlawful-immigrants-and-amnesty-to-the-us-taxpayer

38. DeSilver, D. (2006, September 19). Low-paid illegal work force has little impact on prices. *Seattle Times.* Retrieved from http://www.seattletimes.com /seattle-news/low-paid-illegal-work-force-has-little-impact-on-prices

39. Kershaw, S. (2010, September 7). What if restaurants stopped hiring illegal immigrants? *New York Times.* Retrieved from http://dinersjournal.blogs.nytimes .com/2010/09/07/what-if-restaurants-stopped-hiring-illegal-immigrants/?_r=0

40. Hernandez-Murillo, R. (2006). *Adding up the economic effects of immigration.* Retrieved from https://www.stlouisfed.org/publications/regional-economist /october-2006/adding-up-the-economic-effects-of-immigration

41. Fairlie, R. W. (2008). *Estimating the contribution of immigrant business owners in the U.S. economy.* Retrieved from http://people.ucsc.edu/~rfairlie/papers /published/sba%20final%20report%20immigrant%20business.pdf

42. Bureau of Labor Statistics. (2015, May 21). Labor force characteristics of foreign-born workers summary. Retrieved from http://www.bls.gov/news.release /forbrn.nr0.htm

43. For a more comprehensive view of the causes, character, and consequences of neoliberalism, see Centeno, M. A., & Cohen, J. N. (2010). *Global capitalism.* Cambridge, UK: Polity.

44. See Hayek, F. (1944). *Road to serfdom.* Chicago, IL: University of Chicago.

45. Hayek, F. (1945). The uses of knowledge in society. *American Economic Review, 35,* 519–530.

46. Reagan, R. (1981). Reagan's first inaugural: Government is not the solution to our problem; government is the problem (Heritage Foundation First Principles Series). Retrieved from http://www.heritage.org/initiatives/first-principles /primary-sources/reagans-first-inaugural-government-is-not-the-solution-to-our -problem-government-is-the-problem

47. He launched major military expenditure projects (a non-laissez faire policy) and financed it with debt.

Chapter 5

1. Warren, E. (2005). The overconsumption myth and other tales of law, economics and morality. *Washington University Law Quarterly, 82*(4), 1485–1511; Tyagi, A., & Warren, E. (2004). *The two income trap: Why middle-class parents are broke.* New York, NY: Basic Books; Himmelstein, D. U., Warren, E., Thorne, D., & Woolhandler, S. (2005). Illness and injury as contributors to bankruptcy. *Health Affairs,* 63–71.

2. Beabout, G. R., & Echeverria, E. J. (2002). The culture of consumerism: A Catholic and personalist critique. *Journal of Markets and Morality, 5*(2), 339–383; Schor, J. B. (1999). *The overspent American: Why we want what we don't need.* New York, NY: Harper Perennial; Wright, E. O., & Rogers, J. (2010). *American society: How it really works.* New York, NY: W. W. Norton & Company.

3. Campbell, C. (2004). I shop therefore I know that I am: The metaphysical basis of modern consumerism. In Karin M. Ekstrom and Helene Brembeck (Eds.), *Elusive consumption* (pp. 27–44); Mittal, B. (2006). I, me, and mine–How products become consumers' extended selves. *Journal of Consumer Behavior, 5*(6), 550–562; Zukin, S., & Smith Maguire, J. (2004, August). Consumers and consumption. *Annual Review of Sociology, 30*(1), 173–197.

4. de Graaf, J., Wann, D., & Naylor, T. H. (2002). *Affluenza: The all-consuming epidemic.* San Francisco, CA: Berrett-Koehler Publishers.

5. Baumeister, R. F. (2002, March 1). Yielding to temptation: Self-control failure, impulsive purchasing, and consumer behavior. *Journal of Consumer Research, 28*(4), 670–676.

6. Cross, G. S. (2000). *An all-consuming century: Why commercialism won in modern America.* New York, NY: Columbia University Press; Ewen, S. (2001). *Captains of consciousness: Advertising and the social roots of the consumer culture.* New York, NY: Basic Books; Packard, V. (1957). *The Hidden Persuaders.* New York, NY: D. McKay Co.

7. Beabout, G. R., & Echeverria, E. J. (2002). The culture of consumerism: A Catholic and personalist critique. *Journal of Markets and Morality, 5*(2), 339–383; de Graaf, J., Wann, D., & Naylor, T. H. (2002). *Affluenza: The all-consuming epidemic.* San Francisco, CA: Berrett-Koehler Publishers.

8. Beabout, G. R., & Echeverria, E. J. (2002). The culture of consumerism: A Catholic and personalist critique. *Journal of Markets and Morality, 5*(2), 339–383; Wolff, R. D. (2005). Ideological state apparatuses, consumerism, and U.S. capitalism: Lessons for the left. *Rethinking Marxism, 17*(2), 223–235.

9. Beabout, G. R., & Echeverria, E. J. (2002). The culture of consumerism: A Catholic and personalist critique. *Journal of Markets and Morality, 5*(2), 339–383; Kaza, S. (2000, January 1). Overcoming the grip of consumerism. *Buddhist-Christian Studies, 20,* 23–42; Loy, D. R. (1997). The religion of the market. *Journal of the American Academy of Religion, 65*(2), 275–290.

10. Etzioni, A. (2004). The post-affluent society. *Review of Social Economy, 62*(3), 407–420.

11. Carducci, V. (2006). Culture jamming: A sociological perspective. *Journal of Consumer Culture, 6*(1), 116–138.

12. Schor, J. B. (1999). *The overspent American: Why we want what we don't need.* New York, NY: Harper Perennial.

13. Kaza, S. (2000, January 1). Overcoming the grip of consumerism. *Buddhist-Christian Studies, 20,* 23–42.

14. Juliet Schor in Holt, D. B. (2005). An interview with Juliet Schor. *Journal of Consumer Culture, 5*(1), 5–21.

15. Miller, D. (2001). The poverty of morality. *Journal of Consumer Culture, 1*(2), 225–243.

16. Miller, D. (2001). The poverty of morality. *Journal of Consumer Culture, 1*(2), 231.

17. Bureau of Labor Statistics. (2016). Consumer expenditure survey [Online database]. Retrieved from http://www.bls.gov/cex

18. Data from Bureau of Labor Statistics. (2016). Consumer expenditures survey [Online database]. Retrieved from http://www.bls.gov/cex

19. Note that these figures use different household consumption data than those employed in the previous figure, and these different data are known to generate discrepant results—see Passero, W., Garner, T. I., & McCully, C. (2013). Understanding the relationship: CE survey and PCE (working paper 462). Retrieved from http://www.bls.gov/osmr/pdf/ec130020.pdf. Our primary interest here is in discerning how consumption levels have changed over time, a question for which this figure's data is well-suited.

20. Using CPI-U weights. See Bureau of Labor Statistics. (2014). *Table 1: Relative importance of components in the consumer price indexes: U.S. city average, December 2013.* Retrieved from http://www.bls.gov/cpi/cpiri_2013.pdf

21. Bureau of Labor Statistics. (2015). Consumer expenditure survey [data set]. Retrieved from http://www.bls.gov/cex

22. Clark, K. (2015, November 4). College board says tuition rose faster than inflation again this year. *Time.* Retrieved from http://time.com/money/4098683 /college-board-tuition-cost-rose-inflation-2015

23. Clark, K. (2015, November 4). College board says tuition rose faster than inflation again this year. *Time*. Retrieved from http://time.com/money/4098683/college-board-tuition-cost-rose-inflation-2015

24. National Center for Education Statistics. (2013). *Projections of education statistics to 2021*. Retrieved from http://nces.ed.gov/pubs2013/2013008.pdf

25. See Pew Research Center. (2014, February 11). The rising cost of not going to college. Retrieved from http://www.pewsocialtrends.org/files/2014/02/SDT-higher-ed-FINAL-02-11-2014.pdf

26. Del Boca, D. (2015). Child care arrangement and labor supply (IDB Working Paper 569). Retrieved from http://www.econstor.eu/bitstream/10419/115499/1/IDB-WP-569.pdf

27. These figures suggest that survey respondents are readily including formal child care arrangements (e.g., day care) but not informal or periodic child care or babysitting. This 30 percent figure is roughly similar to Del Boca's (2015) reports of children enrolled in formal care or early education services.

28. Child Care Aware. (2015). *Parents and the high cost of child care*. Retrieved from http://www.usa.childcareaware.org/advocacy-public-policy/resources/reports-and-research/costofcare

29. Leonard, K. (2014, December 9). Workers are spending more of their income on employer health insurance *U.S. News and World Report*. Retrieved from http://www.usnews.com/news/blogs/data-mine/2014/12/09/workers-are-spending-more-of-their-income-on-employer-health-insurance

30. Warren, E. (2005). The overconsumption myth and other tales of law, economics and morality. *Washington University Law Quarterly, 82*(4), 1485–1511.

31. Olen, H. (2013, August 13). Giving up coffee to balance the books: How many lattes to financial freedom? *The Guardian*. Retrieved from http://www.theguardian.com/money/us-money-blog/2013/aug/13/coffee-costs-savings-myth

Chapter 6

1. A recommended overview of the topic is Phillips, D. (2006). *Quality of life*. New York, NY: Routledge.

2. Data from Bureau of Labor Statistics. (2015). *Consumer expenditure survey* [Online database]. Retrieved from http://www.bls.gov/cex

3. Yahoo! (2016). Industry browser [Online database]. Retrieved from https://biz.yahoo.com/p/5qpmu.html

4. Dante, M., Nicholson, S., Levinson, W., Gans, D., Hammons, T., & Caslino, L. P. (2011). U.S. physician practices versus Canadians: Spending nearly four times as much money interacting with payers. *Health Affairs, 30*(8), 1443–1450.

5. Dante, M., Nicholson, S., Levinson, W., Gans, D., Hammons, T., & Caslino, L. P. (2011). U.S. physician practices versus Canadians: Spending nearly four times as much money interacting with payers. *Health Affairs, 30*(8), 1443–1450.

6. See Collins, S. R., Radley, D. C., Shoen, C., & Beutel, S. (2014, December). National trends in the cost of employer health insurance coverage, 2003–2013

Issue Brief. Retrieved from http://www.commonwealthfund.org/~/media/files /publications/issue-brief/2014/dec/1793_collins_nat_premium_trends_2003 _2013.pdf; Long, M., Raw, M., & Claxton, G. (2016, February 5). *A comparison of the availability and cost of coverage for workers in smaller firms and large firms: Update from the 2015 Employer Health Benefits Survey.* Washington, D.C.: Henry J. Kaiser Family Foundation. Retrieved from http://kff.org/private-insurance /issue-brief/a-comparison-of-the-availability-and-cost-of-coverage-for-workers -in-small-firms-and-large-firms-update-from-the-2015-employer-health -benefits-survey

7. Bunker, J. P. (2001). The role of medical care in contributing to health improvements within societies. *International Journal of Epidemiology, 45*(1), 1260–1263; Luce, B. R., Mauskopf, J., Sloan, F. A., Ostermann, J. & Paramore, L. C. (2006). The return on investment in health care: From 1980 to 2000. *Value in Health, 9*(3), 146–156.

8. National Institute of Health. (2010). *Yesterday, today & tomorrow.* Retrieved from https://report.nih.gov/nihfactsheets/default.aspx

9. Kantor, E., Rehm, C. D., Haas, J. S., Chan, A. T., & Giovannucci, E. (2015). Trends in prescription drug use among adults in the United States, 1999–2012. *JAMA: The Journal of the American Medical Association, 314*(17), 1818–1831.

10. Agency for Healthcare Research and Quality. (2016). H-CUPnet [Online database]. Retrieved from http://hcupnet.ahrq.gov/HCUPnet.jsp

11. Henry J. Kaiser Family Foundation. (2016). Hospital outpatient visits per 1,000 population by ownership type [Online data table]. Retrieved from http:// kff.org/other/state-indicator/outpatient-visits-by-ownership

12. Klein, E. (2012, March 3). Why an MRI costs $1,080 in America and $280 in France. *Washington Post.* Retrieved from https://www.washingtonpost.com /blogs/ezra-klein/post/why-an-mri-costs-1080-in-america-and-280-in-france /2011/08/25/gIQAVHztoR_blog.html

13. Noah, T. (2011). The make-believe billion: How drug companies exaggerate research costs to justify absurd profits. *Slate.* Retrieved from http://www.slate .com/articles/business/the_customer/2011/03/the_makebelieve_billion.html; Swanson, A. (2015, Febrary 11). Big pharmaceutical companies are spending far more on marketing than research. *Washington Post* [Blog post]. Retrieved from https://www.washingtonpost.com/news/wonk/wp/2015/02/11/big-pharmaceuti cal-companies-are-spending-far-more-on-marketing-than-research

14. Bureau of Labor Statistics. (2015). *Occupational employment and wages, May 2015: 29–1062 Family and General Practitioners.* Retrieved from http://www .bls.gov/oes/current/oes291062.htm

15. Hamblin, J. (2015, January 27). What doctors make. *The Atlantic.* Retrieved from http://www.theatlantic.com/health/archive/2015/01/physician-salaries/384846

16. Henry J. Kaiser Family Foundation. (2015, October 5). *Key facts about the uninsured population.* Retrieved from http://kff.org/uninsured/fact-sheet/key-facts -about-the-uninsured-population

17. Franks, P. W., Clancy, C. M., & Gold, M. (1993). Health insurance and mortality: Evidence form a national cohort. *JAMA, 270*(6), 737–741; Kirby, J. B., &

Kaneda, T. (2010). Unhealthy and uninsured: Exploring racial differences in health and health insurance coverage using a life table approach. *Demography,* 47(4), 1035–1051; Wilper, A. P., Woolhandler, S., Lasser, K. E., McCormick, D., Bor, D. H., & Himmelstein, D. U. (2009). Health insurance and mortality in U.S. adults. *American Journal of Public Health, 99*(12), 2289–2995.

18. Sirovich, B. E., Woloshin, S., & Schwartz, L. (2011). Too little? Too much? Primary care physicians' views on U.S. health care. *Archives of Internal Medicine, 171*(17), 1582–1585; Welch, H. G., Schwartz, L. M., & Woolshin, S. (2012). *Overdiagnosed: Making people sick in the pursuit of health.* Boston, MA: Beacon Press; Institute of Medicine. (2012, September). Best care at lower cost: The path to continuous learning health care in America. Retrieved from http://www.nationalacademies.org/hmd/~/media/Files/Report%20Files/2012/Best-Care/BestCareReportBrief.pdf; Santa Cruz, J. (2013, December 9). You're getting too much healthcare. *Atlantic.* Retrieved from http://www.theatlantic.com/health/archive/2013/12/youre-getting-too-much-healthcare/281896; Gawande, A. (2015, May 11). Overkill. *New Yorker.* Retrieved from http://www.newyorker.com/magazine/2015/05/11/overkill-atul-gawande

19. Hogan, C., Lunney, J., Gabel, J., & Lynn, J. (2001). Medicare beneficiaries' costs of care in the last year of life. *Health Affairs, 20*(4), 188–195.

20. For example, Bell, M. (2013, January 10). Why 5% of patients create 50% of health care costs. *Fortune.* Retrieved from http://www.forbes.com/sites/michaelbell/2013/01/10/why-5-of-patients-create-50-of-health-care-costs/#3ba01b9e4781

21. Greenberg, M. H. (2007). Low-income families, work, and child care. *The Next Generation of Antipoverty Policies, 17*(3). Retrieved from http://futureofchildren.org/publications/journals/article/index.xml?journalid=33&articleid=67&sectionid=353

22. For more, see Greenberg, M. H. (2007). Low-income families, work, and child care. *The Next Generation of Antipoverty Policies, 17*(3). Retrieved from http://futureofchildren.org/publications/journals/article/index.xml?journalid=33&articleid=67&sectionid=353

23. Greenberg, M. H. (2007). Low-income families, work, and child care. *The Next Generation of Antipoverty Policies, 17*(3). Retrieved from http://futureofchildren.org/publications/journals/article/index.xml?journalid=33&articleid=67&sectionid=353

24. National Center for Education Statistics. (2015). *The condition of education 2015* (NCES 2015–144). Retrieved from https://nces.ed.gov/pubsearch/pubsinfo.asp?pubid=2015144

25. Child Care Aware. (2015). *Parents and the high cost of child care: 2015 report.* Retrieved from http://usa.childcareaware.org/wp-content/uploads/2016/03/Parents-and-the-High-Cost-of-Child-Care-2015-FINAL.pdf

26. See Chapter Two.

27. Hummer, R. A., & Hernandez, E. M. (2013). The effect of educational attainment on adult mortality in the United States. *Population Bulletin, 68*(1). Retrieved from http://www.prb.org/pdf13/us-education-mortality.pdf

28. Devauix, M., Sassi, F., Church, J., Cecchini, M., & Borgonovi, F. (2011). Exploring the relationship between education and obesity. *OECD Journal: Economic Studies, 2011*(1). Retrieved from http://dx.doi.org/10.1787/eco_studies-2011 -5kg5825vlk23

29. Wang, W. (2015, December 4). The link between a college education and a lasting marriage [Blog post]. Retrieved from http://www.pewresearch.org/fact -tank/2015/12/04/education-and-marriage

30. Dolan, P., Peasgood, T., & White, M. (2008). Do we really know what makes us happy? A review of the economic literature on the factors associated with subjective well-being. *Journal of Economic Psychology*, 29, 94–122.

31. Cohen, J. N. (2015, September 13). Slowdown in educational attainment [Blog post]. Retrieved from http://fragilefinances.org/2016/09/13/slowdown-in -educational-attainment

32. Geiger, R. L., & Heller, D. E. (2012). Financial trends in higher education: The United States. *Educational Studies*, 3, 5–29.

33. Geiger, R. L., & Heller, D. E. (2012). Financial trends in higher education: The United States. *Educational Studies*, 3, 5–29.

34. Hiltonsmith, R. (2015). *Pulling up the ladder: Myth and reality in the crisis of college affordability.* Retrieved from http://www.demos.org/sites/default/files /publications/Robbie%20admin-bloat.pdf

35. Hiltonsmith, R. (2015). *Pulling up the ladder: Myth and reality in the crisis of college affordability.* Retrieved from http://www.demos.org/sites/default/files /publications/Robbie%20admin-bloat.pdf

36. Hiltonsmith, R. (2015). *Pulling up the ladder: Myth and reality in the crisis of college affordability.* Retrieved from http://www.demos.org/sites/default/files /publications/Robbie%20admin-bloat.pdf

37. Geiger, R. L., & Heller, D. E. (2012). Financial trends in higher education: The United States. *Educational Studies*, 3, 5–29.

38. Hiltonsmith, R. (2015). *Pulling up the ladder: Myth and reality in the crisis of college affordability.* Retrieved from http://www.demos.org/sites/default/files /publications/Robbie%20admin-bloat.pdf

39. Bailey, M. J., & Dynarski, S. (2011). Inequality in postsecondary education. In Greg J. Duncan and Richard J. Murnane (Eds.), *Whither opportunity? Rising inequality, schools, and children's life chances* (pp. 117–132). New York, NY: Russell Sage Foundation.

40. Elliott, W., & Lewis, M. (2013). *Student loans are widening the wealth gap: Time to focus on equity.* Retrieved from https://aedi.ku.edu/sites/aedi.ku.edu/files/docs /publication/CD/reports/R1.pdf

41. O'Shaughnessy, L. (2011, September 6). 20 surprising higher education facts. *U.S. News and World Report.* Retrieved from http://www.usnews.com /education/blogs/the-college-solution/2011/09/06/20-surprising-higher -education-facts

42. *The Economist.* (2015, March 6) Revenge of the nerds. *The Economist.* Retrieved from http://www.economist.com/blogs/graphicdetail/2015/03/daily -chart-2

43. Perry, M. J. (2014, February 26). Today's new homes are 1,000 square feet larger than in 1973, and the living space per person has doubled over the past 40 years [Blog post]. Retrieved from http://www.aei.org/publication/todays-new -homes-are-1000-square-feet-larger-than-in-1973-and-the-living-space-per -person-has-doubled-over-last-40-years; Timaros, N. (2015, April 28). Why new homes have become more expensive: They're much bigger. *Wall Street Journal.* Retrieved from http://blogs.wsj.com/economics/2015/04/28/why-new-homes-have -become-more-expensive-theyre-much-bigger

44. Dwyer, R. (2007). Expanding homes and increasing inequalities: U.S. hous- ing development and the residential segregation of the affluent. *Social Problems, 54*(1), 23–46.

45. Dwyer, R. E. (2009). The McMansionization of America? Income stratifi- cation and the standard of living in housing, 1960–2000. *Research in Social Strat- ification and Mobility, 27*, 285–300.

46. Warren, E. (2004). The over-consumption myth and other tales of eco- nomics, law, and morality. *Washington University Law Quarterly, 82*(4), 1485–1511.

47. Rich, M., Cox, A., & Boch, M. (2016, April 29). Money, race, and success: How your school district compares. *New York Times.* Retrieved from http://www .nytimes.com/interactive/2016/04/29/upshot/money-race-and-success-how -your-school-district-compares.html; Reardon, S. F., Kalogrides, D., & Ho, A. (2016). Linking U.S. school district test score distributions to a common scale, 2009–2013 (Standard Education Data Archive, 4/2016). Retrieved from https:// cepa.stanford.edu/sites/default/files/wp16-09-v201604.pdf

48. Clapp, J. M., Nanda, A., & Ross, S. L. (2008). Which school attributes matter? The influence of school district performance and demographic composition on property value. *Journal of Urban Economics, 63*(2), 451–466; Chiodo, A. J., Hernandez-Murillo, R., & Owying, M. T. (2010, May/June). Nonlinear effects of school quality on housing prices. *Federal Reserve Bank of St. Louis Review,* 185–204.

49. Whitehurst, G. J., Chingos, M. M., & Gallaher, M. R. (2013). *Do school dis- tricts matter?* Retrieved from https://www.brookings.edu/research/do-school -districts-matter

50. Caldas, S. J., & Bankston III, C. (1999). Effect of school population socio- economic status on individual academic achievement. *Journal of Educational Research, 93*(2), 269–277; Hanushek, E. A., Kain, J. F., Marksman, J. M., & Rivkin, S. G. (2003). Does peer ability affect student achievement? *Journal of Applied Econo- metrics, 18*(5), 527–544; Burke, M. A., & Sass, T. R. (2013). Classroom peer effects and student achievement. *Journal of Labor Economics, 31*(1), 51–82.

51. Ryan, S. (1999). Property values and transportation facilities: Finding the transportation-land use connection. *Journal of Planning Literature, 13*(4), 412–427; Bartholomew, K., & Ewing, R. (2011). Hedonic price effects of pedestrian- and transit-oriented development. *Urban Studies, 26*(1), 18–34; Gibbons, S., & Man- chin, S. (2008). Valuing school quality, better transport, and lower crime: Evi- dence from house prices. *Oxford Review of Economic Policy, 24*(1), 99–119.

52. For example, Linden, L., & Rockoff, J. E. (2008). Estimates of the impact of crime risk on property values from Megan's laws. *American Economic Review,*

98(3), 1103–1127; Pope, J. C. (2008). Fear of crime and housing prices: House-hold reactions to sex offender registries. *Journal of Urban Economics, 64*(3), 601–614; Ihlanfeldt, K., & Mayock, T. (2010). Panel data estimates on the effects of different types of crime on housing prices. *Regional Science and Urban Economics, 40*(2–3), 161–172; Pope, D. G., & Pope, J. C. (2012). Crime and property values: Evidence from the 1990s crime drop. *Regional Science and Urban Economics, 42*(1–2), 177–188.

53. Cohen, J. N. (2015, October 17). Crime rates across U.S. metro areas [Blog post]. Retrieved from http://josephnathancohen.info/2015/10/17/crime-rates-across-us-metro-areas

54. *The Economist.* (2015, December 9). In New Orleans, call 911 and wait for an hour. Retrieved from http://www.economist.com/blogs/democracyinamerica/2015/12/police-response-times

55. Cihan, A., Zhang, Y., & Hoover, L. (2012). Police response time to in-progress burglary: A multilevel analysis. *Police Quarterly, 15*(3), 308–327.

56. Hessick, C. B. (2007). Violence between lovers, strangers, and friends. *Washington University Law Review, 85*(2), 343–407.

57. Gruenstein Bocian, D., Li, W., Reid, C., & Quercia, R. G. (2011, November). *Lost ground, 2011: Disparities in mortgage lending and foreclosures.* Retrieved from http://www.responsiblelending.org/mortgage-lending/research-analysis/Lost-Ground-2011.pdf; Woodruff, M. (2012, January 18). Foreclosure hardest on low-income homeowners. *Christian Science Monitor.* Retrieved from http://www.csmonitor.com/Business/Latest-News-Wires/2012/0118/Foreclosure-hardest-on-low-income-homeowners

58. Lin, Z., Rosenblatt, E., & Yao, V. W. (2009). Spillover effects of foreclo-sures on neighborhood property values. *Journal of Real Estate Finance and Econom-ics, 38*(4), 387–407.

59. Light, J. (2015, June 23). Why the U.S. housing recovery is leaving poorer neighborhoods behind. *Wall Street Journal.* Retrieved from http://www.wsj.com/articles/in-u-s-poorer-areas-have-yet-to-see-housing-rebound-1435091711; Dayden, D. (2015, June 29). The housing recovery has skipped poor and minor-ity neighborhoods. *New Republic.* Retrieved from https://newrepublic.com/article/122202/housing-recovery-has-skipped-poor-and-minority-neighborhoods

60. Environmental Protection Agency. (2015, September). Population surround-ing 1,388 superfund remedial sites. Retrieved from https://www.epa.gov/sites/production/files/2015-09/documents/webpopulationrsuperfundsites9.28.15.pdf

Chapter 7

1. All data except median household income and government revenue: World Bank. (2016). *World Development Indicators* [Online database]. Retrieved from http://data.worldbank.org/data-catalog/world-development-indicators; govern-ment revenue data: OECD. (2016). *OECD.stat* [Online database]. Retrieved from http://stats.oecd.org/#; household income data: Gallup. (2013, December 16).

Worldwide, median household income about $10,000. Retrieved from http://www
.gallup.com/poll/166211/worldwide-median-household-income-000.aspx

2. Gross domestic product, a measure of national economic output. It is used as an estimate of the total amount of economic activity going on in a country or how well-developed or rich it is.

3. The Gini coefficient is a standard metric of income inequality, which measures the degree to which lower and higher income earners in a society have similar income levels. See OECD. (2016b, February 18–19). OECD Income Distribution Database (IDD): Gini, poverty, income, methods and concepts. Retrieved from http://www.oecd.org/social/income-distribution-database.htm

4. This includes subnational governments, such as states and localities.

5. Data from OECD. (2016). *OECD.stat* [Online database]. Retrieved from http://stats.oecd.org/#

6. Figures from OECD. (2016) Social Protection *OECD.Stat.* Retrieved from http://stats.oecd.org/#

7. Data from OECD Family Database. (2016). Table PF2.1.A: Summary of paid leave entitlements available to mothers. In *OECD Family Database* [Online database]. Retrieved from http://www.oecd.org/els/family/database.htm

8. Addati, L., Cassirer, N., & Gilchrist, K. (2014). *Maternity and paternity: Law and practice across the world.* Geneva, Switzerland: International Labor Organization.

9. OECD. (2016). *OECD family database* [Online database]. Retrieved from http://www.oecd.org/els/family/database.htm

10. Cost data from Usher, A., & Medow, J. (2010). *Global higher education rankings 2010: Affordability and accessibility in comparative perspective.* Toronto, Canada: Higher Education Strategy Associates; enrollment and population from World Bank. (2016). *World development indicators* [Online database]. Retrieved from http://data.worldbank.org/data-catalog/world-development-indicators; count of ranked universities from: Times Higher Education. (2016). *The world university rankings.* Retrieved from https://www.timeshighereducation.com/world-university-rankings/2016; Nobel counts from BBC. (2010, October 8). Which country has the best brains? Retrieved from http://www.bbc.co.uk/news/magazine-11500373

11. NAFSA: Association of Global Educators. (2014). Global market share of international students—top host countries. Retrieved from http://www.nafsa.org/_/File/_/global_market_pie_chart.pdf

12. Data from OECD. (2016). *OECD.stat* [Online database]. Retrieved from http://stats.oecd.org/#

13. Klein, E. (2013, March 15). Why an MRI costs $1.080 in America and $280 in France[Blog post]. Retrieved from https://www.washingtonpost.com/news/wonk/wp/2013/03/15/why-an-mri-costs-1080-in-america-and-280-in-france/

14. Figures to follow from Commonwealth Fund. (2013). *International health policy survey in eleven countries.* Retrieved from http://www.commonwealthfund.org/~/media/files/publications/in-the-literature/2013/nov/pdf_schoen_2013_ihp_survey_chartpack_final.pdf

15. Performance Urban Planning. (2015). *12th annual demographia international housing affordability survey: 2016.* Retrieved from http://www.demographia.com/dhi .pdf

16. For an extended discussion, see Rocher, S., & Stierle, M. H. (2015). Household savings rates in the EU: Why do they differ so much? (European Commission European Economy, Discussion Paper No. 005). Retrieved from http://ec .europa.eu/economy_finance/publications/eedp/pdf/dp005_en.pdf

17. For an extended discussion, see Rocher, S., & Stierle, M. H. (2015). Household savings rates in the EU: Why do they differ so much? (European Commission European Economy, Discussion Paper No. 005). Retrieved from http://ec .europa.eu/economy_finance/publications/eedp/pdf/dp005_en.pdf

18. These countries include Australia, Austria, Belgium, Canada, Denmark, Finland, France, Germany, Italy, Japan, Netherlands, New Zealand, Norway, Portugal, Spain, Sweden, Switzerland, and the United Kingdom. For more on the metrics, see Organisation for Economic Co-operation and Development, *Better Life Index*, which is available at http://www.oecdbetterlifeindex.org.

19. Rector, R., & Sheffield, R. (2011). Understanding poverty in the United States: Surprising facts about America's poor (*Heritage Foundation Backgrounder No 2607*). Retrieved from http://www.heritage.org/research/reports/2011/09 /understanding-poverty-in-the-united-states-surprising-facts-about-americas -poor

20. Matthews, D. (2012, September 19). Other countries don't have a 47% [Blog post]. *Washington Post.* Retrieved from https://www.washingtonpost.com/news /wonk/wp/2012/09/19/other-countries-dont-have-a-47

21. Matthews, D. (2013, April 4). U.S. tax code isn't as progressive as you think [Blog post]. *Washington Post.* Retrieved from https://www.washingtonpost.com /news/wonk/wp/2013/04/04/u-s-tax-code-isnt-as-progressive-as-you-think

Chapter 8

1. Olen, H. (2013). *Pound foolish: Exposing the dark side of the personal finance industry.* New York, NY: Portfolio/Penguin.

2. Skocpol, T., & Williamson, V. (2011). *The Tea Party and the remaking of Republican conservatism.* New York, NY: Oxford University Press.

3. For example, New York Times Editorial Board. (2014, March 1). Fear mongering with Medicare. *New York Times.* Retrieved from http://www.nytimes.com /2014/03/02/opinion/sunday/fear-mongering-with-medicare.html; Moorhead, M. (2012, October 3). Romney says Obama cut $716 billion from Medicare. *Politifact.* Retrieved from http://www.politifact.com/truth-o-meter/statements/2012/oct /03/mitt-romney/romney-says-obama-cut-716-billion-medicare

4. Gilens, M. (1999). *Why Americans hate welfare.* Chicago, IL: University of Chicago.

5. For example, see Hayek, F. (1994 [1949]). *The road to serfdom.* Chicago, IL: University of Chicago.

6. For more, see World Bank. (2016). *World governance indicators* [Online data set]. Retrieved from http://info.worldbank.org/governance/wgi/index.aspx

7. Such a view envisions the possibility that the modern market system is an entity that is independent and exists apart from the government. As noted in Chapter Four, the idea of a self-contained, self-managing, government-free market system exists nowhere in reality; modern capitalism relies on the payment systems, ownership systems, contract rules and enforcement mechanisms, public order institutions, and so on that governments deliver. All of these foundational institutions require that someone make a decision about the particulars of these rules and institutions.

Index

Page numbers followed by *t* indicate tables and *f* indicate figures.

About the Author

Joseph Nathan Cohen is the coauthor of *Global Capitalism: A Sociological Perspective* (2010). He is as an assistant professor of sociology and faculty member in the Program for Data Analytics and Applied Social Research at the City University of New York, Queens College. Professor Cohen hails from Canada and earned his PhD in sociology from Princeton in 2007.